Out of Crisis

Great Barrington Books

Bringing the old and new together in the spirit of W. E. B. Du Bois

∾ An imprint edited by Charles Lemert ∾

Titles Available

Out of Crisis

Rethinking Our Financial Markets

David A. Westbrook

Paradigm Publishers
Boulder • London

Copyright © 2010 Paradigm Publishers

Published in the United States by Paradigm Publishers, 3360 Mitchell Lane, Suite E, Boulder, Colorado 80301 USA.

Paradigm Publishers is the trade name of Birkenkamp & Company, LLC, Dean Birkenkamp, President and Publisher.

Library of Congress Cataloging-in-Publication Data

Westbrook, David A.
  Out of crisis : rethinking our financial markets / David A. Westbrook.
    p. cm. — (Great Barrington books)
  Includes bibliographical references and index.
    ISBN 978-1-59451-726-6 (hardcover : alk. paper) — ISBN 978-1-59451-727-3 (pbk. : alk. paper)
  1. Financial crises—United States—History—21st century. 2. Finance—Government policy—United States—History—21st century. I. Title.
  HB3722.W47 2010
  332.0973—dc22

                                                                          2009036129

Printed and bound in the United States of America on acid-free paper that meets the standards of the American National Standard for Permanence of Paper for Printed Library Materials.

Designed and Typeset by Straight Creek Bookmakers.

14 13 12 11 10   1 2 3 4 5

Contents

Preface and Acknowledgments

ONE SHOULD SYMPATHIZE WITH THE JOURNALISTS WHO STRUGGLE TO PROVIDE stories about at least the most striking of the facts in which we seem at risk of drowning, the numbers that "materialize and vanish and rematerialize in a different form."[1] What can be meant by payments reckoned in tens of billions, millions upon millions of unemployed people, trillions of dollars of debt and growth (certainly more than the velocity of money supply, whatever that really is) that might or might not have otherwise happened? Surely the transformation of our world, but perhaps one could be a bit more specific? And so we often read the life and times of the pundit, which can be amusing and even insightful, if the pundit is a good writer.

Another approach to confronting the confusion of our news is historical narrative, usually strongly chronological and explicitly, simplistically, causal. Just months after the crisis began, a stream of books explaining what "really" caused the crisis began to flow; the stream has become a flood with no signs of abating. Such accounts can be delivered at whatever level of detail the reader can tolerate, and we may rest assured that doctoral dissertations on the causes of this crisis will be written by people who are now infants. Narrative and its pitfalls are both further discussed and modestly indulged in what follows, but on the whole this book despairs of telling one convincing story with which blame can be assigned and from which noble policy flows, and so another approach to rethinking our crisis must be found.

A somewhat more muscular approach is suggested by the great mid-twentieth-century corporation law scholar and man of affairs Adolf Berle, who was said to have aspired to be the Marx of the capitalist classes. It would be nice to have a scientific grand theory, with a dynamic akin to class struggle, to explain or at least articulate what has happened to our financial markets over the past few years.[2] But this is not the nineteenth century, and monolithic theories of complex history seem sophomoric or even authoritarian. What might still be possible and even more useful, however, is to work more like some Walter Benjamin of the capitalist classes. Benjamin was the great interpreter of, among other things, Bert Brecht, who wrote *Threepenny Opera,* a scathing attack on capitalism that was a huge hit. That is, the current financial crisis provides us with an opportunity for the critical analysis of established patterns of thought, a chance to ask how are we to (re)think what began as "a housing bubble," went through a period as a "financial crisis," which quickly became "a credit crisis," or even "a liquidity crisis," and finally "a recession," with talk of "depression" in the air. Instead of narrative, this book is an exercise in interpretation, what might be read as a critique of the intellectual history of the present, that asks how we are to engage—think about—the largest financial crisis in several generations and, by extension, political economy more generally.

I teach business and international topics in a law school, and this book is an internal critique of the perspective of financial policy elites. This perspective is expressed in various ways and called different things, including simply economic or financial, law and economics, liberal or neoliberal, Chicago school, Washington consensus, deregulatory, and so forth. The roots of this perspective are old—one might plausibly argue going back to the development of accounting and/or probability in the late Middle Ages—but the "modern finance" with which this book is concerned is probably best understood as a result of development of more "scientific" (and quantitative) forms of economic discourse after World War II. It is associated especially with the development of portfolio theory since the 1950s, economic analysis of law since the 1960s and 1970s, deregulation since the 1970s, financial engineering since the 1970s but gaining speed throughout the 1980s and 1990s, advances in entity architecture since the 1970s over roughly the same time frame, and risk management (often based on both the new financial instruments and special-purpose entities) over the last few decades, but especially since the 1990s, and structured finance in the 1990s and the early years of this decade. As this partial yet long listing of intellectual sources and expressions suggests, modern finance is widespread and diffuse, a powerful yet somewhat unarticulated way of looking at the world and doing policy. It is, in short, both an intellectual tradition and an ideology.

In discussing finance as an ideology, and especially in talking about how this way of looking at the world may be changing under the pressure of current events, I have imagined a fairly sophisticated reader, one attuned to the discourses of the financial markets, especially in the United States. I have not had much choice. Both lack of space and my own limitations prevent me from articulating "the entire edifice," as former chair of the Federal Reserve Alan Greenspan called it, also somewhat vaguely. It is difficult enough to suggest how this ideology, which has been so vital to our political lives, may be entering a time of rupture and transformation. So, for example, the discussion of efficiency in Chapter 1 refers to the Efficient Capital Markets Hypothesis (ECMH) but does not survey the literature, and certainly does not try to teach ECMH to those who do not know it already. At the same time, however,

I have struggled to make my broader argument as clear and accessible as possible. I believe that people who do not have substantial backgrounds in finance will be able to get the gist of my argument, and that people who do have such backgrounds will think that I am being fair, perhaps even generous, in my discussion of how financial thinking has developed and perhaps is being transformed.

Much of this book was written in the form of public talks given in the fall of 2008 and through the long cold winter of 2009. Some of the effrontery of the public presentation no doubt remains, but I find that having to speak—to say something, publicly and soon—forces me to decide what I think. And a question-and-answer session in front of a diverse crowd both encourages boldness of expression and helps to reveal weakness of analysis. ("I'm sounding like an idiot—need to work on this part.") For being great hosts and fine interlocutors, I would like to thank, in chronological order, Frank Partnoy at the University of San Diego, Rosa Lastra at Queen Mary College, Charles Goodhart at the London School of Economics, Christina Garsten at Stockholm University, and Edward Balleisen, David Moss, and others at the Tobin Project. In London, Andrew Haldane from the Bank of England was a very gracious commentator, who not only produced the PowerPoint slides that I should have, but who "translated" my remarks for central bankers (to their visible relief and my grateful chagrin).

My thinking has benefited from talks given under the auspices of the U.S. State Department Speaker Program, both in Brazil, mostly on transparency, and in China, where I spoke to a host of government, academic, and private-sector audiences, mostly on rethinking financial markets. I would like to thank Gretchen Weintraub and the many other foreign service officers who helped to make these trips possible.

In addition to those mentioned, I would like to thank a number of people with whom I have been discussing these ideas, some for many years, including Brandon Becker, David Franasiak, Vitor Gaspar, Phil Halpern, Doug Holmes, Fred Konefsky, Jack Schlegel, George Williams, and Jim Wooten. Patrick Fitzsimmons and Michael Halliday provided excellent research assistance.

I completed this project while teaching at the University of Kansas and at Washburn University, and gratefully acknowledge the warm hospitality of both institutions. I thank Raj Bhala, Chris Drahozal, John Head, and Stephen Ware at Kansas for their interest and helpful comments. Christopher Steadman, Lauren Van Waardhuizen, and especially Pam Tull in the Wheat Law Library were tremendous. My publisher, Dean Birkenkamp, and the rest of the team at Paradigm have continued to be friendly and supportive.

Over the years, my wife, Amy Westbrook, has protected me and sometimes reminded me that there is news outside the scope of my current obsession. My children, Thomas, Sophia, and Peter, reminded me that although "the news happens every day," as Peter put it once, it often should be put aside. I am quite blessed.

Let me close with a vignette. As an untenured professor, and acting on a whim, I sent a copy of an article on what Enron's implosion, and the ensuing accounting scandals, might mean to three old lions, John Kenneth Galbraith, his friend Charles

Kindleberger, and Ronald Coase. All three economists, having cut their teeth before and during the Depression, were concerned with essentially social questions of crashes, confidence, what holds institutions together, and the like—questions that were often dismissed as too fuzzy at the turn of the twenty-first century, but that, not so incidentally, seem far more relevant today.

Galbraith and Kindleberger actually read my article and wrote back. (What, if anything, should I make of Coase's silence?) Galbraith sent me a copy of his last book, *The Economics of Innocent Fraud,* with a scrawled inscription I have yet to decipher (he usually typed, on small pieces of paper). Kindleberger wrote to ask "permission" (!) to discuss my thoughts on Enron in the latest edition of his classic *Manias, Panics, and Crashes.* Our brief correspondence was heady stuff for an obscure young academic, but sadly, both men died before I had a chance to go to Boston and discuss such things in person. Of course, I should have made a chance, but.... Perhaps I know better now. I am at an age when I am beginning to lose my mentors, including, so far, G. P. Cutino, Abram Chayes, and Hal Berman. So this book is dedicated to the encouragement of old men.

David A. Westbrook

An Introduction to the Argument

This modern risk-management paradigm held sway for decades. The whole intellectual edifice, however, collapsed in the summer of last year.
—*Alan Greenspan, former chair of the Federal Reserve*[1]

"CRISIS" IS COMMONLY UNDERSTOOD AS A DRAMATIC AND PAINFUL DEVIATION from a well-established norm. Reversion to the mean is, however, expected, and as soon as the old norm has been reestablished, then the crisis will be over. In this view, the present global financial crisis and concomitant economic recession is an anomaly, and sooner or later (but when?) we will return to "normal" (perhaps represented by the state of affairs in 2005?). We hear this imagination of the crisis every day, in speculation about when the "recovery" of the stock market, and the economy more generally, will occur.

One may also imagine a crisis in a very different way, as the stress that accompanies the birth of a new state of affairs. In this view, the old order no longer exists but is largely destroyed as our circumstances are transformed. It is pointless to speak of the period after the Great Depression as a "return" to the economy of the late 1920s, for example. The world was transformed not only by the Depression but also by the ensuing world war—and when prosperity returned, nobody thought it was a return to the status quo ante. Although it is too soon to tell how significant this crisis will be, as Chou En Lai reportedly said of the French Revolution, the current financial crisis increasingly seems to be historically transformative, more than an anomaly.

The present crisis appears to be important not least as a matter of how the economy is understood by our policy elites. Indeed, the former chair of the Federal Reserve testified to Congress that the paradigm through which he had conducted monetary policy, "risk management," had collapsed. But the understanding of risk management that Greenspan used to conduct monetary policy, and to argue against various forms of regulation, was an expression of what variously might be called an imaginary, an ideology, or *Weltanschauung*, a way of looking at the world that, in its time and place, made sense to a group of people. Not only did this way of looking at the world make sense, it served as the basis for economic policy on both sides of the aisle, and indeed around the world. The understanding of financial markets, and the way various actors participate in such markets, that informs modern risk management and no small amount of monetary policy also informs modern law and economics, and so corporation law, securities law, banking law, monetary policy, much of our foreign policy, and so forth. Without being in any way unkind, there is little reason to believe that this generation of policy thinkers, who were trained in the old, now largely discredited paradigm, really knows how to tackle the problems before it. (Nor, for that matter, is it so clear how to teach finance.) The ways, or many of the ways, (but which ones?) that these problems have been considered are at least compromised, perhaps simply wrong. So for Greenspan to tell Congress that his way of looking at the world, their way, had collapsed was deeply embarrassing, not only to Greenspan but to his audience, and therefore not without courage.

Unsurprisingly, Greenspan was attacked in Congress, largely by people who had neither the intellectual creativity nor the independence to attack him, and more fundamentally, his worldview when he and it were politically strong. Such attacks were distasteful and intellectually dishonest, if hardly surprising, especially during a crisis. More deeply, however, such attacks suggest just how embarrassing Greenspan's admission was. The simple truth is that the Washington elites, insofar as they knew about finance in any formal sense, were trained in the tradition of which Greenspan unquestionably was a master and that he admitted had collapsed. Greenspan in effect devalued not merely his own intellectual capital but that of his audience. No wonder our elected representatives were angry.

As the management of this crisis since Greenspan gave his testimony in the autumn of 2008 has rather conclusively demonstrated, no consensus exists to take the place of "the modern risk-management paradigm." This is a problem, a problem so grave (or hilarious, for those with a mordant sense of humor) that it has not really been addressed publicly. Without a disciplined way of thinking about financial markets, how are our leaders to confront the current crisis? Something must be done, as we are incessantly reminded, but what, exactly? No doubt money must be spent, but how? As of this writing, two administrations, from two different parties, have done a mediocre job, at best, of coping with the crisis. Confidence has spiraled downward. Credit has dried up, except for credit that is guaranteed by the government (ultimately by the power to tax, or, in Max Weber's term, the monopoly of force). Foreclosures have risen, along with unemployment. Productivity has fallen, in the United States and elsewhere. International trade has contracted mightily. In response, the United States and other governments around the world have moved decisively, energetically, and effectively to address this global crisis. Here at home, two administrations have moved boldly, even aggressively, to address our problems. And so forth. The fact that this crisis is not now as bad, and does not at this writing look to get as bad, as the Great Depression is hailed as evidence of our wisdom. Really. One need not be particularly angry or disappointed about these shortcomings in our leadership: Once the dominant structure of thought collapsed (that is, because Greenspan was right), then subsequent actions were unlikely to be particularly thoughtful, even when well intentioned. Learning by experience is often awkward.

With little to replace the thinking in which we were trained that has so signally failed, policy elites have excused their (mis)handling of the present situation by emphasizing how strange and bad the crisis is, as if the financial markets were struck by an act of God, a financial "tsunami," for which no one is to blame, and which was not even reasonably foreseeable. Less dramatically, we read that this crisis is "unprecedented," as we are in "uncharted waters." Such characterizations are too convenient. It is financial policy—the understanding of markets that our elites have constructed with great energy over recent years—that has collapsed. Indeed, the staff has hardly changed. The financial crisis is, in some very deep way, the fault of the very elites who are charged with rectifying the situation. Again, and not to mince words, the situation is embarrassing.

One must hope for new thinking to replace the old, and no doubt some such thinking will emerge in due course. Humans cope. But creativity is unpredictable under the best of circumstances. And Washington policy elites rarely have the skills, the inclination, the time, or the space for real thought, much less creativity. The men and women who tend our bureaucracies, and who give our elected officials their talking points, were, almost every one, astonishingly excellent students and diligent underlings, broadly educated and hypercompetent. As adults they are deeply conventional and, in that sense, conservative. Though we have reasons for hope, it is sociologically and psychologically implausible that our administrative agencies will rethink our financial markets at all well and except under extraordinary circumstances. Such is the nature of mandarin bureaucracy and, unfortunately, the situation of our financial policy bureaucracies in this crisis. And so the crisis arose almost unseen and has been badly managed for several years now.

But coping with this crisis is only the immediate task. Without a considered worldview, it is difficult to think about the reform of financial policy. (The word "paradigm" is inevitable but not quite right, as will emerge especially in Chapter 4.) Clearly, financial regulation needs reforming. In light of the tendency of policy elites to deflect responsibility, it is needful to emphasize that U.S. financial policy failed, and by definition. It seems doubtful that this failure was inevitable, though perhaps it was. But just as a conquered nation cannot claim to have had a successful defense policy, after this crisis we cannot claim to have had a very successful financial policy.

Yet the recent failures of U.S. financial regulation are far from total. It should be remembered that the U.S. financial markets are still the deepest and broadest in the world. Although it would be foolish to claim that wise financial regulation caused the success of U.S. capitalism, surely much of modern financial regulation is correct. We are thus presented with difficult analytic problems: Which aspects of our financial regulation failed, and should be reformed, and which should be preserved? Sorting out such difficulties presumes a perspective, perhaps even a philosophy of regulation—just the sort of confident and reasonably principled understanding that we no longer have.

More broadly, modern risk management was rooted in a host of assumptions that, taken together, formed an idealized but nonetheless powerful view of the public and the private, the government and the market. It would not be too much to say that this view was, in a highly capitalized society such as that of the United States and the nascent global society, a sort of constitutional imagination. Marketplace actors were expected to behave in certain ways, and governments were expected to act in certain ways. Investors, whether individuals or institutions, were entitled to rely on such expectations with their funds for education, retirement, health care, and even operating income. To say that this vision is now substantially fractured is also to say that this is not merely a financial crisis, but a political or even a constitutional crisis—we are not so sure how the pieces of our society fit together or should fit together.

The United States is a profoundly capitalistic society. The lives of ordinary people are deeply and directly involved in the capital markets, most obviously through retirement savings. But Americans also rely on the capital markets to provide savings and credit for housing, transportation, education, health care, and many of the pleasures of life. Much the same point may be made institutionally. In the United States, a vibrant civil sector is largely made up of not-for-profit institutions, which are generally dependent upon endowments, that is, on the ability of the financial markets to store and perhaps even increase value. In a very real sense, the old Marxist division between capital and labor no longer applies. We—at least all of us with fair to middling jobs, and so in the middle class—are all capitalists now. This reconfiguration of the relationship to capital is one of the many reasons that Marxism, that is, the ideology that legitimated both Stalin's purges and Mao's "30 percent mistake," the Cultural Revolution, is not due for a revival.

More deeply, the history of modern (since the development of portfolio theory in the 1950s) finance may be understood as the brilliantly successful collective effort to use contract law (financial instruments) to make property more liquid, that is, more like money. The securitization of bank loans is but one, not unimportant, example of this process. Thus what were once local assets—for example, real property—are now owned globally, everywhere and so in some sense nowhere. We may think of this vertiginous reality as not only the globalization, but also the socialization, of capitalism. More on this in due course. For now, it suffices to note that the American citizen outraged over multimillion-dollar bonuses at companies receiving tax dollars, or the Chinese businessperson worried about the fall in U.S. consumer demand, is correct to be engaged—capital markets are key terrain for contemporary political life. By extension, in rethinking financial regulation, we are in a real sense rethinking what we mean by the social and the political.

To suggest that a crisis might be understood as a birth is also to suggest that the current financial crisis may present an intellectual and political opportunity to re-think our understanding of financial markets, and so our understanding of financial regulation, and, more broadly, our understanding of markets and governments—in short, of the capitalism under which we live. Conveniently enough, the Chinese word for "crisis," *wei ji,* also signifies "opportunity," and so perhaps we should view the current financial crisis not only as a very bad thing, which it is, but also as an opportunity for the renewal of our political economy. Maybe we will learn from this crisis and emerge with a better, more responsible, and more humane understanding of our markets. Probably not, but this book nonetheless pursues this hope for the renewal of financial policy and, more broadly, for the way we global citizens think about markets.

It must be stressed that this is a hope, and hopes often do not come true. The fact that a crisis presents an intellectual opportunity does not mean that the opportunity will be seized and that something important will be learned. Most financial crises are fairly uninteresting as a matter of intellectual history and policy thought, however gripping they may be to the participants. Most crises can be more or less comfortably accounted for within existing conceptual frameworks, or acknowledged (and dismissed) as anomalies. For example, very little was learned by the policy community from the Enron ordeal and the accounting scandals, from the implosion of the Silicon Valley bubble, or, perhaps in the case most relevant to the present difficulties, from the failure of Long Term Capital Management. Until September 2008, it looked unlikely that the policy communities would lose faith in their own understandings and find new ways of seeing things. Even as this book goes into production, in the late summer of 2009, the talk emanating from Washington is in many ways very old-fashioned, well within existing paradigms, however discredited. Not that this is very surprising. Establishments are, by definition, set in their ways. We have no guarantee that as a society we will learn from the present financial crisis instead of merely enduring it.

Today one hears a great many explanations and proposals that may be more or less true or wise, but that are well rehearsed, part of established discourses, and so—to be blunt—irrelevant to the question of whether we stand at a historic moment of financial policy, and so, in a capitalist society, at a historic moment in our constitutional imagination. Arguments about failures of boards of directors, regulatory negligence, the imprudence of government bailouts, the greed of executives, and the like fall into this category. Little is said that has not been said countless times before. More subtly, genealogical explanations of the crisis as a tale of subprime mortgages gone terribly wrong (of crazed lower-class borrowers and/or fantastically successful Shylocks) are like accounts of derivatives markets that begin with farmers selling futures contracts on harvests to come, just true enough to be distracting. Worse, such explanations subtly provide comfort, by rendering familiar patterns of thought barely plausible and sparing us the anxiety of trying, and quite possibly failing, to think anew.

There seem to be two prerequisites for the renewal of policy thought: first, a big event or set of events, and second, the emergence of a substantively new consensus. The week of Sunday, September 14, 2008, should have provided sufficiently big news to occasion rethinking. To recall: It was announced that Lehman Brothers, an ancient firm with global operations, was insolvent, and its bankruptcy filing, and failure to trade, Monday morning triggered a global wave of insolvencies, with many firms saved only by massive government interventions. Meanwhile, Merrill Lynch, the nation's largest securities broker and a huge investment bank, was sold under duress to Bank of America. On Monday, the Dow Jones Industrial Average (DJIA) fell 504 points. On Tuesday, AIG, which recently had been the world's largest insurer, was failing and received the first tranche of many billions of dollars. On Wednesday, credit markets worldwide froze. It must be admitted that, even after the unreal morning of Monday, September 15, we were subjected to a slew of rationalizations as pundits and others tried to preserve the traditional way of seeing things, but these turned out to be like the epicycles that were used to square the Ptolemaic model of the solar system with observations of planets that were not where they were "supposed" to be. The next weeks brought more excitement. The last of the big investment banks, Morgan Stanley and Goldman Sachs, were allowed to become bank holding companies, and Washington Mutual failed—the largest bank collapse in U.S. history. The congressional failure to authorize a $700 billion rescue package nominally agreed upon by both parties was met by one of the largest single day point drops ever in New York Stock Exchange history. Such dramatic events, especially the death of venerable institutions, many of which had survived for a century or more, should prompt all but the willfully obtuse to reconsider our capital markets.

The second requirement for a substantial rethinking of our financial markets—the emergence of a new consensus—has proven elusive. Thinking is hard, and innovation is by nature ephemeral (that much, at least, of the Efficient Capital Markets Hypothesis is correct). The real difficulty with creating a new policy consensus, however, is not intellectual, but political. It is not enough to have new ideas, even good new ideas. Intellectuals can generate new ideas without much difficulty; ideas as such are relatively cheap. But ideas are not politically significant until powerful parties believe them. Thus, in order to rethink our financial markets, we need ideas that the Washington establishment can believe in—even though they were trained and have made their careers on the basis of different understandings of the world. As has already been suggested, such wholesale self-denial does not happen very often; establishments are conservative.

In the abstract, of course, the shock of events, with ancient giants like Merrill and Lehman gone, and AIG falling, would seem to demand fundamental rethinking on the part of policy intellectuals as well as the formation of a new policy consensus, what we teach in schools and place in op-eds and expect to hear in confirmation hearings and professional luncheons, the imaginations that inform our policies, institutions, and laws. But there is no guarantee that a consensus will form, that people will agree on a relatively consistent set of new ideas, especially in times of stress. Losses of faith in shared intellectual frameworks, and the construction of a new frameworks, along with changes in confidence in given markets, perhaps auction-rate securities or commercial paper offered by structured investment vehicles (SIVs), raise questions of collective psychology, how people believe together, and so think and communicate with one another, do business. It is very difficult to know how such questions will be answered. It is therefore difficult to know whether communities of discourse, especially the U.S. Congress, will develop new ways of understanding political economy. As of this writing, the news is not too good.

And yet, even here, there is reason for hope. The pressure of events begs explanation; surprising circumstances may inspire us to rethink our old assumptions. Perhaps events cannot force us to be creative or to reach agreement. But events certainly can give us plenty to talk about, keeping issues "on the table." Intellectual discourse, and hence policy discourse, can be transformed by changing social realities, sometimes quite suddenly. John Kenneth Galbraith's words, from over fifty years ago, resonate today:

> I am not wholly barren of hope, for circumstances have been dealing the conventional wisdom a new series of heavy blows. It is only after such damage has been done, as we have seen, that ideas have their opportunity.
> ... Ideas are inherently conservative. They yield not to the attack of other ideas but to the massive onslaught of circumstances with which they cannot contend.[2]

If Galbraith was right, then we should look for intellectual and political opportunities in the very seriousness of this crisis, and particularly its surprising aspects. This effort to rethink our financial markets is not, at bottom, situated within the United States. It is true that specific aspects of U.S. policy, such as federal encouragement of home ownership through mortgage debt securitization, and easy money as a response to various difficulties, have informed how the financial crisis has unfolded in the United States and so elsewhere. But sticking with these examples, and there are of course others, U.S. housing debt was sold worldwide, and the easy money for which Greenspan is now widely blamed arose in the context of, among other things, a symbiotic and problematic relationship with China, terrorist attacks, and wars—international security concerns. It is trite to say that markets are global, but they are.

More deeply and perhaps less obviously, the scope of capitalist social thought is global rather than national. As Louis Pasteur touchingly said, science knows no country. That is, insofar as we take seriously the proposition that the risk-management paradigm has collapsed, then this is a crisis at the heart of an intellectual tradition, finance. But finance is practiced all over the world, in China and Latin America and Europe and Africa—to name a few places affected by the crisis. The University of Chicago is not just in Illinois, and the financial crisis raises questions of intellectual history, a history by no means confined to the United States. What was the grammar through which we thought, and not incidentally constructed, financial markets? Can we already discern the outlines of a new paradigm, or, more precisely, an emergent aesthetics or imagination of markets, and hence of the conduct of financial regulation?

The stakes are quite high. This book is written in part to help draw the curtain over an era of especially striking irresponsibility on the part of officials in both the so-called public and private sectors. It is silly and unhealthy to rage, especially because irresponsibility is a characteristic sin of both government bureaucrats and financiers, but there is little point in denying that my hope for a revived political economy is grounded in real anger and no small amount of fear. The strategy here is simple enough:

- On an epistemological level, and as suggested above by reference to Benjamin in lieu of Marx, political economy should make the turn to interpretation that the other humane sciences have made. The "rethinking" of this book's title is meant quite literally—we have been thinking about our financial markets, and therefore political economy more generally, in the wrong mode.
- On an ontological level, it is high time that we revive and extend the social understanding of markets, that is, the minor tradition of economic thought running back through Galbraith and Kindleberger (and even Samuelson, to some extent) to Keynes and Knight, Veblen, Maus, Durkheim, Weber, and yes, Marx, albeit in his less than scientific (easily authoritarian) moments. Understanding markets socially, as a way of doing politics, would bridge the division between left and right that deeply structures economic policy across what is uncritically called the political spectrum.
- On the level of political morality, conceiving of financial markets as ways of doing politics should help those on the left to be less squeamish about markets, those on the right to lose their fear of the social, and bureaucrats of all dispositions to take more responsibility for the structures through which our society constructs itself.

This book sets forth an interpretation of the financial crisis as a matter of intellectual history, and then explores what such an understanding might mean for policymakers who understand markets as a preferred mode of governance and who take at least limited responsibility for our social structures. In short, this book is a map, however sketchy, of a third way.

*   *   *

As mentioned in the Preface, the usual way to approach problematic events, for purposes of both analysis and explication, is by telling a story. So books like this generally offer their own versions of what "really" happened. And if the books offer reflections on the revolution, as this one does, then the story is likely to have the following, by now conventional, structure, which serves to make the radically new seem understandable, perhaps even necessary.

This crisis is often said to be the most significant since the 1930s, which begs the question: Will future institutions, law, and regulation hearken back to 2008/2009 as a time of rupture, rebellion, and founding? Is this a time of policy revolution, using "revolution" in a sense like Thomas Kuhn's idea of scientific revolution, a time when an old paradigm is no longer felt, within the relevant discursive community, to be able to cope with contemporary realities, and new paradigms are demanded and constructed? Is this a time for a renewal of capitalism, or at least a revision of the way we understand our capitalism?

Revolutionary thought mediates between three times: the present crisis brought on by the oppressive establishment, mocked as the ancien régime; the future, as represented by the revolutionaries; and a distant past, whose virtues must be recovered. If this proves to be a time of conceptual revolution, then the role of the ancien régime will be played by the policy consensus that arose in the 1970s, and that has dominated economics, business, and law faculties since the 1980s; that has ruled the Federal Reserve since former chair Paul Volcker in the late 1970s; and that has shaped the International Monetary Fund (IMF) and the World Bank for much the same period. As remarked in the Preface, this cultural understanding has different names in different contexts: neoliberal, the Washington consensus, Chicago School economics, the law and economics movement, and so forth. (There is something more than a little funny about Harvard's assemblage of financial luminaries to discuss the present crisis, the academic equivalent of a gathering of nobles to consider that annoying unrest in the streets.)

All revolutions are, as the name says, returns, even if only partially successful. In the present crisis, if the role of the ancien régime is represented by orthodox neoliberalism, then the distant past must surely be the 1930s, when government acted swiftly and surely to restore confidence in the markets. Or so a nation must believe if it contemplates suddenly charging its taxpayers with costs equivalent to the out-of-pocket expense of a medium-sized war in order to provide markets with "confidence." We are all Keynesians now, even if we do not admit it, and even though the world of the 1930s neither can nor should be re-created. So, as discussed below, if this time is revolutionary, it will in many ways resemble, yet be substantially different from, the liberalism that grew out of the New Deal.

Although this sort of story has its attractions, I want to resist the urge to ground our present situation in a revolutionary tale, with an answer ideologically foretold. The purpose of this book, after all, is to begin rethinking our financial markets, and thereby how we understand our capitalism. And in order to get ready to do this, I want to emphasize just how strange our intellectual situation is, how much has changed, and hurriedly, in what we assume, if not necessarily admit, about markets. The game is different; the intellectual goalposts have been moved. The next chapter discusses some of the more salient differences between what has become suddenly obvious, already decided, about our financial markets and the ideology that we believed, and that some of us published and taught, not long ago.

Part I

On Our Situation

Chapter 1

The Suddenly Obvious and the Already Decided

Wₕₐₜ ᴀꜱᴘᴇᴄᴛꜱ ᴏꜰ ᴛʜᴇ ᴏʟᴅ ᴜɴᴅᴇʀꜱᴛᴀɴᴅɪɴɢ ᴏꜰ ꜰɪɴᴀɴᴄɪᴀʟ ᴍᴀʀᴋᴇᴛꜱ ɴᴏw seem compromised, perhaps simply wrong? What are the immediate intellectual consequences of this crisis for financial policy thought? Going forward, how might this rethinking shape our policy and so the reconfiguration of our financial markets?

A caveat: This chapter discusses some general consequences of the crisis for our intellectual situation. Later chapters are more pragmatic, and therefore necessarily somewhat more specific. But the reader who hopes this book will provide definitive answers to the practical problems raised by the crisis will be disappointed. Such a reader is asking the wrong question: There are real limitations on the extent to which an intellectual, operating in the abstract, should offer specific advice to responsible decisionmakers. The world has plenty of armchair generals, Monday morning quarterbacks, and garrulous academics. Instead of second guesses, a book such as this should attempt to take advantage of critical distance to provide cooler analysis and a longer view than is available to those in the trenches, perhaps accompanied by a few tentative and general suggestions by way of demonstrating a desire to be constructive. As a good friend often puts it, "I am not in charge," and I offer my sympathies to those who are.

This chapter discusses ideas that are reasonably obvious, rather immediate consequences of recent events. It may be too much to say that these ideas are already decided—human folly knows few bounds—but indulging the rationalistic delusions common to this sort of book, I would say that certain ideas that were widely held until recently have now lost their credibility, which means that certain ideological issues have been settled, bridges crossed. And it is from the other side of such bridges that we should begin financial policy anew. The bridges themselves, the shocks of ignorance and rejection that accompany the collapse of a worldview, thus serve as prefaces, at most introductions, to a renewal of financial thinking. And so it should also be admitted that as mere prefatory remarks that introduce a possible outlook for financial policy, the ideas discussed in this chapter are not very profound.

If we as a society learn even these likely lessons, however, we will have constituted a substantially new imagination of finance and, thereby, of our very financial society. Although I personally believe these lessons to be true, truth is not exactly the issue. Many propositions are true; few become politically significant. But political significance, in the ordinary sense of the word "political," is not the issue, either. The issue is something more foundational, constitutional for this capitalist society, if not quite mathematically axiomatic. What are the fundamental attitudes with which the next generation might approach capital markets?

These new policy realities should be made explicit so that they can be thought through and discussed. Such articulation is a core, perhaps the core, obligation of the intellectual in democratic life. And in such an articulation it is important to pay serious attention to the embarrassing differences between what is emerging as a new status quo normal and the intellectual and professional (literally, what was professed, believed) life of the very recent past.

Efficiency Cannot Be Presumed; Financial Markets Are Frequently Inefficient

Adam Smith, with the image of the invisible hand, most influentially expressed the idea that the common good was achieved through the competitive interaction of relatively autonomous and self-interested actors in a field called the "market." And the hope that this is the case, or might be the case, underlies every political decision to use a competitive market, rather than some other social mechanism, to accomplish one of society's tasks. Certainly throughout the long struggle with those who espoused Marxism, it was widely argued that markets were superior modes of social, and in that broad sense, political, choice.

In academic finance it was said that markets were informationally efficient. The price mechanism created incentives for, and expressed, vast quantities of information, and did so more rapidly and accurately than any individual, or any bureaucracy charged with central planning, could. In the academy during the 1970s and 1980s, this argument was carried to its logical conclusions. Beginning at roughly the same time and continuing into the present, financial markets have become increasingly automated. Paper records were replaced with electronic records; order flow became electronically communicated; computerized trading strategies were developed; computerized modes of trade execution replaced auctions, so that electronic trading mechanisms replaced open outcry pits; and market participants around the globe were integrated, "networked." So financial markets came to be loosely and more or less consciously understood, on the model of cybernetics as recursive, self-correcting, informational systems. Markets were, in short, social computers, aggregating all of the information available to each market participant. Price thus represented a collective judgment, formed on the best possible data. More subtly, computer science and economics finally seemed to have found ways to account for social phenomena, markets, using the sorts of mathematics that had been so successful in describing physical phenomena. Wall Street started hiring physicists. Even in the heyday of what came to be called the Efficient Capital Markets Hypothesis, however, it was broadly understood that even informationally efficient markets (the model was the U.S. equity market) are not omniscient. Price changes reflect news, which is by definition unpredictable (if an event is predicted, it is not news, but instead is "priced in"). And sometimes microeconomic transactions have effects that are not reflected in the property regime and the price (the transaction imposes externalities). And, although this was believed to be rare, sometimes market actors have the power to set prices ("extract rents"). But, in the main, markets were thought to work very well, because they produce and express the closest thing to truths, especially about welfare and the future, that can be expected in human affairs. All of this became banal after the fall of the Berlin Wall; the unconscious rationality of the market evidently was the way to organize matters. While slightly imperfect, markets were viewed as oracular, and therefore the preferred mechanism for governance, a view espoused even in China and even after the present crisis got under way.

The importance, for contemporary financial policy and the academy, of the conception of "efficiency" caricatured here cannot be overstated. In the United States, the concept of efficiency oriented the single most important legal perspective in generations, law and economics. In politics, as an ideal, efficiency legitimated, and to large degree genuinely informed, the deregulation of financial industries, notably for the Reagan and Thatcher administrations, but also worldwide, if perhaps less enthusiastically. Much U.S. foreign policy, vis-à-vis both developed and developing countries, was organized by efficiency and functionally equivalent terms such as "growth" and "competitiveness."

The idea that a price reflects a fairly accurate collective assessment of the "value" of an asset, or class of assets, is problematic after one's first market correction (perhaps the 1987 market break), but becomes simply implausible after multiple bubbles expand and pop, and as several companies that had been around for more than a century suddenly disappear one week in September, with good weather and no "real" disasters on the horizon. When equity markets worldwide lose something like 50 percent of their value in a short time, the proposition that price discovery had been working in such markets begins to seem silly. Rephrased, volatility undercuts the plausibility of the claim that the price on a given day means anything much.

More important for present purposes, recent U.S. policy tacitly belies the idea that prices are efficient—that is, that a competitive marketplace can be relied upon to use a price mechanism to make sound social choices about which companies survive and which disappear. Consider the following:

1. Many banks have argued that they should not be forced to account for their assets, notably including loans, on a "mark-to-market" basis, that is, at the price the loan would fetch if the bank were to sell it today. The banks have argued that markets regularly underprice assets, especially when, as now, there is no liquid market for much of what banks hold. This may be the case, and perhaps regulators should allow banks to use methods of accounting other than mark-to-market. Such regulation would presume, however, that the market price oftentimes is not the true, sensible price, if by "price" we mean a collective social judgment about value.

As a policy matter, the argument against mark-to-market reflects the fear that, if banks were to account for their assets based upon their daily market price, then many banks would be insolvent. To which the riposte is that both the value of assets and the insolvency of commercial enterprises traditionally have been considered to be matters that, in a free enterprise system, should be decided by markets. In shielding banks from mark-to-market accounting, and hence from insolvency, we are necessarily asserting that some social values (the stability of banks, perhaps) are not best decided by markets. Evidently, price is a partial mechanism of social choice, and therefore not efficient in the grand sense that markets were routinely and publicly proclaimed to be well into the presidential election of 2008.

2. Similarly, the government has acquired bank assets, either directly or as collateral, in exchange for liquidity, at a price far above the market price. (If banks were satisfied with the market price, then the government's actions would be superfluous.) In "overpaying" for the assets, the government implicitly maintains that the assets are underpriced in the market. But if the current market price of the asset is too low, then the market is inefficient—certain values are not reflected in the market price of the assets. Perhaps, but implausibly, the government perceives value in the assets that is invisible even to hedge funds and other highly sophisticated investors. More likely, the government values things that the marketplace does not. The government may well believe that the survival of certain banks and other institutions is in the public interest, even if such institutions have been insolvent or threatened by insolvency. Whether or not the government's judgments are correct is not here the point; the point is that the government has substituted its institutional decision for a marketplace judgment. In so doing, the Federal Reserve and the Treasury have necessarily taken the position that they, rather than market solvency, will be the mechanism that decides whether certain large institutions are viable.

3. As the price of equities in various investment banks and other financial institutions came under substantial downward pressure, the Securities and Exchange

Commission (SEC) suspended short selling in the equities of such companies. Although short sellers are never popular with corporate management (who likes to be bet against?), as a theoretical matter the practice of short selling makes a lot of sense as an aid to price discovery, that is, the process by which markets assign values. Short sellers have incentives to find out which companies are weak, despite what the companies may say to the contrary. Short sellers therefore add to the store of information available to the market, making the price more accurate, hence "price discovery." This, at any rate, was dogma for over a generation. For the SEC to block short selling, then, is for the agency to suggest that markets are not (at least short-selling markets are not) the proper venue for deciding the fate of financial institutions.

The SEC's antipathy to short sellers is nothing new: It has long been argued that short selling can be destructive. Betting against a company may cause other investors to flee the company, not because they have a specific idea of why the company will fail, but because they believe either that the company has some flaw that they do not know about, and they do not want to wait to find out what it is (smart money is getting out, so I better sell), or because they believe that the company cannot survive the wave of short selling. In a world in which investors exhibit herd behavior, short selling may constitute a self-fulfilling prophecy, ruining otherwise sound companies. (Something like this happened to Bear Stearns: Rumors that the firm had liquidity problems caused other firms to deny credit, causing liquidity problems.) So arguments against short selling may be right, but they rest on the assertion that trading may take place on the basis of something other than real information about the company, and to the extent that this assertion is true, equity traders must be characterized as easily persuaded, and their market as something less than informationally efficient.

And yet what we believe and what we say we believe are often very different things. After a few generations of scholarship on the rationality of markets, and perhaps more important, political arguments, regulations, and even laws presuming that markets are efficient, absent conclusive evidence to the contrary, it has become difficult to think about markets without the concept of efficiency. In fact, one way to understand this book is as an effort to begin reconsidering financial policy, and indeed capitalism, without too much reliance on the concept of efficiency. This may not be as difficult as it at first may sound. As a way of reimagining the financial markets, one could do worse than "Mr. Market," the personification of "bid and ask" created by Depression-era finance professor Benjamin Graham. (Poetically enough, in the fall of 2008 Graham's most famous student, Warren Buffett, bought substantial equity in Goldman Sachs, the last investment bank—a literal revolution, that is, a return, in financial thought and action.) Mr. Market is what in Graham's day was called manic depressive, and we might call bipolar—anything but rational. Mr. Market calls every day, buying and selling stocks. On some days, Mr. Market is wildly optimistic about the fortunes of various companies and will pay outlandish prices for stocks, but will only sell at even higher prices. On other days, Mr. Market is darkly gloomy and will his sell stock for a song, but has no desire to buy, since these companies will only fail. There are two tricks: first, to sell to Mr. Market on his happy days, and conversely to buy on his sad days, and second, to remember that Mr. Market will be back again tomorrow.

The image of both individual and collective market behavior as irrational—and pricing as therefore commonly inefficient—is academically buttressed by recent work in behavioral economics (psychologists have never claimed that anybody was very rational). In fact, nobody but economists ever claimed anybody was rational, and a great achievement of behavioral economics is to make irrationality cognizable in an economic idiom.

Corporations Cannot Be Relied Upon to Self-Regulate

In fairness to the lost worldview, it is one thing to argue that individuals are not rational. Reason may be the slave of the passions; the superego may struggle to overcome the ego and id; rationality in a multiparty enterprise may require dictatorship. It is quite another thing, however, to argue that modern bureaucratic institutions—not just corporations, but governments, law faculties, and departments of economics and psychology, too—are not rational. After all, rationality is widely thought to be intrinsic to being modern. And Wall Street is neither an individual nor an institution, but an environment that, it was claimed, was the domain of reason, rationality, because mistakes were corrected, and those who made big mistakes were ruthlessly eliminated, in Darwinian fashion.

As a policy matter, for some decades it was argued that no more substantial regulation of financial market actors (or their instruments or activities) was required, because such entities regulated themselves. (Really.) So accounting firms, credit rating agencies, derivatives, hedge funds, private equity funds, the proprietary trading operations of any number of more highly regulated entities, special purpose entities of various sorts, and sundry private markets (some actually called "dark pools") all escaped substantial regulation. Collectively, these entities made up what has been called the "shadow financial system." By the same logic, even as financial industries evolved and new products were developed, expressing new opportunities with new risks (for examples, collateralized loan obligations [CLOs], collateralized debt obligations [CDOs], credit default swaps [CDSs], and an inexhaustible array of over-the-counter [OTC] arrangements), additional regulation for traditionally highly regulated entities, such as banks, brokerage houses, and exchanges, was deemed an unnecessary drag on innovation. In 2004, the SEC relaxed the capital requirements on the biggest investment banks, largely responsible for the creation and marketing of these new products, and the banks promptly began doing business with leverage ratios of thirty to one. As late as the fall of 2008, after admitting that the risk management edifice had collapsed, Alan Greenspan told Congress that additional regulation was hardly required, because this time Wall Street had learned its lesson about prudent investment, and would go forth and sin no more.

Maybe the idea that economic actors, mostly limited liability entities such as corporations, regulate themselves seems so sensible because we imagine economic actors to be individual people, perhaps even the prudent investors of securities law mythology. (It is worth noting that classical and neoclassical economics, as well as behavioral economics, take the individual as the focus of inquiry—this is known as the virtue of methodological individualism. Institutional economics had to be invented later and has never held center stage in policy consciousness.) Prudent folk run their business affairs, well, prudently, and in the jargon, they are both risk averse and rational. And business corporations, including Wall Street firms, are made up of businessmen (mostly) and -women—so why shouldn't we expect business corporations to be run prudently? Besides, if businesses are irrational, or take on too much risk, then in a competitive market they will be eliminated. Thus the idea that markets self-regulate is based upon a tacit imagination of the corporation as a risk-averse and rational individual, reliably disciplined by its competitors. Let us take these claims in order, to get some sense of why such sensible arguments have been so deeply wrong.

Risk Aversion

Without unduly complicated metaphysics, it is possible to imagine that those who control an organization will so identify with the institution that they cause it to act in its own long-term interest, that is, cautiously. Although neoclassical economics dismissed the phenomenon of devotion (as violative of economic rationality and methodological individualism), we observe devotion every day, in churches, the military, government service, and the academy. In the financial arena, organizations that rely on devotion traditionally are structured as partnerships, or otherwise closely held. They do not tend to be publicly traded corporations with massive bonus plans, a shareholder-driven focus on quarterly earnings, and a great deal of leverage. So we saw the investment banking industry shift its institutional form, from partnerships to corporations, and rather shortly thereafter, disappear. Retail banks, with their insured depositors and regulatory oversight, were precluded from taking on quite so much risk, and some are left standing, though often with government help. Correlation may not be causation, but may nonetheless give one pause.

The traditional purpose of any limited liability entity is to provide a vehicle that can pool capital and take on risk. Corporation law since the nineteenth century has worried that risk-hungry corporations would be underfunded, and that creditors, or in the present instance, the federal government, would be left holding the bag. Much the same could be said about the webs of limited partnerships and limited liability companies (LLCs) through which hedge fund business is conducted. The shadow financial system teaches the rather old lesson that an institutional structure that may be ideal for high-tech startups, in which failures are expected, might need some adjustments—that is, more regulation—for use in the financial system, where failures may pose dangers to society at large.

Rationality

We should have learned from Long Term Capital Management, or certainly from Enron, that an organization of even modest size in which numerous participants are empowered to obligate the organization can quickly develop a web of contingent liabilities too complex for the organization, or its counterparties, to monitor effectively. In short, a company may have no real account of its own position. In such situations, to speak of the corporation acting "rationally" is overly generous.

There is much more to say, of course, about what we might mean by "rationality" and why we do not reliably achieve it in business life (and much more will be said later in this chapter and throughout this book). For now, though, it suffices to say that corporations are mechanisms through which people act collectively. In such a collective, delegation is necessary. It is a considerable feat (and part of what we mean by civilization) to keep the collective moving in the same general direction. And, in the marketplace, outcomes reflect not the collective action of a single organization, but the collectivity (society) formed by the interaction of institutions. To assume that such social action will be in line with some idea of the common good, and therefore that regulation need not be seriously considered, strains credulity. But such was the power of the invisible hand.

Competition

As Adam Smith well knew, life in competitive markets, where prices converge on marginal costs and profits are minimal, is exceedingly unpleasant. Therefore, producers traditionally have been expected to try and secure monopolies, form cartels, and otherwise restrain trade whenever possible in order to protect their positions from would-be rivals and generally make life easier for themselves. Such efforts to improve the life of producers raise prices for consumers. In response, competition law, for historical reasons called "antitrust law" in the United States, traditionally has sought to foster competitive markets in which producers are forced to offer their goods at a low ("competitive") price relative to their cost, or else go out of business. In such markets, it might be said that the market disciplines producers: The power of each producer to set prices is limited by the competition from other producers. (A similar story could be told for the less common case in which a buyer enjoys market power, called a monopsony.)

In recent years, when markets have been presumed to be efficient, it has been assumed that they must be competitive, since competition is the source of market efficiency. Now it might seem to the neophyte that "competition" would require competitors, that is, actual market actors able to deliver a comparable good at an attractive price. Observation of actual markets will reveal that for many goods, such competitors do not exist or, more commonly and subtly, offer goods that are superficially comparable but actually sold in different markets, or are comparable, but the putative competitors do not seem to compete very hard. And yet such markets must be competitive, or else how could they be so efficient? The answer, it was successfully argued for many years, is that would-be monopolists (that is, producers) are effectively disciplined by the threat of new entrants into the market. They do not exercise their market power to raise prices and enjoy enormous profits because doing so would attract competitors, who might, in turn, force them from the market.

Such behavior can be empirically observed. In the United States, corporations generally have tried to keep from making much money and almost never go bankrupt. Since each business niche in the U.S. economy is, and long has been, occupied by a corporation functioning just above marginal cost, Americans rarely establish new companies. And because, in the United States, market actors have almost always been so well disciplined by actual or threatened competition, no government action has been required. As ridiculous as all of this now sounds, since the 1970s a great deal of deregulation, indeed the substantial dismantling of traditional antitrust law, proceeded on pretty much this basis.

Only once a worldview has shifted do its solipsisms become so obvious. If, however, we do not presume that markets are efficient, there is no reason to assume, a priori, that they are competitive or disciplined by the threat of some competition over the horizon. In fact we observe quite a lot of market power, and indeed, quite a lot of entries into markets, presumably in efforts to earn profits considerably above marginal cost, implying the conquest of a bit of pricing power. Which is not to say that competition does not occur—clearly it does. It is to say that competition cannot be presumed; and therefore market discipline cannot be presumed; and therefore self-regulation cannot be presumed; and therefore government regulation may be prudent.

To put the matter slightly differently: In an age enamored of business, it is easy to think that business virtues (and businesses do have their virtues) flow directly from the profit motive. It has been easy to believe that businesses self-regulate (and innovate, efficiently and creatively, and so forth) simply because they are businesses. But this is not, and never has been, the case. Structuring a business on a for-profit basis is not enough to ensure that ownership interests in that business are subject to market discipline, and without market discipline (as corporation law and antitrust law have long taught), corporations will exercise their market power to the benefit of shareholders and managers (who are also shareholders), but not necessarily to the institution's long-term benefit, and certainly not doing the work of the invisible hand.

Competition is in particularly short supply during a period of expanding opportunity, for the simple reason that every firm has work, something to do, and most of all, buyers. Over the past generation, the financial industries have grown in absolute terms and as a share of the U.S. economy. For most of my adult lifetime, with brief and mild interruptions, bull market followed bull market. It now seems obvious that for a variety of reasons the world was awash with liquidity, many of the new opportunities were illusory, and the expansion was to great extent a bubble. Whether an expansion subsequently proves to be a bubble, and if so to what extent, is not at issue here. At the time it is an expansion, an era of plenty and opportunity—and therefore competition, and market discipline, decline. As a Chinese businessman said, speaking of the country's recent wondrous growth, you did not have to be good. You had to be there.

The long bull market running up to the current crisis provides any number of examples of lack of market discipline. The operations of Fannie Mae and Freddie Mac, which were able to borrow at below market rates because they could rely on an implicit government guarantee (a guarantee indeed honored in the fall of 2008), were not subject to market discipline, a fact reflected in their market share. Credit rating agencies formed a cartel and made fine money by telling investment banks what they wanted to hear. The investment banking industry appears to have been run largely for its management and upper-level employees, who routinely received huge bonuses. Shareholders in these firms did not care overly much, so long as share prices rose, which, in a bubble, they obligingly did. It is not clear that shareholders could have done much about Wall Street compensation practices anyway, because despite scandals and new rules requiring disclosure of pay arrangements, executive compensation at even badly run companies continued to rise. And so forth … in short, there is no reason to assume that, in a rather chaotic bubble market, corporations are disciplined by their competitors and therefore can be trusted to govern themselves prudently.

Smart Money Often Is Not

When it was believed that markets were efficient, and efficiency was understood in terms of information, it was easy to be overly impressed with the quantity and quality of information possessed by financial institutions. Wall Street players had the best financial and mathematical know-how, information technology, and legal talent that money could buy. Surely information matters for making wise investments, and Wall Street's systems for the gathering, analysis, dissemination, and exploitation of information are the best the world has ever seen. Information networks span the globe, and now that the transmission of data is instant and, on its terms, perfect, it would seem that little more could be asked—investment has never been so transparent. Similarly, with regard to valuation and risk management, broadly construed, the financial industries are more sophisticated, especially mathematically sophisticated, than ever before—and investment in a global market certainly requires some smarts. Fortunately, the computerization of exchanges, of trading, and of pricing strategies has made financial analysis rigorous, and pricing and therefore trading strategies precise, to degrees never seen before. So when it came, the crisis was surprising, because it was impossible, more precisely, unimaginable. In this one regard, "tsunami" (Japanese for "harbor wave") is a good image, a wave of destruction that emerges in a place of safety, with no cause in sight.

The brilliant execution of a flawed and ultimately vulnerable plan may well be fatal. In 2008, institutions that had survived far worse, most notably the grinding decade of the Great Depression, disappeared in months. Which is not to deny that financial institutions have not suffered in the current crisis; they have. But suffering is no guarantee of virtue. In particular, the fact that fools die does not make them less foolish. The failure of an architect's design, an intellectual edifice, can have real consequences for those who live in the building. Many institutions whose strategies were based upon the risk management edifice failed, and some remaining institutions have had the success, market share and otherwise, typically garnered by survivors of a disaster.

In the 1980s and through the 1990s, old Wall Street firms incorporated themselves and held initial public offerings that netted the erstwhile partners huge sums of money. The New York Stock Exchange itself was converted from a trading facility, which long and bizarrely had been organized as a not-for-profit, into a publicly traded company. The Dow Jones "Industrial" Average began to include representatives of the finance "industry." At some point, investing *in* Wall Street became as common as investing *on* Wall Street. And the money flowed in, from across the United States and around the world. But what was Wall Street selling? Financial expertise. Which Wall Street was uniquely qualified to package and (re)sell. The total value of investments in various financial markets exceeded the value of the things the markets were ostensibly about, oil and corporate debt and whatnot; the financial economy grew larger than the real economy. There was, in short, a bubble in finance, which has been followed in due course by an "epistemological depression," a collapse of faith not just in the market for some asset, perhaps residential real estate, but in a way of looking at markets, modern finance, the soft capital of so many of the institutions and especially instruments that have now failed.[1]

Chapters 3 and 4 discuss information (transparency) and sophistication (portfolio theory and risk management) in some detail, but for now it is enough to note that the problem here is not a lack of information, or a lack of sophistication, in the ordinary sense. The institutions that have been destroyed, or badly hurt, had vast quantities of information and stunning expertise at their disposal going into the crisis. Going forward and as a matter of policy, it would seem to follow that more information, or more sophistication, in the ordinary sense cannot be the answer, just as more debt cannot be the last word. So it is wrongheaded, for example, to blame the collapse of Lehman Brothers on the board's age and lack of savvy. Sophisticated enthusiasm for finance was part of the problem. But how do we (unsophisticatedly?) think about the dangers, for the financial system, of financial virtues? Surely we will need good information and sophistication going forward, just as surely as we are incurring debts in our efforts to stimulate the economy. Such conceptual difficulties are part of what it means to have a worldview in crisis.

At this juncture, however, at least two aspects of "smart money" seem very obvious. First, simply insisting on more information and technical savvy is not the answer. As much as we might like to blame others (the topic of Chapter 2), this crisis is a failure of an elite in the exercise of their virtues, and it is inadequate to address such failures with some version of "be more elite." We need to think about how this elite, of which most readers who have made it this far in the text can fairly be called members, failed.

Second, there is a reason that we speak not just of bubbles, but of "manias" and "the madness of crowds" and even "panics." Even very smart people go crazy, sometimes in their own special way. Intelligence provides no good answers to the wrong questions; it is worth recalling that no less a mind than Isaac Newton lost money in the South Seas bubble.

Moral Hazard Is Academic

"Moral hazard," a phrase with its roots in insurance, has entered public discourse and thereby acquired a broad range of meanings. The phrase is used here in a specific sense that has been influential in U.S. regulatory discourse in recent years: "Moral hazard" is the idea that government should refrain from intervening in markets because the expectation of government aid will cause market actors to take on more risk than they efficiently should. That is, the expectation of government action weakens marketplace discipline. Moral hazard arguments tend to be used to support conservative positions: Government should not regulate and should otherwise stay out of markets, it is asserted, so that markets will be comprised solely by risk-averse and rational actors. In particular, government should refrain from rescuing insolvent market participants, that is, refrain from what is popularly known as a "bailout." Be that as it may, in late 2007 and throughout 2008, the Bush administration repeatedly found itself confronted with marketplace actors that were on the brink of insolvencies that credibly threatened the financial system. In virtually every such situation, the Bush administration intervened in the marketplace, making federal funds available to the troubled institutions. That is, when push came to shove, the Bush administration used tax dollars to intervene in "private" markets—a classically liberal move, in the American sense of the word. In the one case in which the Bush administration did not intervene to save the company, the insolvency of the investment bank Lehman Brothers, credit markets froze overnight. The collateral of many institutions in many places was seized, insolvencies bloomed, and what had been widely regarded as a U.S. financial crisis went global.[2] At least in hindsight, and although the circumstances were admittedly difficult, the Bush administration's failure to intervene decisively enough to prevent the sudden insolvency of Lehman Brothers is now almost universally regarded as a big mistake.

Whether the failure to save Lehman Brothers, or the interventions on behalf of other institutions, was well advised is not the issue here. What we have learned is that when confronted with a credible threat of systemic risk, the most ideologically conservative administration in recent memory in the developed world will use tax dollars to intervene in financial markets. Even though the Bush administration had a strikingly laissez-faire approach to financial market regulation, and so presumably took moral hazard arguments seriously, such general commitments simply did not stack up against the fear of a specific systemic risk, in every case but Lehman Brothers, and not entirely in that case. If the Bush administration was willing to intervene in such circumstances, than any Democratic administration, or any administration in any other developed country, can be expected to intervene in such situations as well. Thus, at least when systemic risk is a credible possibility, moral hazard may become merely an academic argument. Moral hazard, that is, may be a policy consideration, but it does not constitute a politically serious argument against intervention. The financial crisis has changed the intellectual status and political influence of a key element of financial policy discourse.

Uncertainty Is Real, and Different from Risk

When discussing uncertainty, the issue is comfort: Is the investor sufficiently comfortable to purchase? Investors who are not comfortable—who are not at all certain they know what they are talking about—will not invest. And so we have seen credit markets (or the market for Enron stock) dry up almost overnight as investors come to the realization that they have no idea whether their counterparties will be there tomorrow. In December 2008, U.S. Treasuries were for the first time purchased with negative yields—it made sense to park funds, lose a small but known amount, and recalculate in a few weeks, when things had settled down.[3]

The idea of uncertainty is most associated with Frank Knight, a University of Chicago economist (ironically enough, in light of what "Chicago School" has since come to mean) of the 1920s and 1930s. "Uncertainty" is also entailed in John Maynard Keynes's idea of confidence; Warren Buffett seems to mean something similar when he speaks of a "circle of competence." And in 2009, unfortunately after the Lehman Brothers debacle, Ben Bernanke, chairman of the Federal Reserve, seemed to have rather publicly rediscovered the importance of uncertainty for graduating students and, presumably, the regulation of financial markets.[4] The distinction between risk and uncertainty is old, has been suppressed, and is due for a revival.

Uncertainty is often, and somewhat controversially, understood in contrast to risk. In modern finance, risk is defined objectively as the probability of deviation from an expected return. Probable returns are assessed within a framework, a formal understanding of the economic situation at hand, in short, a model. Working within that framework, a number is chosen (on some basis, more or less solid) to represent the likelihood of deviation from the expected return.

Note that there is no normative connotation to "risk"—we are not talking about risk in the ordinary language sense of the chance that a bad thing will happen. In modern finance, there is no distinction between a deviation upward (say, an increase in the price of an asset, when a "long" position would be preferred) and a deviation downward (a decrease in price, for which one would hope to have a "short" position). Understanding risk in this probabilistic fashion allows one to think in terms of both long and short positions, what one might quaintly think of as investment and insurance, or the investment objectives of buyer and seller, at the same time. The only question, for each party, is whether one understands the odds well and contracts (bets) accordingly.[5] For the policymaker and the academic, the quantifiable objectification of risk is the key theoretical move that allows for modern finance—risk management, portfolio theory, financial engineering—the entire edifice of which Greenspan spoke.

But "risk," as used in academic finance and in the phrase "risk management," is also something of a euphemism, indeed very much a product of the ivory tower.[6] One who knows they are playing a game with a fair coin knows quite a lot, more than most people, even most sophisticated investors in precise instruments. Even in sophisticated trading operations, risk is often difficult to understand, and great resources are spent in trying to model it. What is learned is often kept secret (treated as a proprietary trading strategy). And much effort is devoted to shifting risk advantageously—the academic finance picture of "risk" as objectively probabilistic rather willfully ignores the milieu in which it is modeled and traded. Moreover, in operating companies that must make their way in the world, "risk" tends to have a more general meaning that is more in line with its use in ordinary language, the "chance of some bad thing happening."

When things are going well, such difficulties with conceptions of risk may seem mere details of a sociological sort that can be ignored by practical people. When our view of the world is working, then it is natural enough to believe that the conceptions on which our view seems to rest must be more or less correct, subject to stochastic adjustment over time. If our government is performing well, then our philosophy of government must be correct; if banks are making money, they must understand risk management. It is not until our view of the world is understood to be broken that elemental assumptions can be, indeed should be, called into question. The fall of the Berlin Wall did not occasion reconsideration of the venerable question of whether students were to be understood as part of the proletariat. Or, to use a military analogy—after one realized that the Maginot line had failed, debating how many more troops to put on the line (increasing France's odds of defending the line) hardly would have increased the likelihood of French victory. In both cases, more drastic rethinking was required. By the same token, while the breakdown of a risk model prompts the construction of a better model, the tweaking of assumptions, the breakdown of an entire industry's risk models constitutes the collapse of an edifice, presenting a *mise en abyme,* a view of the abyss, the acknowledgment of radical ignorance.

Financial policy, which is philosophically primitive, can no longer suppress a distinction between risk and uncertainty. Uncertainty is a description of a state of mind, a subjective, even moral (in the philosophical sense) concept. "Uncertainty" is a statement about a mind confronting the world, a mind that does not know enough to decide on a course of action, and is aware of not knowing, is uncertain. (To be certain would be to be aware that one knows.) Uncertainty is inherently subjective. As a practical matter, the uncertain mind may refuse to spend money, may "wait and see" instead of committing, investing. And so buyers may not show up at the auction, or on the bourse, or in the showroom. In the academy, uncertainty implies a skeptical stance, an intellectual claim that "you don't know as much as you say you do."[7]

In contrast and recent memory, "risk" is a statement about the probability of outcomes in the world. Risk is a description of the world, an objective concept. In good times, one may speak of expected returns and (more or less expected) deviations from the norm. One may talk with great sophistication about the normal fluctuation in a stock's price (its "beta"), at least until the company implodes and is kept on government life support. (So, what is Citi's beta?) One may, with the bankers, speak of value at risk (VAR), at least until.... As an essentially objective conception, risk is amenable to quantitative discussion. Adepts of modern finance tend to treat uncertainty as the raw material of business risk, grist for the financial mill. Uncertainty is a sloppy lay notion, waiting to be understood as risk, quantified, modeled, and priced. All of which seemed quite doable, not that long ago.

Continuing in this sociological vein, we can say that one way to understand managerial finance, including risk management, is as an effort to make business into an essentially objective, if probabilistic, science that can be taught in graduate schools. Uncertainty has never been very fashionable in the academy, in part because there is not too much to say about it. As a matter of the incentives for young academics, the prevailing preference for mathematical sophistication has made it far easier to build a career on the manipulation of risk models than on acknowledgments of uncertainty. "I don't really know what we're talking about here" hardly enhances a tenure file. And so risk, rather than uncertainty, has dominated both the academy and policy thought. Thus the business model of the business school itself fostered a certain epistemological naïveté.[8] As difficult as it is to think about uncertainty, there are negative consequences of not thinking about it. Despite Bernanke's oft-touted study of the Depression, America's policymakers have not handled the current crisis in a way to suggest any sustained thought about how to address uncertainty or restore confidence. Political and policy elites have repeatedly told the nation that it is necessary to spend money, because this crisis is really important, and there will be no more business as usual. Indeed. Markets, consumers, and most frighteningly, employers, have responded accordingly.

Not to be unduly cynical, but it bears noting that risk—and its taming through quantification, and hence pricing—sounds on the sell side, whereas uncertainty sounds like the prudent investor—Warren Buffett's admonition not to invest in something you do not understand.[9] So in a long and strong enough bull market, we discuss risk, and even some of the most skeptical fuddy-duddies tend to succumb to the siren song of profitable risk management. It takes a substantial downturn, and perhaps a bevy of lenders and consumers who simply refuse to use free money, to make us think seriously about uncertainty. Over a year into what was once known as the credit crisis, bankers still complained that they, and worse, markets, did not know what assets were worth in any terms other than an almost complete failure of present demand, that is, almost nothing. And in response to that uncertainty, the willingness to extend credit evaporated, and the financial crisis lurched into a deep recession.

A final note: Uncertainty is not necessarily bad and is indeed part of the human condition. Hope springs from uncertainty. Acknowledging what one does not know is an intellectual virtue and, through caution and prudence, a practical virtue as well. But when ignorance is suddenly discovered, "certainty" is unmasked as hubris, commitments are abandoned, trusts are broken, and those who retain capacity are too uncertain to act, people may get hurt.

*   *   *

Even at this early juncture, we can see that some things have already been decided. The financial crisis seems to have taught at least the following, which suggest the foggiest of outlines of a philosophy of markets. To review the bidding:

- Markets cannot be relied upon to be efficient.
- Financial markets do not regulate themselves.
- The information available to market actors, and the sophistication of market actors, is insufficient to prevent occasional institutional catastrophe and even systemic risk.
- Confronted with a credible threat of systemic risk, governments will intervene.
- Subjective uncertainty, rather than objective risk, is the problem to be addressed.

Chapter 2

Melodramatic Narratives

Cʜᴏɴꜰʀᴏɴᴛᴇᴅ ᴡɪᴛʜ ᴄʀɪꜱɪꜱ, ᴘᴇᴏᴘʟᴇ ᴛᴇɴᴅ ᴛᴏ ᴛᴇʟʟ ꜱᴛᴏʀɪᴇꜱ, ɴᴀʀʀᴀᴛɪᴠᴇꜱ. Wᴇ have to account for our situation. In particular, hordes of journalists, academics, and government officials must generate stories that enable them to report, analyze, and legitimate—and so, in a knowledge economy under stress, we have seen a gully washer of words. Some of the more notable efforts are cited in this book's bibliography. The narratives that organize the vast majority of these texts, however, are fairly repetitive. While variations exist, we may list narratives that have gained political influence in roughly the following terms.

These stories are not mutually inconsistent, and each of them expresses important truths. It must also be said that each of them has serious limitations, although specifying the limitations would require a careful retelling of each story, with attribution and critical analysis, buttressed by a survey of the evidence, much of it countervailing. This critical assessment would be a waste of time, at least for this book's purposes. For now, it is enough to get the narratives on the table, along with the remark that the possession of one truth tends to obscure other truths. A corpse shot through the heart may have in fact died of cancer. So, in telling one of these stories, we should ask ourselves, which stories are we not telling?

The Housing Bubble

In the most commonly told story, the financial crisis has its roots in a housing bubble. It was long and widely thought that house prices almost always went up. Somewhat more technically, it was thought that the national housing market was inherently diversified. People have to live somewhere, and falling demand in one place, perhaps upstate New York, ought to be compensated for by rising demand elsewhere, perhaps Florida. Thus prices should not fall across the housing market as a class. Or so it was believed.

Recent years, however, saw a boom in home building, eventually leading to a huge oversupply of housing stock. To make matters much worse, many homeowners were in houses they could not afford, or could only afford under nearly perfect economic circumstances. "Subprime" lending, that is, loans arranged by banks or by nonbank institutions outside of the criteria for lending that qualified the loans for securitization by government-sponsored entities Fannie Mae and Freddie Mac, meant that people who never before would have been able to buy a house could and did buy houses. Other Americans leveraged their primary residences to buy investment or vacation properties. When circumstances changed, such highly leveraged borrowers began defaulting. Banks, foreclosing on the mortgages, attempted to resell the houses, exacerbating the oversupply of housing. Real estate prices began to fall, in some markets drastically. Banks found themselves undercollateralized. Homeowners found themselves owing more on their mortgage loans than their houses were worth on the market. If they could not renegotiate their loans (as was usually the case), such "underwater" borrowers sometimes (rationally) chose to default, and even sometimes mailed their keys to their lenders, so-called jingle mail.

Securitization

Rising house prices were fueled by the process of securitization, in which bank loans were bundled together and sold to special purpose entities (SPEs). In turn, the SPEs issued securities (usually debt obligations) that were sold to investors across the United States and around the world. Securitization originally was intended to foster lending. Before securitization, bank loans were paid off over years; most of a bank's assets were promises to pay back principal and interest over time. Consequently, most of a bank's capital was "locked up" in the properties for which the bank had made loans. So, until such time as the loans were repaid, the bank had relatively little capital. Securitization changed this dynamic profoundly. Banks securitized their loans (or, more generally, sold them to be securitized), which meant that banks did not have to wait for years for loans to be repaid, because the banks received their return on the loan shortly after making the loan.

The securitization of bank loans had at least three important consequences. First, and as intended, banks had more capital to make loans, so they could make more loans. Securitization thus made it easier to get a home loan. Second, many banks began to see themselves as "loan originators," that is, they were now in the business of signing up new lenders, selling debt. Third, and most troublingly, banks (and soon, nonbank institutions such as "mortgage companies") were not unduly worried about the credit-worthiness of their borrowers, because they would only hold the loans for a short time. Many loans were made, sometimes without solid information about the creditworthi-ness of the borrower, indeed, sometimes without documents. There was little risk to the bank, because soon, the loans would be sold off, and the risk of default would be somebody else's problem. As a result, an enormous number of bad loans were made.[1]

Imprudent Borrowing

Consider the middle years of this decade: Like the "welfare mothers" of another era, or silly grasshoppers rather than prudent ants, too many Americans simply obey their desires, in this case to own houses. More generally, Americans live in a culture of debt. U.S. savings rates are the lowest in the developed world. American consumers carry far too many credit cards, which they use to buy whatever they want. Many such cards are issued, generally with hidden penalty rates or fees by unscrupulous banks, to people with no real ability to carry such credit responsibly. More affluent Americans also take out second mortgages on their houses in order to spend the equity on vacations, homes, boats, and other personal items. Meanwhile, state and local governments run bloated budgets based largely on property tax revenues and the ability to issue debt on the bond markets. The federal government capitalizes on the dollar's position as the global reserve currency to rack up enormous deficits.

Beginning in 2007, these layers of debt that have structured contemporary Ameri-can culture all became due. With the contraction of the U.S. economy and the drying up of the credit markets, many U.S. individuals and institutions found themselves insolvent or on the edge.

Corporate Greed

The financial crisis was caused by overweening greed, and almost complete lack of prudence, by corporate management at failed institutions such as Washington Mutual, Bear Stearns, and Lehman Brothers as well as at institutions kept on life support by the federal government such as Citigroup, General Motors, and especially AIG. Executive compensation is at record-breaking levels and completely out of line with historical and international standards. CEOs use consultants to cow compliant boards into paying them enormous salaries, with almost no regard for the medium- to long-term health of their corporations or shareholders. The reasoning appears to be that, if business goes bad, then the executives will have been paid. And if they are at an important company, such executives may expect a government bailout.

If anything, the problem has been at its worst in the financial industries, where not only top executives but most managers have received substantial portions of their take ("compensation" implies too much of a quid pro quo) in annual bonuses, substantially reducing the assets of the company and, not incidentally, diminishing the reserves with which such companies might confront hard times. None of this was much of a concern during the long bull market that has now ended. The U.S. economy was growing and, more important, the financial industries' share of the economy was growing, and so the price of shares in companies such as Citigroup and Merrill rose smartly, even if their managers were paid princely sums for, in the event, running the companies into insolvency. At Merrill and AIG, the culture of employee compensation was so deeply ingrained that, even after billions of dollars of taxpayer money had been spent, the executive class tried to pay itself the usual bonuses. (After all, membership has its privileges.) Sensibly enough, the idea that failed managers should be rewarded with millions of taxpayer dollars while the unemployment level soared met with substantial taxpayer disapproval. The executive class rather bizarrely did not understand such disapproval and tended to dismiss it as "populism," no doubt akin to socialism, which is a bad thing.

The desperate greed of fifty-year-old rich guys is outrageous and endlessly amusing, but essentially symptomatic rather than causal. The antics of the executive class (John Thain's $1,400 wastepaper basket was never the property of Goebbels, nor is it made of human skin) demonstrated a near total lack of responsibility and, therefore, the absence of any true leadership. Our executives failed—very, very badly. They failed in part because they were so concerned with their careers (golden parachutes and all) that they did not run their businesses sensibly. These people did not lead their companies well and indeed did not identify with the companies. In particular, because they were cashing out in real time, our executives had little long-term interest in the health of their firms. So it is unsurprising that they took on risks they did not understand, that they did not reserve assets, that they paid themselves too much, and that they engaged in frivolities that made them look ludicrous.

Financial Engineering and the Banking System and a Crisis of Confidence

In the deathless words of the Turner Review:

> The origins of the current crisis ... entail the development of a complex, highly leveraged and therefore risky variant of the securitized model of credit intermediation. Large losses on structured and credit derivatives, arising in the trading books of banks and investment banks, directly impaired the capital position of individual banks, and because of uncertainty over the scale of losses, created a crisis of confidence which produced severe liquidity strains across the entire system. As a result, a wide range of banking institutions now suffer from an impaired ability to extend credit to the real economy, and have been recapitalized with large injections of taxpayer money.[2]

So, all we need to do is fix those toxic assets, refloat the banks, let the banks lubricate the wheels of commerce, and we'll be good.

Inattention by Government and Private Sector Actors

In this view, the financial crisis was caused by a failure of government to fulfill its responsibility to regulate. The oversight of the SEC, as exemplified by its failure to recognize Bernard Madoff's Ponzi scheme, was simply inadequate for the task of regulating the largest financial markets in the world. More profoundly, after each of the crises of the past two decades, Federal Reserve Chair Alan Greenspan and others argued that the government did not need to regulate, because, after all, the crisis was over, the damage had already been sustained, and lessons had been learned. Regulation after the fact was superfluous. Institutions such as hedge funds, or instruments such as OTC derivatives, or even asset-backed securities, it was said, needed little or no further regulation.

Moreover, after each shock to the financial system, the great and the good admitted that although there had been problems, modern risk-management practices made the system "robust." Such arguments apparently carried great weight with market participants, who were making money and who anyway were too young to remember a substantial recession, or to have had professional experience with a financial crisis of more than local impact. Thus, in a permissive environment, risks were systematically underestimated.

Government Zealotry

As the Committee on the Budget of the Republican National Caucus put it:

> Although failures among private sector actors and institutions were significant, the roots of the financial crisis can be traced to flawed government policies. For that matter, the housing sector—where most of the difficulties started—is hardly the kind of unbridled market the term *laissez-faire* suggests: it has substantial government components, including the financial and regulatory roles of large government agencies. In short, the current crisis reflects not a failure of the capitalist system, but the ways in which government distorted the functioning of private markets....
>
> [F]our key factors—which overlapped and interacted with one another—led to the crisis:
>
> Overly loose monetary policy earlier this decade that artificially lowered interest rates.
>
> Actions of two government-sponsored enterprises, Fannie Mae and Freddie Mac, that put taxpayer dollars at risk to chase profits.
>
> The government's push to lend money to those who could not afford it to buy homes.

Private market failures at each step in the "originate-to-distribute" mortgage credit model.[3]

In short, the government is to blame.

The United States and China

The roots of the crisis lie in the relationship between the United States and China. There are various stories here.

1. China manipulates its currency, driving down the exchange rate. China also engages in various forms of trade discrimination. Consequently, Chinese goods are too cheap, and American exports are too expensive. As a result, Americans lose jobs, buy too much stuff at Wal-Mart, and do not save enough. Chinese consumers are not paid what they are worth, are unable to buy goods on the global market, and essentially subsidize American consumption (which is unsustainable, but fun while it lasts).

2. U.S. citizens, companies, and governments borrow too much and do not save or export enough. When its unsustainable work and consumption habits get it into trouble, the United States engages in protectionist rhetoric.

3. China learned the importance of maintaining large reserves of foreign currency from the currency crises of the late 1990s. So China has bought enormous quantities of U.S. paper, enough to make the cost of capital in the United States quite low and to make it rather pointless for Americans to save money. Now that business is bad, however, Americans worry that debt holders are more powerful than debtors (conveniently forgetting the times others have defaulted on U.S. debt). The Chinese worry that the United States will devalue its paper.

4. The Chinese save a lot. The nation has an ancient tradition of thrift, and their social safety net is underdeveloped, even by U.S. standards, and they fear being hurt. As a result, individuals in China save relatively much of what they earn. Conversely, Chinese consumption is relatively low. The result is a savings glut, and—again—cheap capital.

5. Most of the vast wealth generated in China, the world's third largest economy, is funneled through the government, which manages its funds for social stability, specifically, high rates of growth (the number invariably cited is 8 percent gross domestic product [GDP] growth annually), low unemployment, and relatively low levels of economic inequality. This substantial feat was accomplished for years on end after the declaration of "openness" in the 1980s—China started from a low base and proved adept at building factories and becoming the workshop of a growing world. For many factory workers, life is much better in the cities than it is back in the villages. For "middle-class" producers and consumers, life is materially much better than it has been in living memory. And the Chinese are very proud of their accomplishments, perhaps chauvinistically so. So the Chinese do not (yet) complain, even though they do not live nearly as well as their productivity would suggest they should.

As China's economy matures and global growth slows, it becomes harder and harder to keep growth, unemployment, and social equality at expected levels. Moreover, as a result of the success of Chinese modernization, the sums of money that the Chinese government finds itself managing keep growing. Much of this money is earned through trade and therefore is in dollars. Such money cannot simply be remitted to the Chinese people for fear of change, specifically, the outbreak of radical inequality, a spike in the value of the renminbi (RMB), falling exports, rising imports, and locally heavy unemployment. In short, the Chinese government finds itself with an enormous surplus of dollars, which it must reinvest, in government Treasuries, Fannie Mae debt, whatever, in order to retain its hold on power. Not incidentally, demand for the dollar stays high, Chinese exports remain cheap, foreign imports remain expensive, the people remain (relatively) equal, and stability reigns … at least so far. And for their part, U.S. consumers, corporations, and especially governments have been more than happy to buy dollars, i.e., sell debt in order to live beyond their means.

Monetary Policy

The financial crisis was caused by excessively loose monetary policy. Confronted with a host of problems, the Federal Reserve repeatedly lowered interest rates. In particular, after 9/11, money was cheap and Americans did as they were told—they went shopping. Savings rates plunged as we maxed out our credit cards and established lines of credit against the equity in our houses, bought cars and vacation homes for no money down, and so forth. In this version of the tale, for which Greenspan was excoriated by Congress, a host of institutions, led by the Federal Reserve, made credit too easy for Americans. And gluttony has always been one of our sins.[4]

* * *

The foregoing stories are all melodramatic, that is, blame is assigned. Who gets blamed depends on how the story is told. The repetition of such stories is unsurprising, perhaps even unavoidable, because blaming is so useful for political purposes. But there is often less to such stories than meets they eye. The act of blaming presumes a framework for judgment, a framework not only undisturbed but positively affirmed by the action of the villain. Melodramatic stories like those told in this chapter, then, are intellectually conservative: Events may be surprising, people may behave badly, but the structure of our beliefs will be confirmed in the end. In telling such stories, we avoid the challenge posed by Greenspan's testimony to Congress, and illustrated by the preceding chapter, that our frameworks are compromised if not completely broken. And in avoiding the possibility that we do not understand, we foreclose the opportunity for conceptual renewal presented by this crisis.

Chapter 3

Blue Water

The Allure of Modern Finance

How may we begin thinking about the tradition that has failed, and what may arise to take its place, without melodramatically reiterating what we already believe? Critical analysis, the stock in trade of the law professor, is rather easy, especially after a crisis, when people are willing to assign blame. The intellectual problem with such analysis, however, is already implied by the word "critique"—we assume the standard and, on the basis of that standard, make judgments. As remarked in the previous chapter, critical analysis, at least when performed on a melodramatic narrative, thus tends toward foregone conclusions in lieu of new thought. So how are we to begin thinking anew?

If focusing on what went wrong merely leads us back to what we already think we know, perhaps we can achieve deeper understanding—and sometimes new ideas—by thinking about what went right, or at least seemed so right, for a while. Why were the techniques of modern finance that failed so spectacularly so widely adopted in the first place? Why were the problems mentioned in Chapters 1 and 2 not more obvious to all of us? That is, if we ask rather more sympathetically after temptations and blindness, perhaps we will understand more deeply and be able to think better.

The twentieth-century historian of economics and much else Fernand Braudel taught that attention should be paid to the duration of changes, to the various periodicities found in history. Some changes are dramatic but cyclical, revealing, over time, fundamental continuities. The financial crisis exhibits such changes in the form of asset bubbles and accompanying exaggerations in the credit markets, which in classic fashion have been first too loose and then too tight. And some things that appear to be continuities are in fact fundamental, albeit gradual changes, changes over the *longue durée,* in Braudel's famous phrase, or at least the substantial medium run of a few generations. The financial crisis exhibits such long-term changes, too, through the democratization of access to liquidity and the capitalization of the economy, all intimately wrapped up with globalization. Really interesting times, such as the time we are in presently, see the confusing interaction of historical processes of different periodicities.

Cycles

Let us start from the uncontroversial proposition that this financial crisis involves a housing bubble and in fact other bubbles as well, notably in credit default swaps, equities in financial institutions, and a truly bewildering array of complex debt instruments. For theoretical purposes, at least on the first analytic cut, the objects of enthusiasm may not be important: Sometimes tulips, and sometimes housing in San Diego or collateralized loan obligations, become the objects of mania. At a structural level, however, the story remains the same: An idea makes money for an investor; the investor's profits attract more investors; the influx of investors yields spectacular profits; more investors are attracted.... Bubbles always begin as persuasive ideas.

For a while, the bubble continues to expand—until one day, it becomes evident that there are no new buyers, and somebody chooses to sell. Not finding a buyer, our seller lowers his price. Others note the absence of buyers and reconsider whether their assets are worth much. Suddenly, those who bought at the top of the market stand to lose money; in order to cut their losses, they sell, further increasing the supply of a now suspect good, the stock of Citigroup, perhaps. Panic selling ensues, and the price of the once prized asset enters free fall. If the asset is something like a corporate stock, the price may fall to zero. Even if the asset is something quite solid and even useful, such as actual houses in Phoenix, price declines of over 50 percent are possible. As the now fashionable Hyman Minsky argued years ago, investment bubbles have the structure of Ponzi schemes (a proposition recently supported mightily by the shenanigans of Bernard Madoff).

Psychologically, then, bubbles follow a standard narrative: A long period of rising enthusiasm, which may become a full-fledged mania (recall the headier capitalizations of the Internet bubble or Japanese commercial real estate), is followed by the rather abrupt appearance of doubt or uncertainty, and then anxiety that the asset cannot hold its value, an anxiety confirmed and deepened by falling prices. Anxiety may give way to fear or even panic, until the market stabilizes or collapses altogether, but at any rate "finds a bottom." Such an episode is followed by a period of low confidence and reduced initiative among whatever investors remain. The present financial crisis has exhibited all of these stages, although there has been a notable absence of retail panic—for which government willingness to act should be credited.

As both Minsky and Charles Kindleberger famously argued, asset bubbles are mightily enabled by credit markets. Moreover, and much worse, the credit markets, in responding to their injuries from the bubble, are likely to take actions that, in turn, hurt the real economy. To see why, imagine that investors buy only those assets for which they can pay cash. In that case, investors would not be able to bid up the price of some fashionable asset, to inflate a bubble, at least not very quickly. Presumably they would not sell the fashionable asset, in the belief that its price will continue to rise. In that case, although the bubble might grow, it could only grow at a rather moderate pace, as investors earned new money, or as new investors entered the market.

Now consider the much more likely scenario in which investors can borrow. In this second case, investors can buy much more of the bubble asset. Presuming that their expected return on the asset is far higher than their cost of capital, they may multiply their returns, much as a lever multiplies the strength of its user. The demand exhibited by such investors will be reflected in a further increase in prices, further convincing everyone that the asset is a great investment. Indeed, an investor who is truly convinced that he has a sure thing cannot rationally not borrow to maximize his return. So, in the recent housing crisis, but also throughout the regulated and the shadow financial system, we have seen the use of large amounts of leverage to achieve substantial profits, sometimes from rather modest rates of return. (A few hundred million dollars thrown at a few basis points is still a lot of money.) Thus bubbles tend to be exacerbated, if not precisely caused, by the credit markets.

The availability of credit to investors is not constant. Credit tends to become too available as the bubble rises, and insufficiently available when the bubble pops. That is, bubbles are mirrored by the leverage cycle. The leverage cycle is styled after the more respectable "business cycle," rather than the always disreputable and more occasional "bubble," because leverage cycles (interest and margin rates fluctuate) even when nothing so dramatic as a bubble is in sight. For present purposes, however, the key point is that lenders exhibit much the same psychological profile through the leverage cycle as investors exhibit through the life of a bubble.

A borrower makes a convincing proposal; a lender is willing to lend, albeit with conditions designed to protect the lender. Typically, the lender requires rights to property (collateral) and lends less than the full value of the collateral (retains a margin). Assuming the idea is decent, the times are favorable, and luck holds, the deal goes well. The lender is repaid, with interest, which can quickly become habit-forming. Soon enough, the lender's natural anxieties fade. The lender gradually becomes ever more willing to lend and even to require a little less by way of security, that is, to lend at a lower margin. So, in the recent housing boom, the once standard requirement of a 20 percent down payment became more of a ceiling (if you had more than 20 percent in, you would perhaps refinance or take out a second mortgage). Lowering the margin allows borrowers to borrow (and invest) more. So, if a lender requires a margin of 20 percent, a would-be homeowner with $50,000 can borrow $200,000 and buy a house for $250,000. If the lender decides to require only a 5 percent margin, then the same homeowner can invest $1 million in their home (a 400 percent increase in the homeowner's buying power). This "leveraging up" is fine, so long as real estate in San Diego or wherever continues to rise in price—the borrower who runs into trouble can refinance or sell, and clear the loan. More generally, in good times, people are likely to have the capacity to repay their original obligations or be able to work something out. Consequently, risk is estimated to be low, and more credit is extended. Both lenders and borrowers increase their use of leverage, and thereby their exposure.

When the market turns, however, lenders tend to tighten credit. The collateral is worth less; the lender's risk is greater than recently thought. So lenders attempt to limit their exposure, fortify their reserves, and otherwise lend less—to "deleverage." This tightening of credit can aggravate the cash flow problems of borrowers. The classic example is a margin call. For example, in 2007 Merrill Lynch, which lent money to hedge funds run by Bear Stearns, lost faith in the funds' ability to operate and seized their collateral. This not only resulted in the shutdown of the hedge funds, it raised questions about Bear's access to credit, questions that ultimately killed the firm.

More generally, in dramatic leverage cycles, the reassessment of risk within the financial system changes the general business environment. As it becomes suspected that the assets (loans) of banks and other capital-providing institutions are at risk, faith in the institutions is shaken. In an effort to strengthen their positions and reestablish confidence, lending institutions hoard capital, tightening access to credit across the board. Markets (for debt instruments, commercial paper, and even student loans, for examples) dry up. Actors of all sorts flee to safety, often U.S. government paper. For a variety of reasons, including the desire to bolster reserves, the need to meet collateral calls, and the threat or actuality of insolvency, assets are sold into declining markets, further depressing prices. As asset prices continue to fall, some lenders go bankrupt, which causes further tightening of credit. Just so, the "housing crisis" of recent years quickly became a crisis of radically overleveraged financial institutions (and indeed, households, businesses, and governments). Such institutional distress was quickly translated to the real economy: As of this writing, businesses are having difficulty securing operating credit; orders are not being placed; manufacturing is declining, unemployment rising. Without access to credit, businesses may not be able to get out of cash flow difficulties, may find themselves unable to pay their debts when due, and may be forced into insolvency. There is talk of a turnaround, but growth has fallen in the most sustained fashion since 1947, when the federal government began issuing quarterly assessments of GDP.

It might be useful to step back and consider a simple and concrete but quite common middle-class version of this story. Imagine a plain vanilla, indeed conservative, example: A homeowner buys a $250,000 house, with 20 percent ($50,000) down and a Federal Housing Administration (FHA) loan for $200,000. A few years pass, and house prices go up 40 percent. The house is assessed at $350,000, and the homeowner refinances at 80 percent, leaving the homeowner with an obligation of $280,000. Then house prices go down 35 percent. The house is now worth $227,500, but the homeowner still owes nearly $280,000, since early payments are mostly interest. What if the homeowner now needs to sell? The costs of having a real estate agent handle the sale, prepping the house for the sale, undergoing an inspection, hiring a moving company, and so on are likely to add up to at least 10 percent, possibly substantially more—but call it $22,000. So, unless our homeowner has roughly $74,500 in cash (unlikely) or can get credit for that amount (very unlikely), the homeowner cannot afford to sell the house and move. The homeowner can default, though, at which point the bank's losses will be substantial. How many such defaults can a bank sustain?[1]

As a practical matter, our exemplary homeowner is likely to stay put (mobility in the United States is at its lowest level in decades) and will continue to pay the mortgage, honorably, if economically irrationally.[2] For their part, the banks will count such loans as performing and adequately collateralized. The Federal Deposit Insurance Corporation (FDIC) will look the other way for as long as it can. Everyone will hope that real estate prices will gradually recover, and until then, that diligent borrowers will gradually pay down their debts, eventually reducing the principal owed and lessening the exposure of their lenders. If the unemployment rate climbs substantially, all bets are off.

This story is simple, common, and perhaps important to tell because the usual villains are not here. There is no predatory lending; no reckless use of credit cards; no ravening greed; no obvious imprudence. There is no fancy financial engineering, no off-balance-sheet shenanigans or global trades. There is not even much of a bubble—a 40 percent compounded return over half a dozen years is nothing special. The 35 percent fall in an asset value is a bit more unusual, but it is the Case-Shiller index for losses in the real estate market during this crisis to date—a very broad average of actual sales of actual homes.[3] And to refinance at 80 percent, leaving 20 percent equity in the house, is (or was, until recently) quite conservative. As this hypothetical suggests, an enormous number of middle-class houses in the United States are at present underwater.[4]

* * *

A difficulty with this understanding of our crisis is not the internal logic, but the temporal scale. Why is *this* leverage cycle so important? This is the largest financial crisis in generations and therefore must be understood across a longer term. So we might ask, somewhat more specifically, how did the U.S. housing debt market, subprime or not, come to have such great influence in the global economy? And why do we see such an array of admittedly somewhat interrelated bubbles, including houses, mortgage-backed securities, debt securities (many of which had nothing to do with actual houses, or even the housing market), equities in financial industries, and so on? And what does all of this have to do with the "entire edifice of risk management" that has collapsed? In order to approach such questions, it is necessary to see these various bubbles, and even the somewhat broader leverage cycle, as symptomatic of, and in association with, more fundamental historical and intellectual developments, whose general outlines may be traced, albeit not without difficulty.

Modern Finance and the Quest for Sweet Liquidity

To begin simply and, with luck, fundamentally: What makes contemporary capitalism so irresistibly seductive on a personal level, almost regardless of one's political views, is that it gives more individuals more purchase on the future than they have ever had before. Not to put too fine a point on it, money makes good things attainable. Maybe even more compellingly, money makes bad things avoidable, or at least softens the blows of outrageous fortune.

It perhaps needs to be emphasized that what is at issue is not simply wealth, but money or assets easily convertible into money, liquidity. As anyone who has watched a corporate bankruptcy unfold, or who is stuck in a big house that he or she cannot afford to sell, or who happens to be in farming or some other capital-intensive business, should understand, liquidity is not the same thing as wealth. Wealth, as the foregoing examples suggest, is often encumbered. The rich are not always free. Liquidity is the "spendability" of wealth, the ease with which an asset can be converted into some other good, giving the owner the chance to respond, the opportunity to act. Liquidity liberates. The history of modern finance can be understood as the advancement of liquidity; making this sort of freedom broadly available has been a great achievement of financial elites over the past century, and particularly since World War II.

For present purposes, liquidity can be acquired, and should be thought of, in three not entirely distinct ways. First, one's wealth, retained earnings, inheritance, government largesse, or whatever, may simply be in a liquid form—cash or some easily convertible asset, such as widely traded securities, rather than, for example, land or a partnership or personal fame. Second, one may borrow on a secured or unsecured basis. Third, one may capitalize a less liquid asset.

As already suggested, the creation of liquidity is not unconnected to, but is somewhat distinct from, the process of creating wealth. A business may appreciate without throwing off much cash. Or a great deal of money might be made, but plowed "back into the business" or "back into the farm" without creating much additional liquidity. (Indeed, it is at just this point of long-term investment that the human desires for liquidity and for great wealth are somewhat at odds.) And sometimes liquidity is increased—for example, through the payment of higher wages to industrial labor—without much financial innovation. This is no doubt an achievement, but it is not an achievement of finance as such. Thus, to refine a foregoing proposition: A great achievement of modern finance has been to make liquidity available, especially in the United States, through facilitating the extension of credit and developing new ways to capitalize assets.

During the early 1940s, once it was clear that the Allies would win the war, it was worried that demobilization would send the United States back to the economic equilibrium enjoyed in the years before the war, that is, that the Depression would resume pretty much where it left off. And so the postwar period saw the encouragement of borrowing, especially for education (the GI Bill) and homeownership (the establishment of Fannie Mae). Diners Club, the first modern credit card, and BankAmericard, the forerunner of the Visa system, both appeared in the 1950s. The MasterCard system appeared in the 1960s. Merrill Lynch introduced the Cash-Management Account in 1977 (and, with a brokerage firm offering key banking services, Glass-Steagall was doomed). Negotiable Order of Withdrawal (NOW) accounts were conceived in the 1970s (as a way around the restrictions on interest-bearing checking accounts established by the Banking Acts of 1933 and 1935) and were nationally authorized in 1981. Personal lines of credit, often secured by houses (on which the interest was tax deductible), became common in the 1990s. Around the same time, ATM cards (of either a nominally "credit" or "debit" variety) became usable in ATM machines worldwide. In short, at least for members of the broad middle class, it was almost always possible to get access to money.

A roughly similar story could be told in corporate finance: With the passage of time, companies increasingly invested their earnings while funding their day-to-day operations through credit arrangements. Companies from law firms to manufacturers managed cash flow with either short-term commercial paper or credit facilities with financial institutions, or both. (When things are going badly for operating companies, it is often the refusal of money market participants to roll over commercial paper, or a financial institution's demand for additional collateral to back up a credit facility, that turns out the lights.) The details of the history on the commercial side are perhaps a bit simpler—there was less consumer protection law to get around—but the themes are the same: Financial ingenuity has been devoted to getting money into the hands of those who want to spend it.

As interesting as the modern extension of credit has been, more interesting still is the capitalization of assets. A great deal of financial innovation has involved the employment of contract law to make property, and risks to property, and even rights under a contract such as the right to receive loan payments (which banks think of as "assets") more liquid, more like money. A simple example of this is a second mortgage loan on a house. Middle-class Americans were urged (it was financially sensible) not to "leave" equity in their primary residences. After all, your money should work for you, not the other way around. So, rather than attempt to pay off our houses, as earlier generations of homeowners had done, Americans borrowed against their houses and used the money for investments, or bought vacation property (often sold as, in part, an investment) as well as boats, cars, and other pleasures. While borrowing against a primary residence can be sensible as a matter of financial theory and perhaps even psychology (a good memory is often worth paying for and may be satisfying far longer than a mere thing), such borrowing left many homeowners dependent on stable positive cash flow and solid house prices.

As it turned out, this was a vulnerable position to be in. Cash flow is rarely stable for long, and even house prices may fall. In short, once the crisis began in earnest, a strategy that had seemed "financially sensible" was revealed to be a short road to insolvency. The problem here was not financial illiteracy, as is sometimes suggested, but financial sophistication.

A darkly amusing corporate analogy, and there are many, is provided by AIG. As an insurance company, AIG maintained a substantial portfolio of liquid securities, publicly traded stocks and bonds, as a supply of capital that AIG could sell if it needed to pay substantial benefits under its insurance contracts. Until such time, however, AIG's portfolio of liquid securities did not do much. Depending on the nature of the instrument and the fortunes of the marketplace, the securities might draw some interest, collect the odd dividend, or perhaps appreciate in value, but essentially the portfolio was a store of value, a very fancy interest-bearing checking account. So AIG had the bright idea of pledging its securities to large banks and broker-dealers as collateral for relatively short-term loans. AIG would use the money it borrowed to invest in, naturally, the housing and other debt markets, meanwhile rolling over the short-term loans. When it began to lose money on these investments and elsewhere, AIG found its lenders unwilling to roll over the loans and found itself without credit generally. Moreover, the debt markets in which AIG had invested had dried up. AIG found itself unable to redeem its collateral, which presumably left its insurance businesses exposed. Worse, some lenders returned collateral, demanding cash. AIG's securities operation was taken over by the federal government in late 2008.[5]

From the perspective of borrowers (like the homeowners described above or AIG), such transactions are appealing because they yield cash, liquidity. Many of the developments in financial practice over the past few generations can be understood in whole or in part as the effort to use ever more sophisticated capital markets (often spoken of in watery terms, such as "broad and deep") to make existing wealth, property, more liquid.[6] Virtually any asset that produces an income stream over time has been "securitized," that is, rights to the income stream are pooled, and securities in the pool are offered in the global financial markets. So we have seen the securitization of not only housing debt, but also commercial property loans, student loans, car loans, consumer loans, aircraft leases, equipment leases, and royalty streams. As broad as the securitization phenomenon is, it is hardly the only example of the push toward liquidity. Consider, in this regard and in no particular order, how the following classes of transactions make at least one of the parties considerably more liquid:

- The initial public offering of medium-sized corporations (sometimes called a "liquidity event")
- The sale of commercial property into, and the lease of the property back from, real estate investment trusts (REITS)
- The conversion of businesses traditionally organized as partnerships or closely held companies (such as banks, investment banks, and even hedge funds) into publicly traded corporations

- Competition among exchanges for order flow, usually waged in terms of "best execution"
- Debt obligations issued by universities, municipalities, and other entities, secured by anticipated revenue streams such as tuition or fees
- Licensing and franchising agreements
- The conversion of corporate relationships, and associated obligations, into contractual relationships, through various forms of outsourcing, especially of labor

Owners of property are drawn toward cash, seeking the liquidity that will allow them to realize their desires. Virtually every income-producing asset in the nation has been converted into something much more like money. Credit has been extended, or at least offered, to virtually every statistically creditworthy party in the nation, thereby feeding the demand for debt. This a big part of what it means to say that a society, most particularly the United States, is capitalistic.

What about the providers of cash, lenders? What is in it for them? Returning to our examples, the banks making second mortgages, or the broker-dealers making short-term loans to AIG, sought profit (interest) at what was thought to be an acceptable level of risk. Markets for capital tend to be fairly competitive, and therefore banks (and lenders generally) tend to depend on volume. They make more money if they can make more loans, both because they earn more fees and because they earn more interest (they have more assets). More generally, banking and many other forms of capital intermediation are done on very thin spreads and therefore are profitable only if conducted in immense volume.[7] The drive for volume among banks, and in the shadow banking system, notably among hedge funds, is usually expressed as the importance of being highly leveraged. Leverage is the correlative of liquidity. Those with property seek liquidity so they can be free. Those who already have liquidity seek to leverage it, to make it work for them, so that they can live off the interest.

Liquidity thus demands financial products, hence financial engineering. The fund manager who appears one morning at the investment bank with a need to invest millions upon millions will be sold something, even if the bank has to manufacture it. It is difficult to muster too much sympathy for fund managers, but investing large sums of money is not easy, and so the work is often delegated. One of the humorous side notes of the Madoff debacle was that private bankers around the world invested their client's funds in a Ponzi scheme. Who knew what when is not the point here—one can at least imagine a bank manager investing his or her client's funds with Madoff in good faith. After all, Madoff was well respected and had a long track record of paying substantial returns. Again, liquidity demands, and will get, product.

Neither liquidity nor leverage is new (gold has always been negotiable, and banking has been around a long time), but the raw scale of contemporary markets—the intermediation of millions upon millions of actors, electronically linked into globally understood commercial regimes that operate in real time, is new. Bigger markets tend to be more liquid (this is a mantra among stock exchanges). Conversely and traditionally, a house is not a very liquid asset and typically takes an extraordinarily long time to sell (in comparison with a financial product) because relatively few people are potential purchasers of any particular house, for the simple reason that relatively few people want to move to a given place at a given price. The right buyer has to come along and decide to go through the expense and bother of moving to this place rather than somewhere else. In light of the widespread demand for physical inspection, and the practical requirement of living there (or renting it out to someone else who will live there), each house is available to only a tiny fraction of the folks who need houses. Securitization, however, repackaged the value of houses in the United States into a form that could be sold anywhere, providing liquidity to homeowners in the form of lower-cost loans, and to banks in the form of cash for their illiquid assets, such as thirty-year mortgage loans. Investors all over the world bought pieces of houses in Nevada. Wondrous.

It is worth recalling that the New York Stock Exchange, the stock market that crashed in the 1920s, was already to a significant degree a market at a distance, technically intermediated. Order flow came over the telegraph, and capital crossed the North Atlantic with great ease. So for most of the twentieth century the stock markets were already quite modern. That said, much, much more of the same has been developed since then. The achievement of postwar finance is to have made all sorts of economic interests, not just shares of company stocks and bonds, publicly tradable and, at the same time, to make "the public" much more global, if hardly universal (the over a billion folk who live in abject poverty quite literally do not count here). So the Chinese government, taxing its middle class for money made on consumer goods sold at Wal-Mart, bought Fannie Mae obligations, thereby lending money to American homebuyers (who can buy furnishings at Wal-Mart). That is, as with liquidity, so with leverage—the market for lenders is vast.

Illiquidity, Portfolio Theory, and Risk Management

Sticking with our examples of the homeowner with a second mortgage and AIG's securities lending: As a matter of legal structure, the transactions took relatively independent parties and established contractual relations. In such relations, the prosperity of both parties depends on the maintenance of the relationships, that is, the parties rely on the cash flow from the borrower back to the lender. So, if the homeowner cannot make the mortgage payments (or does not want to, because the house is not worth it), he might rationally default. When AIG lost money with its investments in housing debt, and the banks demanded more collateral, AIG had a cash flow problem, and for this and other reasons had to be bailed out for billions upon billions of dollars. As the old joke has it, if you owe $10,000 to the bank and you cannot pay, you have a problem. But if you owe $10 million to the bank and you cannot pay, the bank has a problem.

A well-run bank, of course, would avoid being too dependent on any one borrower; that is, a bank's portfolio of assets should be diversified among borrowers. Constructing a sound portfolio of assets would seem to be central to being a good banker. More generally, in academic finance, "portfolio theory" treats the construction of investment portfolios, whether by a bank or by any other sort of investor. The bank in the joke evidently does not understand portfolio theory, because it has neither diversified away, nor hedged, a nonsystemic risk, the borrower's default. The bank's failing can also be stated more directly: Surely the risk that a particular loan would suddenly become nonperforming due to the insolvency of the borrower is something that the bank should be managing, hence "risk management." Put that way, portfolio theory (a strategy of investing at the core of modern finance) and risk management (a strategy for protecting institutions, or at least appeasing bank regulators) would seem to be equivalent, at least in principle if not in usage. And Greenspan reported to Congress that the "entire edifice" of risk management collapsed sometime in the summer of 2008. If so, then portfolio theory would seem to have similarly collapsed—raising serious questions about how financial institutions are to run themselves (obviously, with government guarantees and occasional massive infusions of cash, but let's not get ahead of ourselves).

Portfolio theory begins from the proposition that risk and return are to be understood together, as flip sides of the investment coin. Investors are compensated for bearing increased risk greater than the risk-free rate of return (for which U.S. government debt is the usual proxy). For example, the bonds of an airline, which may go bankrupt, have to carry a higher rate of return than U.S. Treasury bonds, which are widely presumed to be the safest of investments, because there is virtually no risk of nonpayment. Since there is a substantial risk of nonpayment of (and a less liquid market for) the airline bonds, the airline bonds must offer a greater return—or else no investor would buy them and would simply buy U.S. Treasuries instead. Therefore airline bonds offer greater returns, and investors often buy them. The general lesson is that risk is something to be embraced, at least under the right circumstances. More technically stated: The interest rate of a debt security is positively correlated with its riskiness, understood as deviation from expected return.

For another classic example, an insurance company is paid to bear the risk of a statistically unlikely but quite expensive event, perhaps a fire. If the insurance company can sell enough policies, then when the fire occurs, the company will have money to pay for the damage caused by the fire. We say that the policyholders are shifting risk onto the insurer, for a fee (the premium); the insurer is being paid to bear risk, the chance that a fire will cause damage. Higher likelihood of fire, or greater loss in the event of a fire, requires a higher premium. The insurer is being asked to bear more risk, stands to lose more, and therefore needs a greater return in order to be induced to write the insurance.

Portfolio theory manages unwanted events ("risks" in the everyday sense) through strategies of diversification and kindred strategies of hedging or insurance. The basic idea at the root of both diversification and hedging is now familiar across the middle class, who are asked to insure their homes, set up defined contribution retirement plans, and otherwise manage a household portfolio. The risks of one investment should be uncorrelated, or even inversely correlated (an insurance policy on the house), with the risks of other investments, thereby making it less likely that an investor loses everything. So, from this perspective, risk management and portfolio theory are one and the same—one term is used in banking regulation, and when things go badly, and the other is used in the academy and to sell assets.

And sell assets it did: Because we believed so deeply in risk management, we capitalized our businesses, our homes, our governments, our not-for-profit institutions, our retirements, our health care, and more. Rephrased, the push to liquidity that is such a great achievement of modern finance has entailed the widespread adoption of risk management. But what if, as appears to be the case, risk management fails? And just how did the edifice collapse?

Why Modern Finance Is Modern

A more abstract conception of portfolio theory/risk management—this text will sometimes use "portfolio management"—is critical to understanding what has gone so wrong and, more specifically, to understanding why the problem is so much more vast than subprime mortgages or even derivative toxic assets or any of the other melodramatic problems, implying linear solutions, canvassed in the preceding chapter. Greenspan was right that the edifice collapsed, but we need a more sophisticated description of portfolio management than "what we used to do before this mess started" in order to figure out what should be preserved in the reconstruction of financial markets.

Again, portfolio theory understands investment in the very abstract terms of academic finance, as simply being paid to bear risk. The legal instruments through which this is done come in a vast array, and it is easy to become bewildered by the arcane world of deals out there, somehow equivalent to a rain forest or a coral reef with a dizzying number of species. Indeed, one of the exciting things about the financial crisis is that it has focused scholarly and political attention on financial practices (auction-rate securities, credit default swaps, collateralized loan obligations, synthetic debt obligations of various sorts, portfolios used for insurance payments and collateral, prime brokerage lending and its collateral obligations, monolines, SIVs, and so forth) that heretofore were rather obscure. Although the ingenuity and consequences of such practices deserve considerable attention, for present purposes it is better to think elementally: All of these financial instruments are, at bottom, contracts. Investing, therefore, is the practice of contracting to bear risks, and a portfolio is nothing more than a collection of contracts.

The intellectual consequences of understanding investment in terms of contract, as opposed to property rights in the world, are profound, and the present discussion is preliminary at best.[8] The fact that contracts are often derivative is crucial. A derivative contract is a bilateral contract priced on the basis of another asset, or the occurrence or nonoccurrence of an event, known as the underlying. The underlying might be the price of oil (such as an oil future), the direction of currency exchange rates (perhaps a currency swap), or the default of a major corporation (known as a credit default swap). A derivative contract is, basically and essentially, a bet. The essence of betting is that one need not bet on things one owns, or, in derivatives parlance, one need not deliver the item in question, but can settle for cash (pay off the bet).

One can bet on almost anything; a derivative contract can be about almost anything. More amazingly, a party may participate in the market so long as it has credit (so long as each bettor believes the bettor on the other side will pay in the event of a loss). Thus the supply of contracts (and the size of derivative markets) is limited not by the supply of the good or service at issue; for example, oil or home mortgages, but by the supply of credit-worthy demand. Consider, for simple analogy, a bar full of people betting on the Superbowl. Now double the number of people in the bar, or triple it—one could keep going, and in the last few decades, the global economy did. The market for currency derivatives is far larger than the volume of international trade, and the market for credit default swaps is far larger than the corporate bond market, and so forth. In general, the financial economy became far larger than the real economy, a phenomenon that the historian Niall Ferguson has nicely called Planet Finance.[9]

Planet Finance is not old. Portfolio theory—and hence the fundamental shift in the financial imagination to conceptions of contract—only begins in the 1950s. Although derivative contracts have existed (notably for commodity trading) for centuries, the vast markets that have made it possible for the financial economy to outgrow the real economy were established over the last few decades. Modern derivative markets require mathematical pricing models (the Black-Scholes theorem and its progeny), academic work that was only done in the early 1970s. Using such pricing models to trade requires cheap computing power, which has only been available over the past few decades. The legal and institutional developments that led to the explosion of liquidity are of similarly recent vintage. As a result, financial markets became deeper and wider than their nominally underlying markets—the derivative market for just about everything grew larger than the market on which it was putatively based. Taking these developments together, it seems fair to say that the establishment of modern financial markets itself constituted a relatively short, in historical terms, process that looks to matter over the *longue durée*, that has changed the terms of reference. Echoing the old liberal idea that to be "modern" means to shift from status, associated with property, to contract, it may be said that portfolio theory—as extended through derivative markets that have little need for property at all—is the heart of modern finance.[10]

To be more specific:

1. As mentioned, contract can be written about almost topic, so long as a counterparty can be found. That is, two parties with somewhat varying interests can contract—basically, make a promise—about virtually anything, including things

that may turn out not to be real at all. So derivative contracts are routinely written not just on interest and currency exchange rates, but on the fate of individual businesses (a credit default swap), changes in the weather, the notional price of PVC in China—whatever. Contracts exhibit the sheer reach of language, a dizzying fact that means that portfolio management is in principle infinitely extensible, and therefore *universally applicable*, or even *virtual*. And finance, as a virtual world, is not limited to material reality, at least not much of the time.

2. What is being managed, in a portfolio, is not a business, but a profile of risk and return—achieved by combining contractually articulated abstractions, slices, of a business or set of businesses. Taken together, these slices are designed to provide the investor with a cumulative return in line with the investor's appetite for risk, but the slices generally do not in themselves represent anything identifiable in the world. Investment is rarely in a business as such (that would be a sole proprietorship or a partnership), but in a narrowly defined set of rights in and against the business. Even the broadest common investment, a share of equity stock, gives the investor very few, and quite discrete, rights. More important, the collection of such slices, the portfolio, does not represent anything else—a slice of this company and that default risk and some government paper do not constitute anything other than a portfolio. The portfolio is not a picture of anything, except perhaps an index. It is therefore almost meaningless to talk about the transparency of the portfolio. A portfolio is not an image of anything in the world, though it is composed of pieces of the world. Like a film, a portfolio is *synthetic*.

3. Danger is managed not by having superior knowledge of underlying assets, but by making other investments, that is, through diversification, or hedging strategies, so that the portfolio is constructed in such a way as to be internally balanced. A portfolio is thus, in a very literal sense, *speculative*. The risks of one investment are hedged by another investment. The classic example is of an airline that hedges its fuel costs by buying a derivative. But one or both sides may be derivative, that is, one need not own either planes or fuel. The investment, the thinking, is the bet on the relation between planes and fuel, and whatever else is in the portfolio.

4. Portfolio theory assumes, or contemporary finance creates, instruments that convey bundles of risk and return to investors—hence financial engineering. Again, owing to the nature of language, and of mathematical modeling, such instruments can be highly articulated; indeed, in theory, these instruments can be specified to the degree required by the parties. (As discussed below, this is not true in practice.) As a result, investment is, on its own terms, infinitely precise. Compare, if you will, a sole proprietorship. The owner may understand all about the business, the transactions may be as transparent as can be, but the proprietor remains exposed to whatever the world throws at the business. In contrast, a pension fund buying a synthetic Treasury so that it can meet expected obligations—that must be much more sophisticated, precise. Rephrased, the translation from a world of uncertainty (what do I think will happen to this business in the future?) to a world of risk (what are the probabilities of the circumstances under which this instrument pays?) involves a claim to knowledge.[11]

More generally, in its push toward technocratic articulation, portfolio management is *rational,* in a very Weberian sense.

5. When the noun "security" became a verb, "securitize," we crossed a line. What is significant is not just, as Marx had it, that finance abstracts social relations into property rights, that we think of participation in a collective enterprise (a "share") as an object that can be bought or sold regardless of the wishes of the coadventurers (stock is freely transferable). What matters here is that the institutions of property are transformed. Rights in things, or even in companies, become rights to make financial claims. But claims cannot be answered bilaterally; recourse must be had to courts. And the risk of claims is assessed, and insured against, through third parties, who themselves tend to spin off risks. When there is insolvency, then claimants—and their claimants—are affected jointly. More generally, if a portfolio consists of an array of essentially contractual claims, then the value of the portfolio depends on whether those claims can be made successfully, on who will pay, how much they will pay, and at what cost the transactions will occur. Such questions cannot be assessed by reference to the portfolio or even to its underlying assets. Thus the modern risk-management paradigm, by encouraging the use of contracts to employ and protect assets most efficiently, integrated enterprises and is essentially *social.* (An irony worth savoring: This process of social integration, and the fostering of such radical interdependence, happened even while methodological individualism ruled the finance academy and a devotee of Ayn Rand oversaw banking regulation and monetary policy in these United States.)

In modern financial markets, however, the same point should be made in a deeper sense, one perhaps difficult to think because of the traditional tendency to think of economics, and so of finance, as the aggregation of individual decisions, that is, in fundamentally microeconomic terms. In a financial market of a certain scale, however, all significant actors are dependent on access to liquidity, either credit or buyers for their assets. Rephrased, once the size of financial markets exceeds the real markets, then the sum of (largely contractual) assets and liabilities exceeds the price of real goods and services. In such a world, significant actors tend to be in the position of banks and, like banks, confront liquidity risks—and, as was widely remarked in the fall of 2008, this is a liquidity crisis.[12] But liquidity is an inherently systemic, and in that sense social, concept. The market for credit is defined across the population of potential lenders; the market for an asset is defined by the population of potential buyers.

To recapitulate the foregoing description: A portfolio may be described as *virtual, synthetic, speculative, modern,* and *social.* At least two important things follow from this description. First, risk management is deeply bound up in what it means to be modern; the ideal portfolio sketched above is a simulacrum of modern life, fittingly enough wired in real time over global spaces. If that is true, then the idea that we can simply avoid or escape the sorts of problems revealed by the crisis is a self-deception. Second, and in superficial tension with the first observation, the portfolio is rather groundless, or floating, even fragile. It is merely a web, easily ripped. Or, to shift metaphors, a wine glass, easily knocked over and broken when the wind blows.

Weaknesses of Risk Management

The success and sheer sophistication of risk management—the amount of individual and collective brainpower routinely devoted to the task—long masked serious weaknesses in the enterprise that, taken together, go far toward explaining how the edifice could so suddenly collapse. Such things are difficult to see and harder to say when all is well, and enormous institutions seem to know what they are doing. After the collapse, and often with the benefit of hindsight, however, many of the cracks in the structure are evident. What follows is a brief canvas of some of the ideas, some already mentioned, that now seem to make it so obvious that risk management cannot work as well as was once naively presumed.

Systemic Risk

As is well recognized in portfolio theory, diversification does not work against systemic risk. In particular, many assets that were thought to be unconnected, and hence to offer investment opportunities that were uncorrelated, are in fact connected. (The obvious example is housing prices, which were long thought to be in principle uncorrelated—that is, a rise in prices in one market would be balanced by a drop elsewhere—since, after all, people have to live somewhere. But if housing prices are uncorrelated, there can be no national bubble. Right.) More generally, models that assume diversification, or simply do not consider the possibility of correlation, will tend to underestimate the danger. Especially in massive crises of confidence, previously uncorrelated assets will move in the same direction.

Formal Difficulties in Modeling

Even the most sophisticated models are sometimes wrong (albeit, if they are truly sophisticated, not for some obvious reason), a lesson that should have been learned from Long Term Capital Management, a hedge fund employing brilliant people that nonetheless went bankrupt. Here are some of the reasons why smart people, operating under the best imaginable circumstances, still cannot get the models right (and why risk quantification should never completely allay uncertainty).

1. Some ideas are simply unthought, and so not incorporated into the model—ideas that former Secretary of Defense Donald Rumsfeld called "unknown unknowns."
2. Some events are of low probability, and hence as a matter of business practice discounted into irrelevance or simply left out of the calculations. It is difficult to measure how thick a "fat tail" is—the world seems to have more, and thicker, tails than was recently thought.
3. Although a given event may be exceedingly rare, the number of possible if rare events is very large indeed. Events of very low probability occur quite often. To

borrow Nassim Taleb's image, we may not see a black swan, today or ever, but we frequently see something just as unusual. The likelihood of such an event, whatever it may be, is exceedingly low.

4. Especially in the case of unlikely events, it is difficult to think about the significance of the event or its connections to other events. Singular events can change everything.

Behavioral Difficulties

As already mentioned, people (and many economic decisions are made by individuals) are simply not "rational" in the sense the word is used in economics. The field of behavioral economics has begun to chart some of the many ways in which actual thinking varies from the rather linear rationality traditionally attributed to economic actors. Real people tend to overestimate what they know and their ability to judge; typically weigh relatively recent or otherwise immediate data too heavily; often overcompensate; may require more to surrender a good than they would pay for it themselves, and so forth.

Perhaps most problematical, real people are deeply social—they exhibit what is damningly called "herd behavior" rather than forming independent judgments based solely on objective data. Investors buy on rumor, sell on news, and otherwise go along with the crowd. Hilariously and outrageously, Robert Shiller—a Yale economist noted for his independence, and coauthor of the Case-Shiller housing index—recently admitted that economists missed virtually all the signs of the impending crisis because they, too, exhibited herd behavior, asking the same professional questions in the same acceptable fashion.[13] And if a tenured superstar at Yale with a reputation for intellectual originality feels constrained to be orthodox, it seems a safe bet that most of what passes for financial policy is merely recycled. Real thinking is hard and not always professionally appreciated. If independence of thought is rare in the university, though, why should it be common in the financial markets?

The Proliferation of Credit/Deleveraging

It has long been known that financial crises are enabled by an expansion of credit that turns out to be an overexpansion, though at the time it seemed like a good idea. This principle was famously argued by Irving Fisher, Charles Kindleberger, and Hyman Minsky in their analyses of the Great Depression. One way to analyze the particularities of a crisis, including the one we are in, would be to trace the various streams of credit to their sources. How was credit extended? In addition, and as discussed in this chapter, the present crisis has been fueled by new sources of liquidity, the capitalization of property. (And there is substance to many of the liquidity stories told in Chapter 2.) Examining the processes of liquidity formation that operate in a given time and place may help us to understand how society came to be invested in what ultimately proved to be silly ways.

It should be emphasized that this is a financial crisis, a series of bubbles in financial institutions and products. Liquidity plays an especially central role in financial institutions. It is not merely that, like households and operating companies, financial institutions manage their own cash flow through the extension of credit, that is, capital markets. Banks in particular have always depended on the extension of credit (by depositors who do not make a run on the bank) in order to operate; banks are leveraged. And ordinary trading with clearinghouses or prime brokers requires the establishment of collateral arrangements to guarantee trades that proceed on the basis of credit. And many contemporary investment strategies work by finding small and sometimes ephemeral variations among markets, a few basis points.[14] One could go on with this bill of particulars, but the underlying point can be stated quite simply: A portfolio, understood as a balanced collection of contracts, presumes liquidity in order to match assets and liabilities.

Consequently, financial institutions are all vulnerable to a loss of liquidity. Such vulnerability can be quite acute. For example, ordinary trading with clearinghouses or prime brokers requires the establishment of collateral arrangements to guarantee trades that proceed on the basis of credit. Thus, participation in many financial industries presumes nearly real-time access to credit. To make matters exciting, lenders may rather suddenly decide that their risk modeling is not adequate, that is, that they are uncertain, and that perhaps it would be better not to lend right now. In the case of Bear Stearns, and then of Lehman Brothers, and then of AIG, it was rumored that the firm would not be able to meet its obligations. Who would want to extend credit to an institution that, it was rumored, would not be able to repay? Indeed, perhaps more collateral was required on existing debt. Soon enough, the rumor was proven to be true—denied the ability to roll over their obligations, such institutions were unable to continue operations, at least without massive infusions of cash provided, in every case but Lehman Brothers, by the federal government. The logic is circular, but so are the coils of an anaconda.[15]

Here again, however, the tendency is to think in terms of a particular institution's creditworthiness rather than in more systemic terms. If confidence in a market evaporates, as happened with auction rate securities or collateralized loan obligations in 2008, the entire market may cease to function, may evaporate. In markets ranging from housing to commercial paper to prime brokerage, credit in general—belief in institutions, not this or that particular institution—was lost.

Abstraction

Reliance on ever more extended representations inevitably compromises the transparency of financial instruments. As long as the models seem to hold, investors may assume that what they see—the model—is an abstract but fair representation of some part of the world. But suppose the models do not make sense, either singly or in conjunction? A landscape painting need not represent an actual place; a financial model need not describe a business reality. At some point, the model may reveal itself to be not an abstraction from a complicated reality, but simply a devilishly complex formal structure. Such structures may nonetheless remain obligatory—betting on unicorns does not necessarily mean that one does not owe money.

Hyperintegration

A heretofore hardly recognized cost of systematic reliance on risk management is hyperintegration, sometimes called "tight coupling," which magnifies uncertainty and liquidity risk even as it appears to reduce risk to individual institutions. Spreading risk contractually to those best able to handle it is a good idea, and for many years we heard that the widespread use of derivatives had made the financial system more "robust."[16] If aggressive risk management becomes well-nigh universal, however, and if it suddenly becomes unclear whether a critical party within a network of highly leveraged institutions is solvent, then counterparty risk becomes both widespread and difficult to assess, a lesson that should have been learned from the collapse of Long-Term Capital Management.

Liquidity risk is aggravated by the fact that many trades are involuntary; parties may be obliged to trade. Financial markets are usually idealized as excessively voluntary associations, that is, the participants may trade, or they may sit on the sidelines. Although participants may have the luxury of waiting out a round and being spectators over the medium to long term, they may not have this luxury in the course of day-to-day operations. The trader who is subjected to a collateral call, the entity whose short-term debt cannot be rolled over, the institution unable to find cash and pay its obligations as they become due, or the bond trustee presented with a credit rating downgrade—none can wait. Moreover, within a portfolio, positions are integrated (that is what it means to have a portfolio), and as noted above, it is the portfolio that is managed. Therefore a shock, perhaps the fall of the Russian ruble, is likely to occasion a response in a completely different investment, perhaps the sale of Brazilian positions (contributing to a decline in that country's finances) and a purchase of U.S. Treasuries.[17] So we see shocks proliferate across portfolios, asset classes, currencies, markets.

* * *

To recapitulate: the various asset bubbles that composed the financial crisis were enabled by longer-term shifts in the way contemporary society, particularly but hardly just in the United States, conducts its financial relations, in short, by the triumph of modern finance. And so we have seen more liquidity, more leverage, more integration. By the same token, this crisis should be understood as a crisis of the modern financial system as a cultural system, with its own *ethos*—the topic of the next chapter.

Chapter 4

Tragedy and Law

THE CHEERLEADERS USUALLY EXPLAIN CAPITALISM IN TERMS OF INVESTMENT, growth, and so material progress while acknowledging the hazards of the day, no doubt to be overcome without mishap so long as government lets the market function unimpeded and/or protects asset values, as the case may be. This is an unduly sunny view of the matter. Much of finance is concerned with danger rather than growth or progress. Historically, insurance markets emerged at the same time as stock markets. New parents stop being grasshoppers and become ants, rather suddenly shifting from spending what they earn to investing and insuring. So while the hope of progress and a commodious life is a very real carrot offered by finance, fear is the stick. During a crisis, after the collapse of various manias, thinking carefully about fear, danger, lack of confidence generally, is appropriate. Some dangers come not from the world (the ship sinking, the business going broke, life ending, and who will protect the children), but from the financial system itself—the bubble bursting, the market failing. Let us call such hazards, collectively, marketplace danger, because they arise from within the structure of the marketplace and, more particularly, from the necessity of maintaining cash flow—the vulnerable underbelly of the push for liquidity discussed in the previous chapter. Blue water has its attractions, but it must be remembered that debtors cannot live underwater for long.

Financial policy writ large—including the web of so-called private arrangements that constitute the financial markets—might be understood as three fundamentally different responses to deep, often somewhat unarticulated conceptions of marketplace danger: transparency, portfolio management, and constructed markets. For purposes of exploration and explication, let me suggest that each of these conceptions of, and responses to, marketplace danger dominates and defines an era of modern U.S. finance; that is, I am suggesting a Hegelian tale of U.S. finance. One way to understand the significance of the current crisis is that it marks the end of the second era of modern financial policy and, one may hope, the beginning of a third.

It should be remembered that, at least for present purposes, this is a story, maybe a myth, a perhaps useful way of organizing thought, little more than a hermeneutic device—the reader should hold on loosely. I certainly do not mean to imply anything like a deterministic theory of financial history. The three responses suggested here can be found throughout the history of U.S. capitalism, and, as always, much of significance is unsaid. Indeed, as will be obvious by the end of this chapter, the idea of development, much less "stages" or successive paradigms of financial policy, is deeply problematic. So the romantic and revolutionary perspective with which this book began suggested by Greenspan's perhaps unwitting evocation of Thomas Kuhn's *Structure of Scientific Revolutions,* and seemingly so apt in an age of political turmoil, in which we speak of "the audacity of hope" and look for new paradigms, will be surrendered in favor of a more mature perspective. But tragedies (and indeed, comedies) are built on the backs of simpler stories.

Transparency

Since the early part of the twentieth century, and particularly since the 1930s, the U.S. federal government has responded to marketplace danger with massive amounts of public law and regulation, that is, financial policy.[1] In particular, if we look to the founding of modern securities law in the 1930s, we find a great deal of worry about what was and still is called "fraud." But this is more than fraud in the old common-law sense of a buyer's reliance on a lie told by a seller. The stock markets of the 1920s were national markets, in two senses. Companies had national operations, and investors—shareholders—were dispersed. Thus we had strangers, trading at distances, through intermediaries, with other strangers, in companies that were everywhere and so almost nowhere. The so-called fraud was that investors bought or sold without knowing the economic reality of their investment, and so, under false pretenses. In more linguistic terms, we might say that the representations of companies—stock sheets touting stocks, themselves representing fractional ownership interests (and small fractions, at that) in corporations—had no tight connection to what was being represented, the company. Signifiers were only very loosely associated with signified.

The legal solution was a mandatory disclosure regime, namely, the Securities Act of 1933, regulating the primary market, and the Securities Exchange Act of 1934, regulating the secondary market, and subsequent law and regulation. These laws imposed what today would be called a requirement of transparency. The notion is that people who are buying and selling stock have some idea about how the company is doing and, therefore, what their stock is worth. The mandatory disclosure regime is intended to work like the glass in a telescope: Investors should be able to "see" what they are buying, even though it is a long way away. Prices on Wall Street should therefore accurately reflect the value of activity on Main Street. The function of language, then, is lucid description or representation of the business investment, or, as the SEC has styled it, "plain English."

Obviously, this is a gross simplification, but the basic notion of a mandatory information disclosure regime remains the fundamental idea behind the regulation of U.S. securities markets. The latest grand effort to achieve transparency is the Sarbanes-Oxley Act, passed in 2002 in response to Enron and other accounting scandals. And now, we have a huge financial crisis, in which sophisticated institutions have proven opaque to themselves, which has not played well in the markets. So, since the 1930s, the U.S. financial markets have been about to be transparent. But plain English, much less real transparency, has never quite arrived. Why not?

Now for poets or philosophers or anthropologists, that question is laughably naïve. Think how hard it is to say one true thing, to anybody. Now consider saying one true thing, in writing, about the future of an institution.[2] The problem that transparency is trying to address—how do we know what we cannot see (a certain theological ring is intended)—is enormously difficult. Even in the simple case of common stock, corporations are abstract, distant, and, especially in the case of a financial institution, their holdings largely unknown. Their operations are very complicated, and language is a virus—law can require disclosure, that is, reporting, and can urge that the reporting communicate in effective fashion. However, this is a little like saying "do a good job." Disclosure, as such, is not transparency.[3]

To make matters much worse, in sophisticated financial environments, the bounds, the borders, of the corporation were never so clear and have faded recently. Assets and liabilities are regularly shifted to special purpose entities, or hedged, or otherwise transferred, with intentions of retaining more or less risk, and it can become unclear what risks should be recognized, by whom, and when. As is widely recognized, risk management uses derivatives to shape the risk/return portfolio of the company as a whole. Derivatives, however, "can completely obliterate all transparency" not only to shareholders, but also to the board.[4] (Management no doubt feels it communicates what shareholders and the board need to know.) The property analogue to the derivative contract is the special purpose entity, created to carry out some aspect of the sponsor's business, and which may or may not ultimately be considered independent of the sponsor's business. (This was Enron.) As a result of these financial innovations, the boundaries of a corporation's business, say Citigroup's, are often badly defined, and hence the value of the business is hard to assess. Most intriguingly, and as the SIV mess in the fall of 2007 demonstrated most clearly, the boundaries of a corporate entity can be unclear to the corporation itself. In the SIV mess, Citi could not figure out which of the liabilities of entities that Citi had sponsored, and with which it had various relations, might ultimately be deemed to be Citi's responsibility. Reasonable minds could disagree.

Much more will be said about transparency and its limitations, but for now, it is clear that transparency is at best a partial way to address what was understood to be the fundamental problem of marketplace danger, called "fraud" in securities law, but more deeply, not knowing. Thus, regulatory talk of transparency, like related talk of efficiency, masks epistemological difficulties at the heart of financial policy and, consequently, social choice.

Risk Management

As discussed in the previous chapter, finance offers an approach to the dangers in the world, risk management, that is very different from transparency. With its roots in portfolio theory, risk management looks to the architecture of the portfolio itself to acknowledge and cope with (rather than avoid or prevent) risks. So, for example, the institution of fire insurance accepts the possibility of fire, but relies on a legal and economic structure to cope with a fire if it occurs. Specifically, a stream of payments, the "premiums," is paid to the insurer in exchange for a contractual right that the insurer will pay a large sum, the "benefits," to the insured in the event of a fire. Thus, as discussed above, risk management is not about the fire, it is about the portfolio; not so much about the world as about its legal (and economic and conceptual) model or simulacrum.

Consider, in this regard, a collateralized debt obligation (CDO), that is, a debt interest in a pool comprising debt streams, perhaps auto loans. The risk of the CDO is not assessed by determining a discounted value of the risk of default of the various car buyers, figuring out demographics, likely unemployment rates, interest rates and refinancing, or what have you. Think how hard it is to value a single house or business. Instead, risk is managed (or not) by the structure of the securitization itself. The simplest way of doing so is through diversification within the pool—many car buyers. But the CDO proper relied on a more complex structure. Though the variations are endless, the basic idea is to divide the investments in the CDO into a series of rights to the pool, "tranches" (French for "slices"). Suppose there are ten tranches, A, B, C, and so forth. Tranches are paid in order, so Tranche A gets paid before Tranche B is paid, and so forth. Tranche A obviously has a lower risk of nonpayment than Tranche B, which has a lower risk than Tranche C, and so forth. For Tranche A not to get paid, the entire pool has to fail. Tranche A therefore bears almost no risk, and Tranche J is (relatively) risky. In fact, at least under ordinary circumstances, most of the tranches bear very little risk and therefore received high credit ratings, even if most of the pool was comprised of risky obligations.[5] Thus, and to generalize, in a CDO, the risk of the instrument is managed not so much by attention to the world as by the engineering of the investment structure itself, hence "structured investment," "financial engineering," and similar terms. And institutions all over the world felt comfortable buying products derived from (or sometimes merely modeled upon, a so-called synthetic CDO) the obligations of people they had never met, businesses they had never seen, in places they had never been.

As with transparency, risk management entails a certain understanding of language. And, as with transparency, the understanding of language (and hence law) entailed in risk management is naive. Portfolios are understood as interlocked structures constructed by legal rights dictating the flow of material benefits. In this worldview, rarely held by writers or, for that matter, good lawyers, language is understood to be precise, unambivalent, and analytic—it is possible to determine, ex ante and unambiguously, who gets what under what circumstances. Moreover, for risk management, language is not only analytic, it is also constitutive—it constructs the set of positions, the portfolio itself. Language thus functions like the glass in a drinking vessel, segregating a pool of very specific rights (assets), hedged against loss, on behalf of the pool's owners(s).

Risk management might seem to be a more "private" way to respond to marketplace danger than a mandatory disclosure regime overseen by a government regulator such as the SEC, but this appearance is somewhat misleading. In an age of deregulation, oft-stated government policy is the encouragement of nominally "private" activity. Government has encouraged portfolio management in countless ways. Perhaps most important, the Employee Retirement Income Security Act (ERISA), passed in 1974, had the unintended consequence of shifting retirement from a matter of institutional commitment, defined benefits, to a matter of portfolio management, defined contribution. Fannie Mae and Freddie Mac used portfolio construction to reshape home ownership, retail banking, and a fair amount of asset management by individuals and especially core institutions such as pension funds—rather large aspects of the U.S. economy. Executive compensation was put on a performance basis by changes to the federal tax code; the result was that executive pay and a great deal of corporate behavior were dictated by portfolio-management strategies. In these and other ways, government had a lot to do with the adoption of risk management—and conversely, with the de-emphasis of transparency—as a way to confront marketplace danger.

Most obviously for the current crisis, under the Basel II Accords of 2004, governments worldwide have required banks to understand their positions in terms of risk management. What value is at risk (VAR) is to be determined not so much by reference to the world, but by reference to the portfolio itself. Specifically, banks are required to assess the riskiness of their investments vis-à-vis past performance. Unfortunately, the "past" has been understood to mean the relatively recent past. But the recent past did not provide a representative sample. Some investments are fairly new and have no old history. The recent past in the financial industries, moreover, has been unusually prosperous, a long bull market. For all of these reasons, bank modeling of the downturn has been poorly done. To make matters much worse, risk was also assessed in terms of hedging, which raised any number of cognitive problems, many listed in the previous chapter. For present purposes, suffice it to say that, going into this crisis, bank efforts to hedge and diversify were presumed to be successful and to have reduced VAR accordingly. But in the event, many hedges failed for various reasons, notably including counterparty risk, and many things thought to be diversified were not, as markets fell in tandem. In fact, after Basel II, the industry had very little idea what value was actually at risk. And so the risk-management edifice collapsed.

The fall of the risk-management edifice should not obscure the enormous societal success of the structure. As an expression of portfolio theory, risk management fundamentally changed the meaning of finance and, with it, not only academic economics, not only investment strategies, but also the management of large pools of capital, including all significant corporations and many other socially important institutions, worldwide.

Transparency and Risk Management: A Comparison

We now have enough on the table to compare the two dominant modes in which finance has confronted its demon, the deepwater dangers of markets themselves. What is at issue here are two fundamentally different imaginaries, two different ways of thinking about marketplace danger: transparency and risk management.

The first mode, transparency, avoids or prevents marketplace danger, understood to be *ignorance of possible harm,* by requiring information, and language is understood to be *descriptive* (naïvely representational). As a medium, language is meant to disappear. We speak of understanding: Put all your eggs in one basket, and watch the basket. And we legislate disclosure and other information-driven conceptions of regulation.

Risk management accepts and copes with marketplace danger, understood as *risk* (probability of deviation from expected return), through the contractual construction of diversified and hedged *portfolios.* If we respond to market danger through risk management, then language is used to set up barriers, vessels, and entities and to move economic interests from one to another in mechanical fashion. We speak of putting eggs in different baskets, of financial engineering. And natural language is supposed to be analytic and *contractual* (naïvely obligatory and determinate) and to function with literally mathematical necessity, permitting ever greater reliance on leverage.

It makes some sense, at least by way of heuristic device, to understand these modes sequentially, as the different approaches taken by, and defining, two different eras of finance. It could be said that the era of transparency in the United States ran from the Securities Act of 1933, which required companies offering securities to the public to disclose vast quantities of information, to the passage of ERISA in 1974, which had the unintended consequence of transforming retirement so that most middle-class Americans were turned into part-time portfolio managers. In the same spirit, we might say that the era of risk management runs from 1974 until the passage of the $700 billion congressional bailout in the fall of 2008. We are, then, living after the death of the second era of finance.

Tragedy

The current crisis thus expresses the *success* of risk management, which became so widespread, and which hid its myriad weaknesses for so long, precisely because, most of the time and for a great number of people, risk management was an effective way to respond to marketplace danger. Risk management was stunningly persuasive. In the 1970s, Americans saved in the neighborhood of 10 percent of their income. In the past few years, the average savings rate in the United States was negative. Similar stories could be told in corporate finance.

The financial crisis thus has an essentially tragic structure: Risk management's virtues, carried to excess, constituted a flaw that led to the system's undoing, a tragic flaw. More specifically, the practitioners of modern finance, in the academy, in government, and in business, long exhibited the same hubristic belief in the depth of one's own knowledge, the strength of one's mind, that Oedipus did. But now that the financial markets have crashed, the economy is in shambles, and unemployment is rising—and much worse must be feared even if we hope it can still be averted—and with even Goldman being nursed at Columbia's ample breast (with cash infusions, AIG obligations made good, generous accounting, guarantees in the bond market, and no doubt more, in the land of milk if not yet again honey), the incessant claims of investment bankers and others to be really, really smart leaves a truly bitter taste. By managing risk with unprecedented sophistication, global risk managers left all of us wide open to the far more damaging problem of radical uncertainty, the contraction of credit. Oedipus ended up blind, and appropriately so.

The financial crisis may also be understood on the analogy of tragedy in a deeper way, as a play among conflicting, even inverse, virtues. These imaginaries, transparency and risk management, are not just different. They are antagonistic. The inadequacy of transparency made portfolio management necessary; the widespread adoption of portfolio management made transparency impossible. Portfolio management accepts a degree of ignorance—the evil that transparency was designed to address—as the cost of diversification. Once diversification fails, however, there is no fundamental understanding to fall back upon—and the system violently contracts due to uncertainty and the general need to minimize damage to individual portfolios.

Although the tragic is a more noble, and intellectually rigorous, attitude than the melodramatic, understanding the financial crisis in tragedy's structural terms may be especially difficult in the United States. As already suggested in Chapter 2, Americans tend to love melodrama and to be averse to tragic understandings. We call all sad things "tragic." And if you look for villains hard enough, you will find them. The crisis can be understood in terms of misbehavior: Greed, lax oversight, excessive use of leverage, excessive ability to shift risk, and so forth. It is not that such wrongs were not committed, and that the charges are not true. They are true enough. But such truths tend to obscure more important truths.

It would be simplistic to attempt to "solve" the conflicts between transparency and portfolio management in principle, to declare a master virtue for the conduct of financial policy. One effort to do so, however, deserves some attention here. One might assert that one phenomenon, perhaps homeowner defaults, is correlated with another phenomenon, perhaps the default rate of corporations (the theoretical work was spurred by thinking about the fact that the death of a spouse is strikingly correlated with the death of the survivor). One might also assert that the default rate of corporations is reflected by the market of bets on corporate defaults, the CDS market. If that is all true, then the price of a class of assets, a CDO formed on housing, should be correlated with the CDS market. Or so it was argued, on the basis of a paper published by David Li in 2000; by 2004 the ratings agencies were basing ratings, and securities were being purchased, on the idea.[6]

There are many problems here, but for present purposes note that the CDS price is supposed to convey information about company default rates, that is, the CDS market is assumed to be efficient. But as we have seen, assuming the efficiency of a financial market might not be wise. The beauty of the correlation, however, was that it made it unnecessary to analyze the underlying obligations, the debts that the CDO pooled (or, in some cases, mimicked). For a while, the CDS price data appeared to make the old value investing question (do we know and understand what we are buying?) irrelevant, and therefore to make transparency irrelevant. An old joke is apropos: A man is looking for his keys under a streetlight. A friend asks, did you drop them here? The searcher says, I don't think so, but this is where the light is. Possession of CDS data and some fancy math made disclosure, and even diversification, so 1990s.

But the conflict between transparency and risk management is insoluble in principle—hence tragedy, the sense of being trapped.[7] One basket is not many baskets. Sometimes we are sure, and sometimes we insure. Life, however, is hardly internally consistent. It is difficult to imagine that we can do without either transparency (specific knowledge) or risk management (hedged bets) as ways of handling marketplace danger. Thus the conflict is not soluble for reasons internal to contemporary financial thought and, more important, practice. And for the same reason, reforms of the regulatory structure, even the creation of a prudential macroeconomic systemic risk regulator, one ring to rule them all, as it were, will not make the problem go away.

Law

Some problems are managed rather than solved. The political question implicitly asked by most tragedies is how are conflicts among goods, goods that we cannot do without, to be managed? Specifically, how can we think about financial regulation that encourages both transparency and diversification while understanding that the two are fundamentally in conflict, and neither can ever be fully achieved? What does this tragic perspective mean for restructuring the financial system?

Since Aeschylus, law has been associated with tragedy, in part because law, like tragedy, often deals with conflicts among virtues. So, in understanding the financial crisis on the intellectual frame of the tragedy, we might turn somewhat more seriously toward law; that is, thinking tragically encourages us to focus on the law in "law and economics." In recent years, in attempting to apply a discipline, economics, that understood itself as a science, financial elites have not deeply understood that finance is constituted by law, that is, by politics. As suggested by imagery such as "financial engineering" and "risk management," to say nothing of the great faith in numbers and hence necessity, members of the financial policy community subtly but quite fundamentally forgot that they were talking about legal, that is, social and political, objects. It is unkind but not untrue to say that financial policy has been made by people who in an important sense did not know what they were talking about, who misapprehended the objects of their discourse, and who so far show little signs of learning.

In early 2009, as a few institutions started to recover and things stopped declining quite so badly, some financial elites had the temerity to suggest that the nation should not be too upset by the financial crisis. The industrial revolution hurt people. So the financial revolution may be expected to hurt people, too. All we need is to try, try again, and the ingenuity of Wall Street would bring more prosperity, and more safety, than the debacle might suggest. On its own terms, the argument is bumptious and perhaps even callous, but what is somewhat admirable about it is the very American, "can do" attitude with which such sentiments are offered. Our ideas are right, our heart is pure, we just need a little more practice, or had bad luck.

Such bumptious apologies are a far cry from the tragic (and comic) perspectives urged here, the rueful knowledge that even truly pure hearts are no substitute for serious thought, especially when responsibility for others is concerned. The argument that the present crisis is merely a detour in the triumph of modern finance, the equivalent of a truly horrible nineteenth-century industrial accident, fails to understand the nature of the crisis and, specifically, the reasons why the best information and modeling systems in the world, functioning under the best conditions the world has ever seen, failed so miserably. Because markets are legal constructs, the ability to use transparency to evade, or risk management to cope with, market danger is limited by the legal structure of the market itself. That is, quite apart from what has been said already, the essentially legal nature of financial markets means that neither transparency, nor portfolio management, can be completely successful strategies. Specifically:

1. *The precision of contracts, and hence of portfolio management, is limited.* Contract law is often implicitly and not implausibly understood as a predictable set of relations, much like the laws of mechanics, which is why we can model derivative obligations with mechanical precision. And people can rely on such modeling. Except when they cannot. The laws of contract are considerably more flexible than those of nature. The idea that a bunch of engineers and physicists should have been effectively writing contracts that they fundamentally did not understand—not being lawyers, much less bankruptcy lawyers, or even corporate managers—may be remembered as one of the more amusing follies of our time.

Again, from the perspective of a transactional lawyer, the proposition that the precision of contracts is intrinsically limited should have been banal. Except that it was not—for a long generation, we seem to have forgotten the simple fact that derivative contracts are *contracts* and hence inescapably rather imprecise. In particular, whether a set of documents contains a legal, valid, binding, and enforceable obligation is a question that lawyers are regularly asked to opine upon. Indeed, lawyers are asked to be liable for the substance of their opinions. And as any transactional lawyer knows, the largest standard exclusion in such an opinion letter is for bankruptcy, insolvency, and equity generally. Even a simple bond may change in bankruptcy, as creditors of Chrysler and GM have been recently reminded. The law, even in places where law is thought to rule, bends, but how far?

To put matters in very English fashion, contractual documents establish social relations reviewable both "at common law," in which a relatively rigid rule system predominates, and "in equity," in which individualized decisions must be made because rules are inconsistent or unjust, or—as is often the case in bankruptcy—simply unworkable. Traditionally, at least until the nineteenth century, law and equity were handled in different court systems. The different courts were characterized by different remedies. Law courts gave money judgments. Equity jurisprudence, the idea of doing the right thing in particular situations, required more tailored remedies, so courts of equity issued orders. Now, in both Britain and the United States, the systems of jurisprudence have been for the most part unified, and many courts sit in both law and equity. So as a very practical matter, the unwinding of Lehman Brothers is a matter of no little complexity and uncertainty, in which it can be expected that rules will be broken (that is what equity is for), and therefore to be worked through—not modeled.

To generalize: The legal character of financial markets imposes theoretical limitations on the possibility of risk management. This is a fundamental ontological problem: The discipline of finance has misunderstood the nature of its objects, with serious consequences for financial regulation.

2. *The legal rights of financial actors limit the possibility of transparency.* Consider, by way of example, the municipal debt chapter of the present crisis. A municipal bond issuance is insured by a monoline with a good credit rating and sold on that basis. If, due to its other investment activities, the monoline loses its credit rating, the bondholders' trustee is legally required to protect the interest of the bondholders. This may be done in various ways, all of which cost the issuer, the municipality, a lot of money in a short amount of time. As a result, the municipality runs a risk of insolvency, even though it has never defaulted on a payment.

Transparency is not much use here. As a practical matter, the municipality is not in a position to monitor its insurer's other investments. Even if the municipality could somehow negotiate the right to monitor the investment activities of the monoline, another creditor of the municipality could not, because the monoline would have no particular obligation to the third-party creditor (the creditor would not be in privity of contract with the insurer, in the old language). A party to a transaction cannot, as a matter of due diligence, demand to see the books of the other party's insurers and debtors. Hence the widespread if now obviously foolish reliance placed upon credit rating agencies.

To generalize: A networked web of contracts among discrete entities cannot be fully understood on a bilateral basis; we cannot know everything about our partners' partners. (The semblance between the old common law notion of privity and contemporary conceptions of the private, especially proprietary knowledge, is instructive.) Consequently, as already suggested, legally and in principle, a risk-sharing network cannot be fully transparent to its actors. This is a fundamental epistemological problem, again with serious consequences for financial regulation.

* * *

When we focus on law, markets more clearly appear to be what they have always been, a form of social organization, political contexts understandable only in terms of their legally defined constituent parts. If modern financial markets are social, if the quest for liquidity led to hyperintegration and systemic risk, then marketplace danger should be understood socially, too. It seems implausible to hope that individual action, even aggregate individual action, will be an adequate response to such a danger. The most candid of registrants cannot be asked to disclose the social; the most carefully hedged portfolio, for all of its virtuosity, tells us little about the world. How, then, are we to begin thinking about market danger in specifically social terms?

We might start by abandoning the image of financial law and policy as "a regulatory response" to the failure of a market, in which an always belated sovereign sorts out the squabbles of the peasants. We should instead think of law and marketplace activity at the same time, and we therefore should think through more contemporaneous metaphors.[8] One such metaphor is glass—the ideas in this and the previous chapter first appeared as "three-glass tragedy," with apologies to Brecht's *Threepenny Opera*. When law seeks to ensure the provision of information, transparency, language functions as the glass in a telescope, as perfectly representational as possible. When law seeks to construct portfolios, containers for the wealth of households and enterprises, through the conclusion of contracts, then legal language functions like the glass in a drinking vessel. And now, law confronts marketplace danger through the construction of edifices, the chartering of institutions and the regulation of their interconnections, and we may think of legal language in architectural terms, like the glass that fronts skyscrapers or, for that matter, typifies Gothic cathedrals. We have witnessed a shift from *descriptive* to *contractual*, and now to *constitutive* uses of legal language to confront marketplace danger. (Constitutive metaphors of finance as a game, as a network, or even as sculpture or as gardening will be discussed at length in Chapter 7.) Financial regulation should not be so bashful as it now is—not because markets fail and the state must step in, but because reasonable minds can be expected to disagree about good architecture.

If we think of the coming era of financial policy in architectural terms—of self-consciously building markets—we should remember that architectural glass—in either skyscrapers or cathedrals—retains some of the characteristics of telescopes and drinking glasses. We still need to be able to see through the windows. We still need a sense that we are investing in something real. We want governments, as well as corporations, to be accountable. So we will not outgrow transparency. And a building's windows define spaces, separate the inside from the outside. We need to separate ourselves from one another, so that we may contract and allocate responsibility. So we will not outgrow risk management, either.

Rethinking the Discipline of Finance

Much financial policy has been philosophically and linguistically naïve, simply unaware of what has been happening in much of the rest of the world of ideas. Unlike most all the social sciences and the humanities—and if financial policy is neither social nor humane then we have problems indeed—financial policy did not take what is sometimes called the turn to interpretation. Perhaps more bizarrely still, and especially in the U.S. legal academy, financial policy has been willfully insensitive to law. Mistakes were made, not only practically, but intellectually.

However, this is a new day. Greenspan was right; the edifice collapsed. And understood as an intellectual crisis, this is a time of tremendous opportunity, a chance to think anew amid the ruins. The opportunity is nothing less than the effort to think, seriously and publicly, about finance as a form of politics, indeed socially constitutive politics. This shift in how we think about finance, from the objective science to which Karl Marx and Milton Friedman aspired to the cultural awareness exemplified by Walter Benjamin, entails a shift in the role and the self-consciousness of both the scholar and the regulator. Experts should talk to one another, and not just at conferences, because that is how imaginaries are socially constructed, especially now, with our vast distances and instantaneous communication.[9] Language is neither transparent nor determinate, but endlessly subject to interpretation and construction. And there is a certain comfort here, in the necessity of conversation among experts rather than the objective demonstration and forceful argument to which financial policy has long aspired. Worldly philosophy may remain dismal, but as we build new buildings, those of us fated to think about money and its failings should become less lonely.

Part II

On Rethinking

Chapter 5

Policy Thought, Regulation, and Innovation

IF WE THINK OF THE RECONSTRUCTION OF OUR FINANCIAL MARKETS AS A POLICY mountain to be climbed, then how we approach the mountain depends on where we start our ascent. To shift imagery slightly, the stance of a thinker matters. Therefore, in considering how to reimagine financial markets, attention should be paid to the differences among different kinds of thinkers, and so different kinds of thought. In particular, thinking in the abstract is not the same as governing however reflectively, and governing, in turn, is quite different from understanding the social role of one's business.

*   *   *

A great deal of political thought assumes the existence of power and endeavors to limit its abuse. In administrative law this enterprise traditionally is conducted in terms of how to limit the power of government officials. Since the formation of the modern administrative state—which had precursors but that we associate with the same New Deal that gave us the structure of financial regulation in the United

States—generations of judges, academics, and other policy-minded folk have worried about how to limit bureaucratic discretion (under the motto that this is a government of laws, not of men) while still leaving government officials with power sufficient to accomplish their missions and serve the people. This construction of the problem presumes that where power exists, it will be exercised, summoning to Acton's dictum that power corrupts, and absolute power corrupts absolutely.

But despite its importance for political thought generally, and for the U.S. constitutional tradition in particular, the proposition that those with power will use it is not an iron law of politics. In fact, administrators, like many corporate bureaucrats, are well known for covering their asses, or, as the Japanese are reported to say when teaching conformity, the nail that sticks up gets pounded down. In a related thought, Hannah Arendt worried that bureaucracy was rule by nobody—and "nobody" could be horribly effective, as in the Nazi Germany that was on Arendt's mind. But in other situations, nobody may come, nobody may help, and then nobody is to blame. Government inaction is a problem, too, a problem brought home to many Americans by the federal government's enraging lassitude when Hurricane Katrina drowned so much of New Orleans.

In this vein we can understand the poverty of "the modern risk-management paradigm" that collapsed in the summer of 2008. To exaggerate only slightly, under the Basel II accords, big banks are supposed to determine what their risks are and what reserves are adequate to confront such risks. Counterparties regulate one another. Corporations self-regulate. All of this is enforced by presumptively well-informed investors in highly efficient capital markets. The system runs itself; the players referee their own games. Nobody, certainly no federal regulator, has to be responsible at all. (As long as this crisis does not lead directly to war, we might be able to continue to overlook the extent of our well-financed abdications of responsibility. My cohort and especially our elder siblings may yet get away with their fecklessness, unlike the generation of 1914. So pray for peace, and be thankful that the risk-management paradigm collapsed.)

And now, as a Democratic administration took numerous very expensive steps to address the financial crisis—which is also an unemployment crisis, a productivity crisis, and so forth—that left important institutions intact and did not seem to do much for growth or unemployment, people began to ask whether this administration was facing its "Katrina moment." As of this writing in July 2009, whether or not that judgment proves apt remains to be seen, but a more general point should be clear: The power to regulate implies an obligation of responsibility, an obligation that government officials may not meet. Tyranny is hardly the only political problem. In an uncertain world in which the powers of government are not absolute (nor should they be), government bureaucrats, like kings and other fathers, will of course fail, but their virtue and their effort is to be responsible, to try.

To be responsible is also to be responsive to a particular situation, to exercise situated judgment. So, in the common law tradition, the figure of the judge represents not the automatic operation of the law's rules, but the moment and exercise of the faculty of educated and faithful judgment, what Daniel Boorstin, writing of Blackstone, called the "mysterious science" of the law. In a rather different arena, wartime leadership, Clausewitz spoke of the ability of the great commander to understand and operate upon the essentials of his particular battlefield, to understand which forces are critical right here, right now, and therefore, to be able to make the right decision when it counts.

The role of the official is thus quite different from that of an intellectual, who need not be accountable for the situation of which he thinks, speaks, or writes (the *vita activa* is not the *vita contemplativa*). The intellectual's glory, and his weakness, is that he is not limited to particulars at all—he is free to discuss "rethinking our financial markets" or some such nebulously general topic.

This rather traditional disjunction between the man of affairs and the man of ideas, the mandarin and the philosopher, has always been a problem for both sides, both politics and philosophy. The problem has been even worse since the Enlightenment, since when it has been publicly asserted (more than a little hypocritically) that politics is based upon Reason. The problem has been further aggravated by the bureaucratization that characterizes modern life, in which men legitimate their rule not by the grace of God, hereditary rights, and their strong right arms, but by vague reference to organic statutes that nobody has read and by expertise demonstrated mostly by youthful attendance at a succession of prestigious schools. Since power has come to be legitimated in such rationalistic and institutional terms, the problem of bureaucratic irresponsibility has loomed.

(On the intellectual's side, the triumph of reason, the idea that government is based upon ideas, is obviously attractive, not least because it appeals to the strengths and indeed the vanities of intellectuals. And intellectuals are rarely, and as such, never, solely responsible. Still, as this book has suggested throughout, the current financial crisis—which as of this writing is merely very painful, but which raises truly serious fears for the historically anxious—cannot be understood without the contributions of finance intellectuals since the 1950s. No doubt World War II would have occurred without Martin Heidegger, Carl Schmidt, or other Nazi intellectuals, but it is not so clear that this crisis could have occurred without the Chicago school of neoclassical economics. It is clear that decades of teaching modern finance to legislators, corporate managers, and individuals, and legislating much the same, had an effect. So the question of intellectual engagement, and even the possibility of real academic responsibility, is hardly simple.)

Over the past two generations, bureaucratic irresponsibility has been legitimated, indeed demanded, with regard to the financial markets. In the regnant Manichean view, government and market are monolithic and reciprocal modes of social organization. Government is identified with the forces of order; markets are identified with the forces of productivity, creativity, indeed happiness. The relationship is zero-sum: Power exercised by the government equals liberty lost in the market. The dead hand of regulation, the imposition of rules, stifles innovation, and conversely, in the absence of rules, progress is expected to flower.

For example and as already mentioned, Basel II provides an object lesson in irresponsibility. It is one thing for regulators to admit that they do not know how much capital to require banks to hold in reserve. Indeed, it is not clear that we can ever know precisely what capital requirements are adequate to confront an uncertain future. It is quite another thing to defer the decision to big banks, as does Basel II. After all, big banks have incentives to undercapitalize themselves, are doing business through limited liability structures, are "too big to fail," and for these and other reasons can be relied upon to make sensible decisions in the general interest, even if the reasons for whatever reserve requirements are ultimately decided upon are never really demonstrated. Enough sarcasm: it was quite literally irresponsible to shift these decisions onto banks, which by and large have made bad decisions.

This is not to argue that government regulators necessarily would have gotten global banking right. (Indeed, in light of the performance turned in by the Fed and other central banks, there is little reason to believe that government organs would have insisted on the responsible management of financial institutions, even though bank regulators presumably do not personally or institutionally have great incentives to reduce reserve requirements.) The point here is that government regulators would have been fulfilling their responsibility to make the call, and would be accountable for their failure, at least within the bounds of central bank and other forms of official independence.

But accountability has not been a strong suit of late. Even after the crisis was well into its second year, Greenspan argued that no new regulation was necessary, because (1) such regulation would crush out innovation, and (2) chastened companies would return to the path of virtue. That is, in a world imagined to be bifurcated between "the government" and "the market," where the government is stifling and inefficient, the market is creative and efficient, and power is a zero-sum game, any new rule must result in a net loss of creativity and efficiency. And even after the marketplace tumult of September 2008, Greenspan argued against regulation because marketplace actors had learned. So there was no need to stifle economic activity, the looked-for recovery, with new government regulation. There was still no need, in other words, to take responsibility.

This Manichean view of the relationship between markets and governments (*eros* and *thanatos*) has deep appeal. Weber was hardly wrong; much of bureaucracy is indeed an iron cage and experienced as constraint—and the multiplication of constraints is pretty much the decline of liberty. There is much more to be said about why deregulation was and to some extent still is so compelling, but this entire book should be read as an effort to wean us off such sophomoric bifurcations, *Atlas Shrugged* and all that, in order to express a more capacious and sophisticated understanding of political economy.

Mere explicit statement reveals the stunningly simplistic worldview on which we based our financial policy for decades. When building markets, the question is the soundness of the market, or, to shift metaphors, how the game plays. For pertinent example, one of the reasons that commercial banks survived, and investment banks did not, was that investors (both equity investors and especially depositors) had more confidence in commercial banks. Compared to investment banks, commercial banks were more highly regulated, had more access to government funds, had larger reserves and lower levels of leverage, and, in the case of depositors, there was substantial insurance against losses in the event of collapse. At least under the circumstances of this crisis, the commercial banks took a terrible beating, but they did better than investment banks.

For those on the political right, it perhaps needs to be insisted that in many circumstances, regulation encourages confidence and so spurs economic activity. For all the talk of the joys of deregulation, little business is done in undeveloped countries or failed states, where intrusive bureaucracy is hardly the question. Institutions like bankruptcy, or federal deposit insurance, for example, make it much easier to find the courage to start a business or leave one's cash in the hands of a stranger. Government action may even spur innovation, as we have seen with the Internet, among other examples, although innovation is admittedly difficult and somewhat unpredictable. The practical (and indeed more philosophical) intellectual frame for political economy, and hence financial regulation, is not "the government" versus "the market," but what kind of market?

From this perspective, justifying regulatory irresponsibility (not failure so much as absence) in the name of business freedom is a fundamental mistake. Economic activity, including competition and innovation, the struggles of the marketplace, can only be *politically* justified (argued to be in accordance with a society's virtues) in public terms—such activity must promise a worthwhile way of life. Thus the argument for some new regulation, or indeed the abolition of some existing regulation, must always be that the new market will be an improvement over the current market, the new game will play better. Such an argument is always already political in nature. Such an argument is also impossible to prove *ex ante*—the future is uncertain—but may be more or less plausible, depending on the situation. We must work our way forward, and in that endeavor, business folk and policymakers alike are central actors, not somehow exempt from the construction of their worlds.

Those things said, perhaps those on the left should be reminded that there are serious limits to what bureaucracy, however democratically legitimated, is likely to know—hence the fundamental unseriousness of misty-eyed nostalgia for a viable Marxism, or even the Keynesianism of postwar British Labor governments that one encounters nowadays. (Talk of the rise of a Chinese model is unserious for this and many other reasons, including the sheer unattractiveness of Chinese authoritarianism.) But if regulation is unavoidable, yet the world is uncertain and bureaucrats acknowledge their limited capacities, then how are we to think about financial regulation?

As has been suggested, the previous generation fundamentally avoided this question and devoted itself to deregulation, that is, did not think too much about how to approach the problem of regulation. Regulation should be put in place when markets have failed (in situations where market activity has imposed negative externalities).

For example, in *Regulation and Its Reform*, Stephen Breyer, now a Supreme Court justice, influentially argued that regulation should be eliminated unless it effectively addresses market failure. Such argument did not confront the question "what sort of market" in any positive sense; "the market" was assumed to be what would remain after deregulation.

In response, those on the political left argued that the deregulatory approach produces socially unacceptable outcomes. In particular, leftist (or "liberal" or "progressive") social analysis tended to focus on people, understood as distinct from, and often victimized by, the market. Tactically, leftist arguments often focused on the (bad) arguments for deregulation made from the political right. Such leftist arguments, however, were overly abstract because doubly parasitic—theories about theories about markets and their regulation. Thus, as a substantive matter, critiques on the left were very rarely about the markets, the collective social phenomena, in question. Unfortunately, antideregulation does not produce a deep understanding of how to build markets.

Now that the need for serious thinking about regulation has become apparent, and indeed politically required, we discover that, after a generation or more of deregulation, neither the folks active on the political left nor those on the right have thought very much about how to regulate. We do not have much positive and contemporary, much less new, thinking about regulation. In this regard, it is worth noting that the last major effort to regulate financial markets, the Sarbanes-Oxley Act (SOX) of 2002, was largely a rehash of 1930s' ideas about disclosure. SOX was immediately and widely attacked as being anticompetitive, the dead hand of regulation, and so forth. Indeed.

The great exception to the antiregulatory ideology of the past few decades has been monetary policy. Provision of liquidity engineered soft landings, now criticized; or, to put it more cynically, monetary policy protected asset values, which is something that most of the upper middle class can support. That said, in a time of considerable rancor between red states and blue states, right and left, monetary policy was all things to all people, hence the enormous influence and popularity of Greenspan for so long. Traditional liberals liked monetary policy because it was government action. Market conservatives liked it because it seemed to be working through, rather than against, the desires of investors (which conservatives often simply equated with the health of the market or even the good of society writ large). But throwing money, either narrowly through intervention, or broadly through monetary policy, is strong medicine and often the wrong medicine. Only very rarely should great quantities of money be administered over time in large doses, as demonstrated within living memory by the monetary loosening of the late 1960s and early 1970s.

So, in a world of substantial uncertainty, where efficiency cannot be presumed, and we have little understanding of bureaucracy, much less the possibilities of intervention, although we know that lots of liquidity is rarely the answer, how are we to rethink our financial markets? More to the point of this book, what can we intellectuals, who both benefit from and are limited by our distance, contribute to democratic discourse?

Sometimes the view from the ivory tower is good. With intellectual distance, we may think more clearly about the human significance of marketplace events than the actors themselves. Specifically, policy always rests on perceptions of (usually recent) history. Recent financial disasters teach specific lessons about the failings of existing regulatory approaches, thereby suggesting ways forward. Realizing these ways forward will require a great deal of political work, for which the republic may not have the stomach. Be that as it may, interpretation of this crisis, even a hermeneutic understanding of the character of our failure, how it went down, and what may be learned, and imaginative articulation of what may be hoped are prerequisites to a reasonable policy and hardly useless contributions.

The next chapters approach the problem of substantively rethinking our financial markets in some detail, but a few general points should be made here.

1. Financial regulation has heretofore been dominated by microeconomic concerns; much regulation has sounded in consumer protection. Systemic risk has been a concern, but it usually has been addressed indirectly. This has changed: Systemic problems are now front and center, and social costs borne by individual humans are seen to be the adverse consequences of systemic problems. This shift in focus, from individual harms, easily understood in private terms, to systemic health, inherently social, is part and parcel of understanding markets as ways of constructing politics.

2. There has been a great deal of talk about a prudential systemic risk regulator. The concept of "systemic risk" (like "toxic asset") risks being reified by policy discourse. If systemic risk were readily identifiable, then systemic risk would not be such a problem. But "systemic risk" is a way of talking about a constellation of relationships that threaten the social covenants at the heart of any economy, and the number of such constellations is indeterminate. Political proposals for a systemic risk regulator may not be unwise, but certainly indulge our hopes for living in a much more certain world than we inhabit.

3. Regulators should unapologetically take responsibility. In an era of deregulation, when marketplace efficiency was assumed, regulatory activity (and certainly proposed regulation) tended to be apologetic, abashed at interfering with the no doubt innovative and therefore good operations of the marketplace.

4. Regulators should not presume that they can prevent all damages. Cars are designed to crash, even though the builders hope "their" car never crashes, and presumably the drivers seek to avoid wrecks. Sooner or later, however, for some reason that cannot be specified with regard to a particular vehicle, cars will crash. And so we build cars to survive most accidents. Similarly, if we are going to allow autonomy among economic actors and have markets, we can rest assured that mistakes will be made, and there will be crashes. The fundamental issue for regulators is not preventing problems, but ensuring that the problems are not fatal—that is, preventing disasters.

5. Regulators should not presume to possess perfect knowledge about how to do things. Play with a net, but allow for experimentation. More specifically, where possible, regulation should aim at specifying performance rather than designs. Innovation—discovering new and better ways to do things—is important. And the fun of markets is playing the game, a question to which we now turn. So although regulators should insist on helmets, they ought to let 'em play.

Chapter 6

Constructing Healthy Markets

IT MAY BE HOPED THAT THIS CRISIS WILL PROMPT US TO THINK ABOUT MARKETS in more profound ways. Specifically, we may begin to think of markets as a mode of governance. Like other modes of governance, indeed like the United States itself, markets need to be constituted. Markets do not simply arise like mushrooms after the rain; they are built by people working together. Considering markets as something that we have constructed—built—raises the question of whether a given market has been designed, and is working, well. One of the many infuriating things about the present crisis is that financial policy elites have not had the balls (in light of the macho rhetoric of the past few years, the gendered image is entirely intended) to admit that they, along with the rest of us, built bad markets.

In thinking of markets as things we build, like houses, we will become much more conscious of markets as objects of judgment, as in some sense aesthetic objects. Do we think this market is working about right? Is it the kind of market we would like to see? Self-consciously imagining markets as aesthetic objects is difficult, and much of the rest of this book will begin putting conceptual tools for such an imagination into place. One place to start, however, might be with markets that have been working very, very badly—such as banking in the United States at present. The unwilling nationalizations, or as some wags have called it, "preprivatizations," of banks and other financial institutions raise in rather pressing terms the question of what sorts of markets we wish to have in not unimportant sectors of our economy.

Consider the following sequence of events and their consequences.

1. The current administration, like the last one, has intervened in the financial markets by providing government money to troubled institutions in a variety of financial industries and in auto manufacture.[1] The administration presumably believes that these institutions must be saved in order to save their industries (a dubious but perhaps politically inescapable proposition discussed in Chapter 8).

2. The administration has received a variety of legal rights from these institutions, presumably because it would be politically impossible simply to give the money away.[2] This quid pro quo, rights for cash, has made it possible to document many of these transactions as if they were essentially commercial in nature. Under these "deals," the administration has made grants, received various kinds of shares, extended guarantees, and provided loans of various sorts, some of them nonrecourse (that is, if the borrower does not repay, the lender, the government and ultimately the U.S. taxpayer, has no legal recourse). Complex contracts have been drafted that do not secure much that is enforceable.

3. The administration has explicitly stated that it does not wish to nationalize the institutions it seeks to help. When possible, and not without effort, the interventions have been structured as guarantees, or forms of insurance, so as to avoid having the government take ownership of a controlling equity stake. Even when the administration has been unable to avoid acquiring control, the administration has been slow to exercise the government's proprietary interest.

4. The reasons for the administration's determination not to nationalize are no doubt various and rather unclear. Federal Reserve Chair Ben Bernanke and others have claimed (somewhat implausibly) that the insolvent institutions receiving taxpayer largess have substantial "franchise value," that is, brand value, that would be destroyed if the companies were nationalized. (Why would we be any less fond of our national brands if we actually owned them? We are fond of the national parks or the armed services.) Presumably, such franchise value will have an actual monetary value once happy days are here again.

   More plausibly, the administration has argued that it does not want to run these institutions and therefore does not wish to acquire them. Here the administration is on sound political ground, even though government regularly hires people to run businesses in receivership of one sort or another, notably failed banks. Almost all Americans believe that a wide variety of society's tasks, including almost all of what the financial markets do, should be done through market mechanisms as opposed to bureaucratic agencies, and therefore tend to support the administration's stated desire to stay out of business.

5. However, there are only so many sticks in the bundle of rights that constitute the institution of property. As troubled institutions receive more and more government money, and therefore transfer more and more rights

to the government, at some point the government gains operational control and even de jure ownership. This process has been called "creeping nationalization."

6. The administration has worked hard to preserve the management structure and personnel of institutions that were very badly managed in order to maintain the appearance that these institutions remain independent. Unfortunate circumstances have made the administration's conceit implausible, including the following.

A. First, various institutions that had received emergency transfers of federal funds embarrassed themselves by paying their executives bonuses and otherwise conducting themselves in the ostentatious fashion that has been normal in the past few years. Dennis Kozwalksi's $6,000 shower curtain (Tyco, 2002) was replaced by John Thain's $1,405 wastepaper basket (Merrill Lynch, 2008) as the emblem of the rococo tastes of the executive class. Widespread political outrage ensued, and the administration had to act to stop further bonus payments, encourage the return of bonuses already doled out, and the like.

B. After the initial government payments, it quickly became clear that recipient institutions could be saved from immediate insolvency by the infusion of liquidity, but that mere cash does not buy meaningful reform. In several but by no means all cases, the administration has grudgingly and haltingly exercised its ownership rights to install new and probably better management (doing worse would take considerable effort).

C. By mid-April 2009, it was clear that, despite the first few infusions of cash, banks were not lending. More money, the administration reasoned, was necessary to solve the problem, but Congress was unlikely to authorize more money. Note that past government payments, structured as debt or in some instances as preferred stock in order to avoid the appearance of control (or responsibility?), were considered liabilities for regulatory purposes. Beginning with Citigroup, the administration began converting its "debt" holdings into "equity," thereby giving the banks more money that they could, under applicable regulations, lend, should they decide to do so. Note also that, at least in theory, the administration thereby took on more risk (shareholders are paid after creditors). The government became the controlling shareholder of Citigroup, but note, finally, that the government (and so the taxpayers) received no additional benefits from Citigroup and similarly situated institutions for taking on such extra risk—not that this really matters, since the taxpayers appear to be as liable for Citigroup as is required to secure the continuance of the firm.

D. In the second quarter of 2009, Chrysler and General Motors both declared, and were rushed through, bankruptcy. Over the objection of superficially secured creditors, who were pressured by the administration, Chrysler was sold in a fire sale to Fiat. With no plausible buyer for General

Motors in sight, the U.S. government acquired near total ownership of the corporation.

E. Because of its repeated infusions of cash, the government acquired some 80 percent of AIG.

Nonetheless, the administration continued to downplay its controlling role. In June 2009, the Congressional Budget Office maintained that the operations of Citigroup, General Motors, and AIG were not part of the federal budget, in part because it was not clear that the administration would exercise its power over the companies.[3]

7. The administration thus found itself in the odd position of taking action for a public purpose and, as a rather strange result, *unwillingly owning* banks and other financial institutions. The unhappiness of taxpayers—and Congress—about this state of affairs ranged from resignation to outrage.

8. Unwilling nationalization pointedly raised the question of how to (re)establish markets. The widespread discomfort over nationalization indicated a broad-based political, one might even say constitutional, consensus that certain enterprises ought to be conducted through markets. How are banks and other financial institutions to be induced to run their own affairs in sensible fashion?

9. Rather than supporting the traditional opposition between economics and politics, in which government responds to the failure of markets, the problem of starting markets again suggested a different worldview, in which markets are understood not to be opposed to politics, but as an expression of political life, governance mechanisms appropriate for numerous social enterprises. Politics, here, preceded markets, not the other way around. This was a 180-degree turn from the philosophical assumptions of the age of deregulation.

10. As the administration sought to reestablish markets in which competitive businesses worked, its position echoed, in a smaller way, the epochal shifts in the Soviet Union and China during the 1980s, when the powerful decided that some things needed to be done through market mechanisms, the competitive interaction of relatively autonomous actors, rather than through central planning.

11. A great deal of money was provided to banks and other financial institutions. Precisely why these institutions were recapitalized is less than clear.

A. It was widely believed and often said that a well-functioning credit market is critical for the maintenance of a healthy economy. It seems to have been presumed (without much discussion) that if banks had money, they would lend it, because that is what banks do, lend money. But much of the money given to banks was used for various things apart from making loans: the acquisition of weaker banks; the payment of bonuses; the renegotiation of hitherto unrecognized balance sheet weaknesses; the strengthening of reserves. In short, there was no direct connection between the liquidity provided to banks and the extension of credit, which, after all, requires not only money in the bank, but also willingness to lend. Unfortunately, this unconfident time saw hesitancy to borrow and far greater hesitancy to lend. So the federal government provided banks with unprecedented amounts of money, but the credit markets were slow to thaw as unemployment and deficits mounted.

B. It is more than a little possible that the purpose of recapitalizing important financial institutions was simply because they were important—the commercial fabric of the nation should not be subjected to the sudden death of too many of its most important firms. So the government gave institutions cash, guaranteed their obligations, and took a soft line with their regulation (not very stressful tests, very accommodating accounting). As of this writing, the administration continues to do what it can to get our teams through these trying times. This is perhaps politically necessary, but unfortunately less than egalitarian—and so, for "populist" reasons, we spend a great deal of time talking about the social benefits of a well-functioning credit system.

12. Now that it is clear that the administration is willing to ensure the survival and substantial market share of financial institutions it deems vital, these favored institutions appear to be somewhat more plausible investments, and so the price for stock in some once troubled financial institutions has seen a modest increase, and a number of surviving institutions, operating in a world of guaranteed credit and with little competition, have made large profits. (Once again, Warren Buffett wins—with a 10 percent guaranteed annual dividend, only further damage to Goldman [unlikely, considering its new market dominance and explicit and implicit government guarantees] coupled with truly devastating and sustained inflation would seem to threaten his position.) For various reasons of their own, the government and the press across the political spectrum have hailed stock market increases and profits as proof of the fundamental soundness of the financial markets, and even "green shoots" for the economy as a whole, once again confusing the few with the many.

*   *   *

It seems clear that the federal government will be much more involved in the operations of the capital markets in the near future than they were in the past. As noted in Chapter 1, it has become clear that the federal government, when confronted with a credible threat of a systemic meltdown, will provide liquidity to the financial markets. The government has in fact provided so much liquidity that some recipients of the largesse have been more or less purchased—that is, nationalized. Moreover, and as has been widely remarked, if the government is expected to act in a crisis, then the government may be expected (and it would be more prudent) to act before a crisis arises—that is, to regulate. Government regulation of the financial markets will continue to increase for some time. So, as in the New Deal, we see organs of the state deeply involved in the financial markets, and it is now again silly to talk of a financial market somehow "free" from government activity.

As a jurisprudential matter, none of this is new, though a lot of it has been rather willfully forgotten over the past generation. Ever since the American Legal Realists of the 1930s, lawyers have pointed out that markets are constructed upon and through laws—property law, contract law, securities law, banking law, law regulating the payment system and the working conditions of the janitorial staff—for these purposes, law is basically the formalization of social relations and is everywhere. (It bears mentioning that perhaps the most prominent Realist, Karl Lewellyn, ended up drafting the Uniform Commercial Code, and a fellow traveler, William O. Douglas, was chairman of the SEC before becoming a Supreme Court justice.) From this perspective, "the Market" is an abstraction that is pretty much only useful for philosophical discourse, like "the State." In the real world, however, we have markets, in the plural, just as we have governments, and within governments, executives, agencies, courts, and so on; and in the real world, the forms of political life jostle and interpenetrate one another, as hard as that is for intellectuals to remember.

It is true, if perhaps a bit too easy, to note that the bifurcation between state and market continues to survive due both to a lack of imagination and to the fact that the bifurcation is convenient for partisan politics. At a much deeper level, however, the problem is agency. Governments, on one hand, are inevitably personified, thought of as the will of the sovereign, and judged in essentially moral terms: Did the king act as a good father to his people? (Liberals, in the sense the word is used in U.S. partisan politics, tend to trust in the father, to be paternalistic. Conservatives traditionally worry about the power of the sovereign, with due exceptions made for times when the president is nominally conservative.) Markets, on the other hand, are imagined as realms of self-interest, competition, and disunity. (Liberals see markets as immoral, or at least uncharitable, whereas conservatives tend to portray markets as spaces for honest toil and freedom.)

So the problem posed by the political desire to establish markets is this: How are we to think about a structure, even as we think about competitive struggle? The ideas seem incompatible. Or how do we think about government policy, if at the same time we want marketplace actors to act autonomously, and therefore in some (limited) sense to be "private"—to act on their own behalf? Although we expect business folk to act in their own interests, we also hope that markets serve society's interests, and although we expect government to act in the public interest, we also know that government officials, politicians, tend to protect the power of their positions even when they are not personally corrupt. So how are we to think about these conflicts when we know (or should know) that the intellectual position—the position of the author and of most readers of this book—is neither responsible nor necessarily pure of heart? We may wish for a politics of markets, but how do we think through and construct such a politics? The next chapter considers these questions in more detail.

Chapter 7

Metaphors for Thinking Socially about Capitalism

AN ESSENTIALLY TRAGIC AND SO LEGAL CONCEPTION OF THIS FINANCIAL crisis, Chapter 4 argued, teaches that marketplace danger should be confronted with the understanding that finance both is socially articulated (with its characters and logics legally defined) and, conversely, constitutes social spaces. Capitalism is always already social.

But what does this statement—that capitalism is social—mean? After all, the "social" traditionally has been understood in politics on both the left and the right as antithetical to the marketplace, hence the term "socialism," which we all know is rather antagonistic to capitalism, concerned with "the social costs" of "unfettered markets" even when not about seizing the means of production. So "thinking socially about capitalism" simply does not compute very well; it does not parse in the political grammar of the past few centuries as other than an awkward compromise (the resigned view of modern European social democratic parties).

Be that as it may, a directly political understanding of capitalism is a better way to understand not only our society but also the practical measures taken by the United States and other governments to shore up financial markets. Presuming that governments act in the public interest, at least until proven otherwise, and that even in the face of corruption, it may be worthwhile to think about what ought to be done in our circumstances (that is, we may try to be both principled and realistic), then one of the things that has been already decided is that the capital markets are themselves essentially public—or else why would we tolerate giving so many tax dollars to a bunch of rich financiers? If we understand capital markets to serve the public good, though, and so are willing to spend public money to aid private entities, then we are entitled to ask specifically how these markets help society and how they can do still more good. So, practically put, if government is going to spend money to save financial institutions, how can it do so in a way that best facilitates the broader social benefits generated by the operation of the capital markets? Answers to such questions should be considerably more specific than hazy invocations of the invisible hand.

If, however uncomfortably, we no longer deny the social character of our capital markets, then we must confront considerable intellectual difficulties. We do not have a very well-developed conceptual tool kit for thinking socially about markets. The bifurcation between left and right, between solidarity and competition, has ruled our imaginations and our political discourse for so long that it is difficult to think in other terms in sustained fashion. What passes for political thinking about markets in these hard times tends to tip over into a damp moralism or a libertarian zealotry, depending on the character of the thinker. An intellectual task for the present, then, is to find terms through which social capitalism can be articulated. In discussing how we govern ourselves through markets, we should bear in mind the somewhat conflicting propositions (1) that we are thinking about markets, so that there will be winners and losers, and messiness, some of which is creative, and (2) that markets are ways of organizing people, and so humane concern is demanded. In order to do this, we need new metaphors, new conceptual grammar, through which to talk about markets and hence about financial regulation. Such metaphors should allow us to think structurally and synchronically about the role government might play without—and this is critical—destroying the autonomy and energy, the animal spirits, that make markets so fecund. Such metaphors should help us to think more clearly about governance through markets.

It should immediately and truly be objected that we have always governed through markets. In particular, the financial markets are finely wrought, incredibly elaborate contexts for the management of capital. The housing market, especially securitization, is the product of explicit government policies. Environmental law—for example, carbon trading—often understands the importance of creating markets in order to do society's work. And so forth.

Indeed. Such thinking, however, tends to replicate the dichotomy between government and markets even as it gets much more sophisticated about the details of the relationship in this or that context, such as broker-dealer regulation or carbon trading. So, in the environmental context, thinking about "markets" is fairly instrumental. Policymakers should use the market as a tool to achieve policy goals (known a priori, or else why bother going to graduate school?), especially at low cost and with a high chance of being effective. In the financial context, we frequently speak of regulators setting "bounds" to markets. We worry about social costs, and government is expected to provide a safety net. Government is expected to "respond" to crisis and other market failures. And so forth.

Games Metaphor

We might imagine markets dynamically through the metaphor of games. Like a market, a game is played by, happens among, competitors, actors who struggle against one another. The players in a game, again, like the actors in a market, are autonomous: They decide how they wish to play against one another, or do business, as the case may be. And like games (even individual sports, if we consider training), markets require cooperation as well as competition.

A game is not independent of its rules; the game can only be understood in terms of its rules. The rules shape and inform how the players play even if they do not determine who wins, or by how much. This, too, is like a market. Theft is not business. More generally, expectations, customs, and laws organize how business is done, how parties cooperate and compete.

More interesting still for present purposes, changes in the rule structure may change the nature of the games we play or the results of competition. For example, before the introduction of the three-point shot in basketball, the game was largely about controlling the space under the basket, a space that therefore was frequently very crowded. The addition of a three-point line meant that more points would be scored from outside the line. Since three points can be quite significant, and some players can consistently hit shots from that distance, such players need to be guarded. But guarding such players away from the basket opens up space under and around the basket, which changes the nature of the inside game. In short, adding the three-point shot changed the "shape" of basketball.

It would be strange to say that the rules providing for a three-point shot (in addition to the old rules, providing for two points for a field goal and one point for a free throw) respond to some "failure" of basketball. The old rules worked just fine for decades. Basketball, with or without a three-point shot, is still basketball. But, as suggested above, one might prefer the slightly different dynamic of basketball played with a three-point shot (or a shot clock, for another example, a rule that forces the ball to be turned over more often). And for that matter, the distance of the three-point line from the basket can be moved, for different levels of play (college or professional), with subtle effects on the guarding calculus made by players in real time—the variations are endless. By analogy, the widespread tendency to understand regulation as an effort to prevent market failures—the orthodoxy that underpins regulatory thought after the age of deregulation—wrong-headed thinking. There is no market, as there is no game, without rules. Changes to the rules, efforts at regulation (always experienced as a modification of the status quo ante), thus always reflect what may very broadly and too philosophically be called an aesthetics, a sensibility that inspires us to want to see something different when we watch a basketball game.

The actual practice of regulation (to be distinguished from the contemporary ideology of regulation based on market failure) is much like setting the rules of a game: Both are driven by an aesthetic speculation of how the efforts of the players might work out under the new circumstances. So, for example, in granting monopolies (to colonize foreign lands or, these days, to profit from inventions) in order to spur innovation, or in breaking up monopolies in order to spur competition, law speculates on how business folk will play through the new situation. A striking and very relevant example of this interplay between field and game, stage and play, regulation and business is the quite conscious effort, by the federal government in the postwar era, to craft a housing market that made home ownership widely available. The government fostered the securitization of home mortgages, so that banks had more money to lend, thereby increasing the volume of home lending. Moreover, the government allowed an income tax deduction for interest payments on money borrowed to buy a primary residence, and people borrowed more to buy homes and bought more homes. In so legislating, the government was not responding to market failure; the government was shaping a market.

From this perspective, the idea that regulation should address the negative externalities of a transaction (at least where parties cannot be expected to bargain at relatively low cost) can be understood as a sense that certain consequences of a given transaction should be incorporated into the property regime. Rephrased, the orthodoxy of the deregulatory era is a special case of the broader point made here, the idea that, in regulating, we imagine a marketplace that is different in some ways from the marketplace we currently have, with a different set of likely plays

Turning to the left, to imagine markets in terms of games is substantially different from socialism, of whatever degree, precisely in its embrace of competition, not as an unfortunate necessity, but as an arena for certain sorts of life, with serious rewards, both for individuals and for society as a whole.

The image of the game is particularly apt at present, when the crisis has produced many losers, but some big winners, too. Participation in games presumes trust. Teammates obviously have to trust one another. Athletes have to trust their trainers and managers. Players have to trust that the sport will be administered, and competition will be officiated, fairly. Players have to trust that other players will abide by the rules. Especially in physically risky sports, players must be able to trust that other players will not endanger them, at least not beyond expected bounds. For example, football presumes tackles, but it includes stiff sanctions against unnecessary roughness. Likewise, business practice includes trust—that is, more than rational self-interest. Coworkers must trust each other in countless ways. Parties to a contract, who often have opposed economic interests, each must be able to trust that the other will abide by the terms of the contract and, oftentimes, by its spirit. Such trust is rarely absolute; contracts may be enforced judicially and otherwise. That acknowledged, few contracts are entered into upon the expectation of judicial enforcement, which is expensive, slow, and uncertain. And most important, nobody wants to play a game that has been fixed against them; nobody wants to be a patsy. So when trust completely evaporates, games end, and financial markets—which are markets in credit, that is, trust—simply cease to exist.

The speed with which a financial market can evaporate—recent examples include markets for short-term commercial paper, CLOs, and auction rate securities—is astounding. Even "brick and mortar" markets can go soft within very short periods of time. It is odd to think of markets as avoidable, perhaps because economists have taught that markets follow necessary laws, as does nature, and scarcity is part of the human condition. But as the Depression or the current crisis should have taught us, markets must be attractive or people will not participate, and the market will wither and die.

Trust is so important for both games and businesses because, in choosing to enter the arena, players must believe they have a chance. Players must continually choose to enter into the arena. The arena is understood to have its dangers, and other ways of life have their attractions. There are few things that one needs today. Water, perhaps. But for most things, most of the time, we can, like Bartleby, prefer not to do business. We may refuse to extend commercial credit; to make home loans; to buy a new car; to buy anything made in China—to take obvious recent examples of some social significance. It takes something to go forward, to decide to participate, as opposed to doing nothing, waiting. Whether we speak of the individual investor's uncertainty, of the trust between business partners, or of the confidence of an entire marketplace, the question is the same: Will the game be played? In a commercial society, this may seem an unusual question. But those of us who have forgotten the history of the Depression might pause to consider buying a house, or rebalancing our retirement funds, or making almost any other large investment. At least as of this writing, uncertainty stalks the land, and people and institutions hang back to wait and see.

In such circumstances, government should attempt to inspire confidence, encourage people to "get off the sidelines" and "get in the game." This is, admittedly, not an easy thing to do. Once upon a time, it was believed that simple government spending would restore confidence. People would be paid; they would buy things; opportunities would become evident; people would invest … and happy days would be here again. Now we know that matters are not so simple, but the focus of government action—and the criterion by which proposed responses to the crisis should be judged—should remain the reestablishment of confidence.

Tensegrity Metaphor

Kenneth Snelson's tensegrity sculptures provide a marvelous image for a social structure composed of self-aggrandizing parts and, as a bonus, help us to imagine the failure of such a structure, in finance called systemic risk. Although the rigid elements of Snelson's towers are discrete, and indeed pull against one another, the structure stands so long as the cable remains taut. The building is integrated by tension, hence the term "tensegrity." In contrast, conventional edifices are built on the principles of compression. The solid masses push, together, against the force of gravity. Think of a load-bearing wall, in which the weight of the building pushes down, and the wall pushes up, or supports. Higher parts rest upon, are built on, the foundation of the lower ones. Those social edifices known as markets are much like towers built according to principles of tensegrity. Just as the tower's cable pulls, members of *Homo economicus* are said to be self-interested, acquisitive, grasping. The building stands, however, because the cable's pulling does not move anything: The cable's tension, mediated by the bars of the tower, opposes and hence balances itself. Thus it is the balanced tension among the distinct parts that makes the structure stand—an architectural and rather static expression of Adam Smith's argument that individual self-interest forms a collective, a marketplace (an even more precise expression of Marshall's dream of markets in equilibrium).

Tensegrity is a particularly apt conception of financial markets, especially if we shift the metaphor slightly to see the cable's tension as representing that particular form of self-interest known as credit. Virtually all financial institutions are leveraged, that is, the sum of their obligations vastly exceeds the sum of their capital (indeed, what counts as "capital" is always a more concrete form of credit, but let us bracket that ontological difficulty). So long as highly leveraged institutions continue to pay one another, individual institutions, and the system, function. But what if, as with Bear Stearns, some question arises about whether an institution can meet its obligations as they come due? It is often unclear precisely why, how, or from whence such questions arise, but nevertheless, somehow it comes to be rumored that there may be a problem. Institutions tend to deny such rumors, of course, but then they would, wouldn't they? Hearing such rumors, institutions might be slow to pay, or might demand extra collateral, or might refuse to roll over credit, or might cut a credit line, as JPMorgan did to Bear Stearns. And so a rumor might become fact.

Credit is crucial. Without credit—the trust of other financial institutions, and hence willingness to lend and trade—participation in the financial system is impossible. Since all financial institutions are leveraged, not least in their trading arrangements, no financial institution is in principle invulnerable to a sudden loss of creditworthiness. In the grim fall of 2008, even mighty Goldman Sachs, ostentatiously well connected and the last man standing among investment banks, found itself embarrassingly denied access to the credit markets.[1] This despite the money borrowed directly from the federal government, the infusion of tax dollars received from AIG, and the elimination of meaningful competition in most of Goldman's enterprises. And still, unreasonable investors, perhaps ignorant of just how oligarchic the state of play was and is, would not lend to Goldman. Fortunately for the firm, the federal government guaranteed its commercial paper, so that Goldman was able to borrow from the "private" markets, continue operating, and indeed make a profit. As of April 2009, Goldman sought to raise additional capital (and what could the risk possibly be, having secured a federally funded mandate—the sort of monopoly once enjoyed by the East India Company?) and to return money borrowed directly from the Treasury (why borrow when being guaranteed is so much more liberating?).

Network Metaphor

Consider the basic architecture of the Internet: Information is divided into packets, distributed over a network, and recombined at its destination. The destruction of a particular pathway would cause data to be rerouted. Perhaps data transmission would slow down, but it would not be stopped. More generally, the destruction of a part of a net does not destroy the net itself. A net with a hole in it retains most, if not all, of its integrity. A more centralized system, which might be pictured as a wheel, is contrastingly vulnerable. If the hub of a wheel is destroyed, the wheel ceases to exist. There are lessons here, more than metaphorical, for the construction of financial networks. A system should be relatively decentralized, enough to survive the sudden incapacitation of a nodal point (such as AIG). Institutions may be key, but they should not be vital. Connections should be redundant and pathways multiple.

At the same time, like all structures, nets have their own vulnerabilities. A surge in the electrical power grid may do widespread damage. A computer network is vulnerable to the propagation of viruses, and so to spying, precisely because it is a network, with nodal points in communication with one another. (The military operates computers offline.) And in a financial network, rumors of counterparty risk can propagate across chains of obligation, leading highly leveraged institutions to suspend payment in precautionary anticipation of nonpayment, bringing the system to an abrupt halt.

So the challenge, for financial regulation and practice, is to build a financial network that is sufficiently robust, and perceived as such, that sudden failure of important institutions does not cause the system to lock up. Techniques that may help with this effort are discussed in Chapter 9.

Ecology Metaphor

The intellectual history of economics might be understood as a succession of ways to socialize conceptions of nature, so that implicit imaginations of what nature is inform our understandings of economics and financial regulation. In particular, Thomas Malthus was concerned with breeding. For Malthus, the drive to procreate set in place implacable social logics, at least among the lower classes, who were doomed to poverty by their irresistible urge to fornicate, and its foreseeable issue, population growth. Even for Aristotle, long before the development of modern economics, *oekonomica* is the art of household management, and households are fundamentally concerned with feeding and breeding, a domain of necessity, but merely biological. And at this point it is trite to note that both classical and neoclassical economics view the world in essentially, and literally, Darwinian terms. (At least until real asset values are threatened, at which point arguments about improving the breed tend to be replaced by humanitarian concerns for systemic risk and the virtues of the lender of last resort.) More generally, science is by definition the study of nature. Therefore, if we are to have a science of trading, markets will be understood naturalistically.

Assuming that we will retain a science of markets, then we may expect our economics to continue to track our changing imaginations of, and stances vis-à-vis, "nature." Even at this relatively early date, two fundamental developments seem relevant.

First, nature is increasingly studied and understood in terms of ecosystems—that is, as a system or network. The nineteenth-century emphasis on a relentless struggle for survival has shifted somewhat to an interest in how multiple types of organisms (or organisms within organisms) work in some web—often competitive struggle, but sometimes cooperative or symbiotic relationships—with each other within a given setting. In contrast to the nineteenth-century imagination, which saw the world as tightly organized by stable patterns of necessity enforced by death, the life sciences now chronicle periods of evolutionary stability, in which species survive relatively unchanged for substantial lengths of time, and there can be mass die-offs that kill indiscriminately without "selecting" much. There is a greater emphasis now as well on sex—mutation, speciation, cross-fertilization (or not, leading perhaps to genetic vulnerability)—and on accidents, ranging from the appearance of new predators to asteroids. The resulting organisms must of course be viable in order to be evolutionarily significant, but the circumstances and hence the viability of such organisms may in substantial degree be random, or informed by exogenous factors, often human in origin. Invasive species may move with relative ease into new environments, by which they were not shaped, but in which they do just fine. In the right circumstances, "weaker" species may survive. One could go on, but to generalize, the imagination of the life sciences has become considerably more contextual, holistic, and complicated, but by the same token, more accidental, less deterministic, less able to trace the lines of a priori necessity internal to the system, than the mind of the nineteenth-century thought it discerned.[2]

Second, in an age of both global warming and neurobiology, nature is not understood to be completely distinct from humanity. This is hardly the place to attempt to resolve the relationship between the two, but it is important to note the widespread sense of responsibility for the natural, for the environment. This is, after all, our home. At the same time, we also understand ourselves as part of nature—indeed, in natural terms, as at least also, animals. By analogy, one might think that we would come to feel responsibility for the shape of our markets, for it is our markets that sustain us, that form our way of life and indeed ourselves. In doing so, we might shift our image of markets from "a jungle" to older images of "a garden." Gardens are fascinating places of *both* planning and necessity, dependent on fortune, somewhat bounded and set apart from the broader environment, governed by the gardener, who is dependent on the garden's produce.

Part III

On Policy

Chapter 8

Restoring Confidence after a Crash

Reconstruction and Development

$\mathbf{A}$GAIN, LET US TAKE IT AS A GIVEN THAT IN A FINANCIAL CRISIS ADMINISTRATIONS will intervene, that is, spend tax dollars in an effort to stabilize the markets in question. It is an article of faith in certain circles that an expectation of such intervention will cause captains of industry to engage in even riskier behavior than they would otherwise, so-called moral hazard. Perhaps this is true, but as discussed in Chapter 1, in a crisis, governments often let the future fend for itself, and intervention proceeds. But how should government act?

Let us also take it as a given that the activity in question ought to be conducted through a market rather than through some other social mechanism. If markets are like games, a serious crisis may cause people and institutions to stop playing, to stop participating in the market. So, for example, bad investments by banks have recently led to a loss of faith in banks, which in turned caused banks to hoard what capital they had—that is, to stop lending. To quip, banks stopped being banks. In addressing the crisis, then, government needs to find ways to encourage potential market actors to enter the market, to get the players to play. And here we are at the marvelous, and somewhat frustrating, problem at the heart of market regulation: The game cannot be forced. Business cannot be commanded, or else it ceases to be a game—or a market. So, in intervening in distressed markets, a government seeks to rebuild a field of dreams, and hopes they will come again and resume play.

Confusion in the Aftermath of the Crisis

Many of the federal government's efforts to address the current economic crisis have been compromised by a failure to make important distinctions among different aspects of society: (1) the people, or society writ large; (2) particular industries, such as banking, insurance, and car manufacturing, that may be critical to the well-being of the society; (3) workers within these industries; (4) corporations, such as Citigroup, AIG, or General Motors; and (5) the managing officers of these corporations.

In particular, the managers of dominant corporations have been treated, for example, as if they themselves *were* the industries they dominated and (unsurprisingly) claimed to represent. It is said that the severity of the crisis left the administration no choice—the actions taken had to be taken. One must be on guard, however, against sloppy thinking justified as political necessity. Distinctions undrawn, the administration's appropriate desire to do something to protect the economic health of the nation has meant, in practice, bailing out ships with great tears in their hulls and often even rewarding their captains. The confusion between "industry" and "corporation" is somewhat understandable, not least because "an industry" cannot appear before Congress or cash a check. Corporate officers can and do. As a practical matter, it is difficult to help "the auto industry" or "the banking industry," as such, because an industry is an abstraction. So, being pragmatic, surely it makes some sense to help leading (or once leading and still large) enterprises. But we should be clear: The government's responsibility is to its people, and hence to the economy, sometimes including the well-being, or at least the orderly demise, of specific industries. The government owes no special responsibility to specific corporations, their managers, or even their employees.

The benefits of government interventions into financial and other industries—indeed, the benefits of almost any government effort—are unevenly distributed. At some point, however, using public means to favor specific private interests becomes unseemly and tips over into corruption. And so a government that determines that it must bail out key corporations in order to counter systemic risk is faced with the necessity of engaging in noble corruption, like the noble rot of winemaking fame, but harder to manage.

Government bailouts can lead, and in this crisis have led, to a number of more or less familiar problems. The simple and serious problem up front is not moral hazard, but old-fashioned "throwing good money after bad." Who believes that the acquisition of certain "toxic" assets was Citigroup's only mistake? It seems far more possible that Citi acquired, indeed created, bad assets because it was badly run. In that case, buying, or guaranteeing, Citi's losses does little to reestablish the institution's credibility, let alone the viability of the industry. And so one request for money is followed by another, at Citi, at AIG, at GM. But how is flooding General Motors with liquidity going to teach the company how to be good at what it used to do? Confusing a corporation with an industry fosters the generally mistaken idea that improving the cash flow of a corporation will restore that institution's place in the marketplace and even revive the marketplace. In central banking jargon: Government bailouts tend to treat fundamental solvency problems as passing liquidity problems. In its efforts to convince the markets that leaking ships are in fact seaworthy, the government assumes large, and indefinite, exposure: More and more money is required to make a case that few find convincing. By and large, investors do not buy for good reason: The business model makes no sense. Only after the stock price has crashed, and the government has made clear that the company will not be allowed to fail, and that equity holders will not be altogether wiped out, is one likely to see investors returning to buy, but what they are buying is essentially a government security.

The confusion has other dire consequences. As discussed in Chapter 6, because the government does not want to give taxpayer money away, it must insist on rights from the corporation in return for the provision of liquidity. Soon enough, the corporation in question is nationalized, in legal fact or in effect. But the government has little expertise—or even desire—to run such companies on an ongoing basis. To make matters worse, taxpayers are placed, as owners, in the position of hoping that their (badly run) company does better than a (presumably better run) company that was not nationalized. For example, we are placed in the awkward position of having to hope that the banks that received Troubled Asset Relief Program (TARP) funding take business from banks that did not need the funding in the first place. In the same vein, new businesses that might enter the marketplace are discouraged from competing with the now national company, and Schumpeter's creative destruction does not happen.

Nationalization also raises questions of security. The creation of national corporations is fundamentally in tension with the liberal trading regime that the United States has struggled to erect since the end of World War II, a regime that grew out of the belief that protectionism lay at the root of the national wars. We may complain about globalization, but we should not forget the very real peace and prosperity it has brought. The difficulties of contemporary global politics are dwarfed by the nationalist horrors of the twentieth century, and the surest way to return to those horrors is to redefine economies in aggressively national terms.

And, probably not last but definitely not least, bailouts rarely work.[1] There is no reason to assume that the money provided to bail out a corporation, and thereby reduce some social harm—for example, to counter a dearth of credit—will in fact be used for such purposes. Dollars are fungible, and TARP money has been used for many things besides easing the credit crunch: for corporate acquisitions, for executive bonuses, and, more justifiably, if still not for the stated purpose of the funds, to strengthen reserves. More generally, the news, for the institutions in question and for the economy as a whole, has gotten worse, not better, since the Treasury and the Fed began moving so "aggressively" to address the problem(s). Bracketing our immediate situation, the general issue for a liberal government is how to intervene (spend tax dollars) to prevent widespread social harms caused by the hasty insolvency of failed businesses, without assuming the burden of running such businesses. Here is a way to begin thinking about the problem.

Nationalize, Liquidate

Suppose that some markets for certain goods (very broadly understood) within a given society are in crisis, so that the goods in question are scarce. The crisis in these markets imperils other markets, and even the well-being of the broader society. Further suppose that, despite the failure of these markets, the society in question remains committed to providing these goods through market mechanisms. Suppose, in short, a situation like that of the United States at present.

How might such a society begin to think about reviving its markets? Surely some attention must be paid to the market institutions, corporations, that are failing? And surely it must be clear that, despite recent disasters, the same or similar businesses can be, and indeed will be, profitable?

Resolution Authority

To recapitulate from Chapter 6: In its bashfulness over taking equity stakes, its insistence that Lehman Brothers failed because no buyer presented itself one Sunday afternoon, and so on, the administration has attempted to present the restructuring of the financial industries in excessively "private" terms. A degree of analytic and even democratic clarity would be gained by dispensing with this charade. Any given Sunday that the Federal Reserve and the Treasury get together to transfer billions of dollars, the public has an interest in the proceedings.

At issue at present, therefore, would be to create a legal mechanism through which the government can take direct legal control over insolvent institutions, not just banks, that are deemed to present systemic risks—the social equivalent of a bankruptcy filing by creditors, but on behalf of the nation rather than debt holders. Although the government already has the authority to seize banks, new legal authority is needed to provide for the honest and timely nationalization of nonbank institutions rather than the creeping nationalization we currently enjoy. (In light of the insolvency of the institution in question, issues of just compensation for the taking of private property should be minimal and manageable after the fact.)

Minimizing Social Harm

Intervention, nationalization, and government expenditure of tax dollars on behalf of an industry are (correctly) justified not by the pain of a discrete group of economic actors, but by broader reactions to the failure of such actors. Having seized legal control of the entity, the government's first order of business is to ensure that the specific social danger that justifies the intervention is directly addressed. During a time of institutional transition, government should take the economic place of the failed firm, on a temporary basis, in order to fulfill the social function that had been fulfilled by the failed institution and that the government is seeking to protect.

The Financial System. In many crises, including those involving Bear Stearns, Lehman Brothers, Merrill Lynch, AIG, and arguably the short-term paper and money markets, as in the late 1990s case of Long Term Capital Management, the public goal is to maintain the financial system, specifically, to maintain the flow of funds through the financial system despite the emergence of counterparty risk and concomitant uncertainty. If a financial institution is unsure that its counterparties will perform (because the counterparty is insolvent, or widely believed to be insolvent and hence illiquid, or merely exposed to an insolvent institution), then the institution may rationally and preemptively refuse to roll over credit (as JPMorgan did with Bear Stearns), withhold payment, or simply fail to execute trades. Much like a bank confronting a run, lack of faith in a trading institution may render it insolvent (unable to pay its debts as they become due) even if the institution is fundamentally sound (that is, has a positive balance sheet), because it will be denied access to liquidity. For government seeking to address such situations, basic principles of central bank intervention on behalf of banks apply: Provide liquidity, guarantee that trading positions will be honored, and sort out the long-term position of the institution. Specifically, in the case of a prime broker, such as Lehman Brothers, the government should have done more to reassure Lehman's trading partners, many of whom had substantial collateral at Lehman, that trades would be conducted on an orderly basis. (In the absence of an international law governing emergency resolution, discussed briefly below, it is unclear how this could have been done, except by keeping Lehman alive.) Much as deposit insurance has made runs on banks rare, knowledge that governments are prepared to seize and operate other financial operations should make structurally similar liquidity crises similarly rare.

Resolution of a financial institution thus involves an inescapably somewhat hazy distinction between an institution's short-term "trading" obligations and its longer-term "debt" obligations and equity interests. Roughly speaking, the first set of obligations pertains to the firm's position within the financial network, that is, to systemic risk, and to the reason for government intervention in the first place. The second set of obligations, along with the net of trading positions, determines the institution's worth to its owners, its equity position, in which the government has no real interest—this failed company is just a company like any other, and dealing with its insolvency is the domain of bankruptcy law.

Moreover, because they are not due immediately, longer-term obligations, in general, may be considered on their merits, renegotiated, discounted, and so forth. The ramifications of such payments (or nonpayments or partial payments) may be worked out by all concerned without forcing institutions to suspend trading operations. To return to the metaphor of tensegrity, the function of government intervention is to occupy the position of the failed institution in the financial system, to maintain the tension in the cable, while new arrangements are structured. Simultaneously, the affairs of the failed institutions are restructured or wound up.

A difficulty: Systemic risk, or more broadly, the social harm that occasions the government's action, cannot be equated with the scale of the institution. Neither Enron nor Worldcom presented immediate risks to the financial system in the way that much smaller institutions, such as Bear Stearns, did. That said, a succession of Enrons does present risks to the financial system, namely, loss of faith in accounting, and hence disclosure, and hence equity positions. Similarly, despite their sometimes enormous scale, most troubled insurance companies do not seem to present risks to the financial system, because the relatively slow speed with which their funds are managed allows counterparties to react in measured fashion, that is, to continue trading. By the same token, however, a sustained set of failures in the insurance industry, leading to loss of faith in the activity of insurance, would be a matter of public concern, for which government intervention would be appropriate.[2]

Employees. In a very few cases, most notably the U.S.-based auto industry, but perhaps certain other distressed sectors (agriculture in a drought), the social danger justifying the government use of tax dollars to intervene on behalf of certain players is sudden unemployment. Although the issue in such cases is not uncertainty and the unwillingness of counterparties to trade, the appropriate government response is structurally analogous to the intervention on behalf of a failing financial institution: The government should *temporarily* take the economic position of the failing institution. So, in a case like that of General Motors, suppliers and existing employees should be assured that their existing contracts will be honored. In order to allow an orderly transition out of the corporation, it may be necessary to use tax dollars to pay base salaries, for example, for some substantial period.

Orderly Liquidation

All parties should understand that the corporation in question will not survive long. Practically, this means that managers will lose their jobs and will need to seek new employment. Managers are not thereby disadvantaged; they would have lost their jobs if the government had not seized control of the corporation. Perhaps more important as a political matter, letting managers go would largely avoid the problem of using taxpayer money to pay stratospherically high bonuses to defeated managers. Managers who are kept on to help with the liquidation should be smartly compensated, as should the various administrators hired by the government, because liquidation can be complex work. And perhaps good managers will find work with solvent firms, which will pay them bonuses—but that will not be the affair of the government or the taxpayers. Similarly, equity investors should expect to be wiped out—that is the cost of making a bad equity investment, and the reason why equity investors should be diversified. For their part, debt holders should be grateful to get away with a haircut. Remember, the patient here is the industry, not the corporation.

The government should bundle the corporation's assets in relatively small, exceedingly transparent pools and auction such pools off. That is, instead of a "bad bank" that somehow purges existing institutions of their impurities, supposedly leading to investor enthusiasm for companies that only yesterday were run into the ground, the government should create—and sell—very simple "good banks." More generally, in an extension of the approach used by the Resolution Trust Corporation to (eventually) resolve the S&L crisis, good companies should buy good assets. So, for example, an insurance company might be interested in a pool of AIG insurance contracts.

Residual Assets

In many cases, including the resolution of banks, the government would be left with certain odds and ends, "toxic waste" CDOs and the like, for which no market might exist. The government may simply hold title to such things (society was on the hook for their ultimate cost, anyway). Perhaps some such assets might be worth something, someday, perhaps not. The government's losses on such assets would not be indefinite, but would be capped by the cost of the nationalization, less the proceeds of liquidation. (Under the current approach, taxpayer losses keeping AIG or GM operating as a going concern are, to put it gently, indefinite.)

Benefits of Nationalization and Liquidation

Apart from avoiding the perils of nationalizing going concerns suggested above, the approach suggested here has three benefits worth emphasizing: closure, prudence, and confidence.

First, within a relatively short period of time after an announcement that an important company presented a systemic risk, the surviving economic actors, and society as a whole, would be back to business. No talk of lost decades. Closure.

Second, corporate governance ought to become more prudent, once managers, shareholders, and even debt holders realize that they could lose everything, that there is no such thing as too big to fail, that they work for dispensable institutions.

Third, after losses have been taken, the survivors move on, knowing what they have purchased. New entrants, fresh players, could enter the business arena, knowing that the game is not rigged. That is, in complete distinction to the current approach, an aggressive program of nationalization and liquidation could help marketplace actors regain their confidence.

Public/Private Partnerships
(Using Markets to Avoid Responsibility)

The nationalization and liquidation of corporations that pose systemic risks are probably politically unrealistic. Despite the many years in which the political right preached the "nexus of contract" theory of the corporation, perhaps believing that loose talk of the corporation as an entity might lead to undue solicitude for employees and other "stakeholders"—virtual communism—most Americans across the political spectrum regard corporations as important entities and therefore want to see them survive. Many corporations trace their institutional histories across generations. We believe in our big commercial institutions, if perhaps not yet as devoutly as the French or the Japanese believe in theirs (but wait). And so neither this administration nor any other is likely to have the stomach to send major corporations to the wall, to start a new game, even when it is both economically sensible and socially more humane to do so.

There is of course a darker version of this story. So long as a corporation remains afloat, and so long as the market is understood to be different from the government, then the intervening administration is in an ideal position: It can use tax dollars to "help" the institution but is not really responsible when (as is often the case) the institution fails to perform very well. And so AIG testifies in front of Congress as if it is a private corporation; Citigroup runs its affairs without interference from the administration; officials at Goldman dismiss the extent of the firm's troubles (do not most healthy banks sell off shares at 10 percent in perpetuity?) and of the help the firm received from the government. One suspects that the government does not exercise its power because it does not really want to be responsible for these institutions, for the same reason the government so long denied responsibility for Fannie and Freddie: Better to keep problematic operations off the balance sheet as long as possible and intervene only when and as required.

In this regard, the Democratic Obama administration is following in the footsteps of the Republican Bush administration. Not that political parties matter too much here; the civil servants doing the work at both the Federal Reserve and the Treasury under this administration are largely the same people who ran these institutions under the last administration. Moreover all were trained in modern finance and so find themselves equally at sea after the failure of risk management as an organizing philosophy for financial regulation.

So, in the fall of 2008, with Bush still in office, the Treasury forced major banking institutions to take TARP loans. Some, perhaps most, needed the money, and since the money was distributed to all of the industry leaders, receipt of the money did not particularly taint any one institution. It is difficult to know exactly what would have happened if such institutions had not taken the money, but presumably a fair number would have failed and would have been resolved by the FDIC. Probably, the FDIC would have run out of funds and would have had to be recapitalized. Directly or indirectly, failed banks, and their assets, would have been brought onto the government's balance sheet. It would have been a very expensive mess. But it probably would have been over within a year or so—the major surviving banks would be sound. Instead, over half a year later, after even the government's gentle stress tests, banks are being forced to raise capital. Many banks are able to do so, of course, because their stock is trading at a fraction of its former cost, and the government has made it clear that it is guaranteeing the existence of these banks, thereby lowering the cost of capital. The Fannie Mae problem has metastasized.

The Bush administration's commitment to the appearance of marketplace trans-actions ran so deep that it took, and lost, a terrible gamble. After months of rumors and a worsening position, one fine weekend in September 2008 it became obvious that Lehman Brothers would not stay in business the following week. So the Federal Reserve and the Treasury attempted to find a buyer for Lehman Brothers, as they had done for Bear Stearns some months earlier. Bank of America was a possibility, but Bank of America decided to buy Merrill Lynch, the world's largest brokerage and a substantial investment bank, too, which was also collapsing that week, along with AIG, until recently the world's largest insurer. For a day, maybe even longer, Barclays looked like it might be willing to buy Lehman Brothers, but Barclays declined to do so. By Sunday, there was no buyer for Lehman Brothers, and the firm failed Monday morning. (In the next days, Barclays would acquire the pieces of Lehman that it wanted before sailing off into heavy weather of its own.) After Lehman's precipitous, and actually unexpected, bankruptcy (everybody had assumed that the administra-tion would somehow engineer a rescue), what had been seen as an essentially U.S. financial crisis became undeniably global. In light of the consequences for the system, it is doubtful that the Bush administration would have made the Lehman Brothers mistake a second time, but it is indicative of the administration's commitment to the appearance of markets—and one has to say, its hardly atypical unwillingness to take full responsibility—that the Lehman Brothers debacle happened at all.

Shortly thereafter, Secretary of the Treasury Hank Paulson, presumably with the knowledge of the Federal Reserve, allegedly refused to allow Bank of America Chair and CEO Kenneth Lewis to back out of the bank's pledge to buy Merrill Lynch, the world's largest broker and a major investment bank, whose failure posed substantial systemic risk. Bernanke and former secretary Paulson subsequently testified to Con-gress, maintaining that they did not do anything improper. Bracketing the game of he said/she said, the administration's issue cannot have been, in the immediate sense, eco-nomic: The ostensibly laissez-faire Bush administration in fact provided financing and assumed much of the risk of the transaction, as it had done with JPMorgan's acquisition of Bear Stearns, and various other fire sales, in lieu of takeover. The administration's problem was political. The administration seems to have deeply wanted its interven-tion to look like an ordinary marketplace transaction, as if major financial mergers were routinely negotiated over a weekend, with costs paid by the government.

More troubling if slightly more subtle, however, the administration appears not to have wanted an *actual* marketplace resolution of the matter at all. Paulson allegedly or-dered Lewis not to disclose the financial state of the acquired company, Merrill Lynch (file an 8-K, in the jargon of securities law, which requires publicly traded companies to disclose news of major importance). This, too, is disputed. What is not disputed, however, is that an 8-K was not filed until much later. Surely the administration was aware that Merrill Lynch was deeply distressed (or else why was the administration involved?) and that Bank of America's acquisition of such distressed assets would be something that a reasonable investor might find of interest? To bracket the issue of whether a senior government official ordered the breaking of the law, it is clear that the Bush administration was not, at bottom, committed to markets—to letting economic actors price assets on the basis of the best available information. What the administration was committed to was the appearance of markets, even if that meant (no doubt temporarily and for good reason) rigging the game.

Although hardly so egregious as ordering a violation of securities laws so that investors would misprice a major bank, if that is what happened, the Public-Private Investment Plan (PPIP) announced by Treasury Secretary Timothy F. Geithner in April 2009 raised similar questions about the Obama administration's commitment to constructing a healthy banking market rather than a Potemkin village of the same.[3] By that time, the Treasury had an alphabet soup of plans at various stages; it had even started a new website, "financialstability.gov," devoted to promoting them—a simply textbook example of transparent government. PPIP was designed to recapitalize banks by buying their bad investments, so-called toxic assets, which the administration, in an Orwellian turn, suddenly took to calling "legacy assets" (Love Canal was a "legacy" of chemical production).

As was widely remarked when the plan was announced, PPIP was essentially a fancier version of the plan that Secretary Paulson had taken to Congress in September 2008. The original Paulson plan, famously proposed via a three-page memo asking for $700 billion to be used to buy assets at the Treasury's discretion, was abandoned in favor of a somewhat more complex program of injecting capital directly into banks, which of course caused banks to begin lending aggressively, thereby jump-starting the economy and leading to the strong recovery of mid-2009. Direct recapitalization, however, left the toxic assets on the balance sheets of banks, hence the desire for PPIP.

From its inception, PPIP was deeply flawed in two fundamental ways: It was unfair, and it was highly unlikely to work.

PPIP was unfair because the government proposed to provide risk-free loans, and matching funds, to private parties such as hedge funds in an effort to entice them to do two things: (1) to put up some money (less than 10 percent equity), and (2) to set some price at which the federal government would buy toxic assets. Thus, the administration seems to have hoped that the government's funds would be multiplied by the magic of leverage. As was immediately and prominently noted, not least by Nobel laureates Paul Krugman and Joseph Stiglitz (both sympathetic to the Democratic Party), the U.S. taxpayer provided almost all of the financing and assumed almost all of the risk of these transactions, but received very little upside of any value that the assets might recover over time. In short, PPIP was intended to be a transfer of taxpayer money to (badly managed) banks, first and for sure, and to a few wealthy investors, second and possibly. As a business matter, this was a terrible deal for the U.S. taxpayer.

The deal was said to be justified, however, because broad economic recovery requires that banks begin lending again, which is probably true. Thus it was asserted, mostly implicitly, that taxpayers would ultimately benefit from PPIP, as bad as the deal was, because it would help the economy as a whole. More specifically, if we taxpayers financed the purchase of private investment in the banks' toxic assets, the cash that banks would receive for their toxic assets (assuming the program worked), combined with the absence of the same toxic assets from the bank balance sheets, would make bank balance sheets more transparent, thereby helping to restore investor confidence in the institutions. (Presumably potential investors also would be pretty happy about the direct capital injections, favorable accounting treatment, guarantees, and whatnot the banks had received.) Feeling better about themselves, banks would go back to providing sensible finance to the real economy, which provided jobs and so forth. Or so it seems to have been hoped—the actual logic was sketchy. But perhaps sketchy was intentional, as from the beginning there was almost no reason to believe that this plan would work as advertised.

Why not? Banks hold assets of widely varying quality that, under current conditions, were only marketable at very deep discounts, if at all. Under PPIP, banks chose which of their assets to sell and were expected to sell the assets that they believed to be truly bad while retaining relatively good assets. Critics pointed out that if banks contributed nearly worthless assets, then PPIP had almost no chance of recovering its costs.

Supporters of PPIP argued that, since the price was set by an auction, the government would not overpay. This argument was hollow: If the participants in an auction bear little of the risk (if they are spending somebody else's money), they can be relied upon to inflate the price. So, under PPIP, taxpayers overpaid banks for bad assets and simultaneously financed a low-risk sale of the same assets at a stunning discount to investors who might be enticed to make money on the spread (it's garbage, but really, really cheap). None of this seemed to bother Treasury officials, perhaps because the fundamental intention was to recapitalize banks, and PPIP was essentially smoke and mirrors: With its talk of private participation, however fractional, and of asset "purchase," however inflated, it was designed to allow the government some cover for what it was doing—transferring taxpayer money to banks that had been badly managed, while allowing the banks to maintain their nominal independence, thereby sidestepping both the mess and the direct responsibility of nationalization. Tactically elegant, if intentionally irresponsible—and this quite apart from the consequences of taking on so much government debt. And if a few of the rich got richer in the process, well then the more things change.

That was April. By August, as this book went to press, it was unclear whether the PPIP would happen at all, though a description of the program remains on the Treasury webpage, in a sparklingly vague future tense. But enthusiasm is waning. Important banks are not failing; some have been recapitalized by TARP money; some have even returned money to the government. Many financial institutions have taken advantage of various government guarantees. Implicitly, the stress test showed the extent of regulatory rigor. Balance sheets remain inscrutable; reliance on the government is fairly direct. The economy is not good, but the tsunami seems to have passed, and the surviving banks hardly need the PPIP. Moreover, even though hedge funds and other investors would bear little of the risk, for many months it has been unclear whether such investors would participate. As a practical matter, prices contemplated by the government in its announcement of PPIP seem to have little chance of any real upside, especially if banks contributed truly worthless assets. So, as of this writing, it is worried that the auctions—and hence the transfers of money—will fail not because of internal flaws, but, more simply, because the auctions are undersubscribed, or simply will not occur at all.

Assuming, however, that the auctions take place eventually, and that investors buy bad assets from banks, how would such recapitalization restore medium- to long-term confidence in the institutions? The Obama administration simply asserted that a well-functioning banking system is really, really important. This proposition, repeated quite a bit, is unobjectionable, but it hardly addresses the question of how buying some bad assets from some badly managed banks creates good banks or a good banking system. Or, most fundamentally, do the contemplated transactions induce the financial system to provide sensible finance for the real economy?

The short answer—perhaps on its way to becoming the final answer—is that there is no reason to believe that PPIP will help the economy at all. PPIP missed the forest (How do we get the financial system running properly?) for the trees (How do we "sell" toxic assets that nobody wants to buy? Or perhaps, How do we avoid declaring these insolvent banks insolvent? Or even, How do we avoid taking the financial system's liabilities onto the government's balance sheet?).

Despite its declared intentions, PPIP would do little to make bank balance sheets transparent. Under PPIP, banks only transferred some of their assets; banks still would own lots of more or less toxic assets. How many, and how toxic? Who would know? Would the banks themselves even know? Recent experience has demonstrated that banks are not good at valuing their own portfolios. To make matters worse, as 2009 wore on it emerged that banks were systematically overvaluing their performing loans. In many cases these loans were collateralized by assets, notably residential and commercial real estate, whose values had declined below the loan amounts. In short, neither PPIP nor anything else done by the government to date has ensured that bank balance sheets are at all transparent, and apart from rather explicit government guarantees, there is little reason to believe that investors know what the banks are worth.[4]

Redeeming Toxic Assets: A Better Way

There is something to be said for a reasonably transparent banking sector, subject to market discipline, as well as being subject to regulatory supervision and the beneficiary of various government assurances. If the administration found it necessary to keep major financial institutions afloat by redeeming their bad investments at taxpayer expense, the administration should act in a way that has some chance of helping the economy, restoring confidence in surviving institutions, and, if at all possible, being fair to the taxpayers who are funding it. Here is a possible approach.

1. The federal government could establish a special purpose entity, perhaps called Angry Maiden, and give it an open line of credit at a very low rate. (Maiden Lane runs next to the Federal Reserve Bank of New York's building in Manhattan and has been used in the names of the government-sponsored special purpose entities [which should be called "GaSSPE"] used to bail out Bear Stearns and AIG.)
2. For a limited time, maybe a month, Angry Maiden would use the federal money to buy *any* assets offered by a bank for a significant portion, perhaps 60 percent, of book value, up to some substantial portion of the bank's assets, perhaps 30 percent, thereby replacing the worst of a bank's "trash with cash."
3. After the offer had closed, all remaining bank assets would be accounted for at their market prices. A public auction could be held if there was some doubt as to what the going rate was.
4. Any assets for which no market truly existed would be essentially written off and accounted for at some arbitrary low rate, say 20 percent of book.
5. Angry Maiden would be professionally managed to wind down its assets over the next decade or so, much like the Resolution Trust Corporation eventually did with the assets acquired by the government during the S&L crisis.
6. Nonvoting preferred shares (or an equivalent legal interest) in Angry Maiden would be distributed to ordinary Americans. This could be done in any number of ways. For example, they could simply be added to the retirement accounts of servicemen and -women, or distributed to the next million immigrants and babies to receive citizenship. In the event that Angry Maiden were to make money, over and above the cost of its financing, the benefits should flow back to the American people. (Obviously, the government could just retain ownership for the benefit of the fisc, but what would be the fun in that?)

What would be the costs of the Angry Maiden plan be? First, like PPIP, Angry Maiden would be essentially "cash for trash," the taxpayers paying for the folly of banks. Second, under the Angry Maiden plan, the government would extend 100 percent of the financing, instead of over 90 percent, as under PPIP. But, because the government would simply set a price at which banks were free to participate rather than subsidizing bidders at an "auction," assets purchased under Angry Maiden could be much cheaper than those purchased under PPIP—it is not at all clear which plan would cost more money up front.

Although Angry Maiden would be far less elegant than a serious program of nationalization, liquidation, and reasonable wealth transfers to facilitate social transitions, as sketched above, Angry Maiden would have three huge advantages over PPIP, and for that matter over what appears to be the likely alternative, opaque balance sheets combined with government guarantees.

First, under any such plan, the American people are asked to rescue a fundamentally irresponsible industry. If there is any return on their massive provision of liquidity, it should flow back to the American people.

Second, and even more important, if we really believe that banks are central to the functioning of our economy, within a few months we would know what a bank's balance sheet was really like—banks would be much more transparent than they are today. We might even be confident in such institutions. They might even be confident in themselves and begin (prudently!) lending money. The bank credit freeze would thaw, and that part, at least, of the crisis would pass.

Third, the Angry Maiden plan would be more honest than PPIP, which, in its sponsor's willingness to pay for the illusion of noninvolvement, recalls not just Citigroup's dalliance with structured investment vehicles, but Enron's balance sheet. Or we can pretend that the loss of confidence in our financial institutions did not happen in the fall of 2008 and continue to back our banking system with the full faith and credit of the governing class.

*   *   *

Lehman Brothers will not be the last complex multinational institution to fail suddenly. The moral of the Lehman Brothers collapse has become that while companies do business globally, they die nationally. Lehman Brothers has been the subject of over 70 separate, and often antagonistic, insolvency procedures. In general terms, the source of the multiple proceedings, and the antagonism among them, is this: Global businesses like Lehman Brothers are complex structures, with different business functions, and assets, located in different places, where different courts have jurisdiction. When the music stops and insolvency is declared, there is no reason to believe that the assets available to creditors will be proportionally distributed among jurisdictions. Similarly, in order to restructure or preserve any of the business, different aspects of the enterprise, which happen to be in different jurisdictions, must be combined. In short, the fragmentary nature of the insolvency of global enterprises presents huge challenges.

In certain circles it has become commonplace to remark on the need for an international insolvency regime. The widely recognized difficulty is that international agreements are hard to reach over relatively simple issues and at the best of times. Insolvency is complex, and these are trying times. Moreover, insolvency involves tax, and few things are nearer to the heart of sovereignty. And so pleas for an international insolvency regime are generally made with an air of hopelessness.

Arbitration may suggest a way forward. Commercial contracts often include an arbitration clause, in which the parties agree to arbitrate disputes that may arise, and specifying the rules, law, and place for such arbitration. The vast majority of the world's states are parties to the convention on the Recognition and Enforcement of Foreign Arbitral Awards, also known as the New York Convention. Under the convention, states agree that their courts will enforce arbitral awards made elsewhere, subject to certain very limited exceptions.

In the same vein, although the successful negotiation of a substantive insolvency convention may be unattainable, one might imagine a treaty setting forth minimum procedural and substantive standards for the administration of insolvency, and guaranteeing equal treatment to parties (mostly creditors) from any signatory state. Under the treaty, corporations could elect to be governed by the insolvency rules and courts of any qualifying jurisdiction, and so state in their articles of incorporation. Signatory countries would agree to consolidate insolvency proceedings in the jurisdiction so designated.

Chapter 9

Confronting Systemic Risk

WIDESPREAD GOVERNMENT INTERVENTION—GIVING TAX DOLLARS TO FINANCIERS while unemployment and foreclosures rise—has been justified as necessary to combat "systemic risks" to the financial system. This reasoning leads to demands that systemic risk be regulated and avoided in the future, and to the deceptively simple question, What is systemic risk?

Systemic risk is a rather loosely defined term in academic finance, specifically portfolio theory. Once upon a time, meaning the long fat years before this crisis when minds were concentrated on profit, the academic quasiunderstanding of a nonconcern was good enough. Most risk, understood as deviation from expected return, can be diversified away—a diversified portfolio should converge upon expected return. Investors therefore should not invest in only one or even two companies, which might be successful or might not. Instead, investors should invest in a diversified portfolio, a "basket." But on rare occasions worth academic contemplation, during a depression or even the mysterious stock market break of 1987, perhaps, the class of assets—the entire stock market, for obvious example—declines. In such a situation, as in the current market, diversification across an asset class—owning a basket of different stocks, or even a collection of stocks, debt, and real estate—is pretty meaningless. The entire system suffers, hence systemic risk.

Humorously enough, and crucially for present purposes, this now much more relevant understanding of systemic risk is literally derivative. Systemic risk is defined in terms of diversification, as the risk that cannot be diversified away. While we might (barely) understand diversification, that does not tell us much about what diversification is *not*. The problem is rather circular. If we understood what presented a systemic risk, then we could either (1) invest in something that was not correlated with the risk, or, even better, (2) invest in something that was inversely correlated with the risk, that is, hedge the systemic risk. But in that case, and by definition, such a risk would not be systemic.

One can see why, in an age of widespread enthusiasm for portfolio management, systemic risk received little sustained attention. The problem is akin to that of uncertainty—How do we think about that which we can only barely name? Confident ages have little time for such questions. In our own, less confident era, political calls for a "systemic risk regulator" seem to be ignorant, disingenuous, or just whistling past the graveyard. That said, we must respond in some fashion, and so address the question, How do we even think about confronting systemic risk?

Prime brokers and other institutions with large-scale trading operations, for whom "systemic risk" has acquired a more specific meaning in recent years, suggest a way forward. The sudden incapacity of a critically important player in a web of highly leveraged institutions may cause such institutions to cease trading with one another, which then leads to insolvency in the simple but devastating sense of being unable to pay obligations when they are due. So Long Term Capital Management, or Bear Stearns, presented systemic risk because, if those firms had suddenly stopped trading, then other institutions might stop trading, not only with the failed firms, but with firms believed to be exposed to the failed firms. Such secondary firms, not receiving cash, might then in fact be unable to fulfill their obligations, and defaulting, place at risk other firms, and so on. The spreading sense of uncertainty regarding who was a viable trading party would mean that no trades would be done, and the failed trades would push firms into insolvency. But the problem is even more mechanized, entailed in the system, than this account suggests. As remarked in Chapter 3, to speak of modern finance as a web of contractual obligations means, in part, that many trades are not voluntary, that is, an actor may be legally and practically obliged to trade. Perhaps the most obvious, and an important, example of such an obligation is a collateral call.

At least three points bear mentioning at this juncture. First, the problem here is not with the firms that fail per se, but with the inability of other participants in the system to take account of what the failure means and continue to do business. Second, this inability is aggravated by hyperintegration of the system—that is, in conditions in which many deals are done at great speed among relatively few players. So, as noted above, questions arise, and are multiplied upon themselves, of the form: If X does not pay Y today, will Y be able to pay me? Third, an institution's inability to assess such questions, in the context of very limited time, a large number of transactions, and uncertainty, makes it rational for the institution to delay paying Y (or demand collateral from Y, or refuse to extend credit to Y, or simply reduce exposure to Y), thereby exacerbating Y's cash flow problem (and perhaps dooming Y).

The financial system is, to put it mildly, rather central to the operation of a commercial society. It must be admitted, however, that lots of enterprises are central to the operation of society. And so "systemic risk" has acquired another, even sloppier, but truly important meaning: the broad social and human implications of the functionality of the market in question. Quite apart from commercial banks and their love children, mortgage companies of various sorts, we have seen investment banks, broker-dealers, insurance companies, car companies, and lately, a trucking company repair to Washington to argue that they, too, are of systemic importance, and their sudden and imminent insolvency would hurt the U.S. economy writ large, and so they should receive tax money. Conceding that market failures are painful, how are we to begin thinking more carefully about when government should intervene? And given that systemic risk can hurt people in unexpected places through no fault of their own, how are we to confront systemic risk?

Appropriately enough, proposals fill the air. This chapter and the next attempt to organize some of many proposals for the regulation of systemic risk currently in circulation. While there are many good ideas, there is no "magic bullet" here, no one proposal that will end the crisis, fix the economy, and prevent the next crisis. Many of the proposals in this chapter are commonplace, and even the less common suggestions follow rather straightforwardly from widely accepted understandings of the crisis. As of this writing, some of the proposals are being incorporated into legislation; they may be law by the time this book goes to press. The point of this chapter is to use this book's conceptual framework to structure the plethora of policy ideas abroad in the land, and, conversely, to use various more or less viable, but real, policy proposals to help us think through our emergent political economy.

It is important for both author and policy-minded reader to remember that political thought is not political action. Intellectuals, operating as intellectuals, are almost always quite limited. Even with the best will and the deepest mind imaginable, thinking is simply not the same thing as getting a group of people to say yes. It makes little *practical* sense to imagine more than the political system will bear (though speculative political thought can be worth doing for its own sake), and it would be foolishness to pretend that the particular solutions offered here will be the way our issues will be actually resolved. That said, it may be that an enlightened republic requires a certain kind of intellectual performance, texts that operate through rationalistic tropes, as if politics consisted of no more than the play of ideas. Discourse requires its objects. Rethinking financial markets requires us to have images of the markets before us— images that this book has struggled to sketch. And in that spirit, how may we begin to confront systemic risk?

Protecting the System

Recall that Chapter 4 argued that the ages of transparency and portfolio management had passed, and that the present crisis might be understood—or mythologized—as the death throes of the age of portfolio management and the birth pains of the age of constructed markets. Recall also that in constructed markets, the key is to realize that *ex ante* efforts to prevent harm will never be entirely successful, and therefore to pay attention to the extent of potential harm. How may we allow for failure without disaster? How may we, understanding that failure is part of social life (of life, full stop), protect the system itself?

Two approaches present themselves. We may worry about the stress within the financial system, which we might think of in an electric network as voltage, but in a financial network will be expressed (and caused) by radical shifts in price, that is, volatility. We might ask, How can we make the network stronger, or, How can we reduce the stresses on the network?

Or we may ask, What happens when a significant nodal point fails? How may we ensure that the failure of such points is gradual, and so may be accommodated or compensated for, rather than violent, beginning a sequence of unfortunate events and ultimately imperiling part or all of the system itself?

That is, to shift metaphors, we may try to protect habitat and, in doing so, protect species. Or we may focus on the health of significant species, with confidence that if important species are doing well, then their environment is healthy. In fact, both approaches are required.

The Network

Hyperintegration and Segmentation (Glass-Steagall Revisited). At the level of the firm, "risk management" is a misnomer. Risk is not managed; risk is shifted via contract. Contract, however, increases the number of players involved in a business and thereby tends to increase the mutual interdependency among players. So, for example, in the municipal debt aspect of the current crisis, a downgrading of credit ratings of the monolines (insurers) led to constructive default on the part of municipalities who had issued debt, even though the municipalities had not missed payments or otherwise acted in breach of their obligations.

Moreover, such transfers tend to reduce transparency. As in the municipal debt crisis, it may be difficult, if not impossible, to assess the risk of a particular company or transaction, because doing so would require assessing the risk of the companies with which they were doing business, and indeed, the general risk of the environment. A buyer of a municipal bond has neither the right nor the time to analyze and then monitor the portfolio of the monoline insurer, or to assess the business practices of the credit rating agencies. This lack of transparency breeds uncertainty. If Company A cannot assess its counterparty risk in a transaction with Company B because it cannot assess the risk of all of B's counterparties (including, perhaps, a few credit default swaps issued by AIG?), then Company A is fundamentally uncertain about its exposure. In such circumstances, and presuming a shock to the system (surprises are unknowable by definition, but seem to be plentiful), then it might be logical for Company A to refuse to extend credit to Company B, or to call whatever could be called from Company B. At this point, Company A is likely to become a cause, not just a potential victim, of a liquidity crisis. In short, the widespread adoption of the best risk-management practices is positively correlated to liquidity crises.

Failure to see the dangers entailed in the adoption of risk management practices, especially across industries, was a fundamental error in finance that infected public policy, corporate management, and even the management of households. Risk management, empowered by financial engineering, preached by business schools and hence regulators, encouraged the tight coupling of financial obligations and ostensibly alleviated the need for reserves against uncertainties (because risks were planned for, managed). Risk management has thus in practice reduced cash reserves, thereby magnifying the constraints imposed by leverage (the need for cash flow) on management. When something untoward happens, management has little room to maneuver and is forced to "deleverage."

If we were confronted with the failure of a few firms, or firms that were somehow unsophisticated, the failure of risk-management procedures could be dismissed as poor execution of a good idea. So, it was said, of Lehman Brothers, but Goldman Sachs was said to be well managed and therefore safe, until Goldman's exposure to AIG became known. Risk-management failure has been ubiquitous, and it has damaged the most sophisticated firms, some fatally. The idea itself, at least in its present form, is bad.

As we have seen, a firm with risks properly shifted onto the grid does not suffer, and certainly does not die, alone. After repeated government interventions for incredibly sophisticated firms that—it was feared—could not fail, or could not fail suddenly, without sending a shock through the system, we have to conclude that their risk-management practices were simply inadequate for the firms, and worse, for the system. The microeconomic enterprise of risk management thus seems to be positively correlated with the macroeconomic problem of systemic risk (and government intervention).

Recent economic history appears to bear out this rather startling proposition. As "risk management" has become more "sophisticated," and indeed has become required as a matter of "responsible" corporate governance, we have seen an increase in the number of government interventions (going back at least to LTCM and including judicious lowering of interest rates after Enron); systemic risk appears to have actually increased in tandem with the adoption of risk-management practices. The financial system seems to have been at risk even when the economy has boomed.

Although the last long generation of financial theorists has stressed autonomy and freedom of action in the marketplace, a host of practical developments (financial engineering, data mining, advanced modeling, and computer-driven trading, for example, all linked together by instantaneous communication) has created a very tightly integrated financial network, or ecology, in which parts are interconnected in myriad subtle and (until they break) generally unnoticed ways. This kind of interdependence is not entirely new—financial contagion is an old idea and a well-observed phenomenon. The New York Stock Exchange crash of 1929 had consequences worldwide. That said, in recent years the financial markets became more tightly and profoundly linked than ever before, even as financial market ideology became even more (ridiculously) committed to the proposition of institutional independence wrapped up in a libertarian tortilla. Arguing with recent madness is a waste of time. For now, it is enough to note that publicly traded institutions leveraged at over ten to one (at twenty and thirty to one) have given many, many hostages and should never speak of independence.

To recall the discussion of tensegrity and network integration from Chapter 7, the challenge is to allow communication among disparate actors (at bottom, to allow globalization) without making continuous communication vital to the continued operation of the financial system. Can we communicate in such a way that interruption of a given communication does not mean the destruction of our linkages, of the possibility of future communication? Can we design a financial system that can sustain disruption?

Which brings us to Glass-Steagall or, more properly, to the second Glass-Steagall Act.[1] Passed as part of the Banking Act of 1933, Glass-Steagall required investment banking and commercial banking to be conducted as separate enterprises, which meant that a company had to choose what kind of business it was in, and conversely, what business it would leave to other firms. The law was passed to address the concern that commercial banks, which took deposits and in which ordinary folks placed their trust, had become overly engaged in the securities markets, both through underwriting and through the lucrative practice of lending for securities trading (margin lending). As a result, it was worried, ordinary depositors from across the nation were funding Wall Street's excesses. Insurance was added to the mix, and the complexity of state and federal banks, to say nothing of bank holding companies, made things much more complicated, but by midcentury it is fair, if a simplification, to say that investment banking, commercial banking, and insurance were conceived of as separate businesses, regulated by different government agencies.

The received wisdom developed in two important ways after the passage of Glass-Steagall. First, the Depression largely was blamed on factors other than the commingling of investment banking and retail banking, notably inappropriate monetary policy. Second, and more important for present purposes, the development of modern finance knocked the conceptual underpinnings out from under Glass-Steagall. As noted, from the perspective of modern financial policy—dating from portfolio theory in the 1950s—the essence of investing is the bearing of risk, defined as deviation from expected return, over the risk-free rate of interest. At this level of generality, there is no fundamental difference among various financial industries. Investors are all playing the same game; only the fields change. But there is no difference, in principle, between investment banking, proprietary trading, commercial (or consumer) banking, and the issuance of insurance. Rephrased, business schools teach the theory of "finance," not "securities trading" or "insurance underwriting." Distinctions among the financial industries are artifacts of history and practice, but are not really essential. From this perspective, Glass-Steagall was a perhaps understandable overreaction to the crash of '29, but was not respectable on its own terms.

The commercial expression of this thinking was the construction of Citigroup via the merger of Travelers Insurance and Citibank, a deal that was illegal at the time it was consummated. The parties were reasonably confident that their lobbying efforts had been successful and that Glass-Steagall would be repealed, as indeed it was by the Gramm-Leach-Bliley Act of 1999. By the time it was repealed, however, Glass-Steagall was so weakened as to hardly deserve being called a law. Aggressive regulatory interpretation by government agencies that no longer believed in the act's efficacy meant that bank holding companies were engaged in substantial investment and commercial banking activities.

In the wake of the financial crisis, however, former chair of the Federal Reserve Paul Volcker and others have called for a resuscitation of something like Glass-Steagall. Against this, it has been said, rather truly, that the mixing of financial activities has had little or nothing to do with the risks undertaken by financial institutions. Glass Steagall by its terms would not have prevented the mistakes Citigroup actually made, to say nothing of AIG or Bear Stearns or other firms. Nor should it be denied that, at a certain level of generality, portfolio theory, and hence modern finance, is correct: Commercial banking is like insurance is like investment banking. Finance is finance.

Moreover, calls for a new "Glass-Steagall" may be somewhat counterproductive, because the phrase "Glass-Steagall" invites us to reenter debates over legislative responses to what were believed, rightly or wrongly, to be root causes of the Great Depression. Such debates are interesting, but the Depression was different from the present crisis in important ways. The real issue raised by renewed discussion of Glass-Steagall is not whether lack of segmentation caused either the Depression or the current crisis, but simply: Should the financial markets be segmented?

Yes. Not because lack of segmentation caused the present crisis (in general, it did not—business units such as AIG's Financial Products Division drank the Kool-Aid all by themselves, without help from sibling subsidiaries), but because lack of segmentation makes it far harder to value institutions, especially under stress. A financial conglomerate is a bit like an apartment building built without internal fire doors. When all is going well, the conglomerate functions well. But when there is a fire, it is impossible to say that the fire will not spread, or even, from the outside, exactly where the fire is. So AIG had more than twenty divisions, in numerous businesses, but was brought down by a few divisions, notably Financial Products and AIG Investments. Similarly, much of Citigroup's business was sound.

Volatility. If we believe that capital markets are almost always efficient, then volatility, sudden and substantial repricing, is not much of an issue. If, however, we believe that assets are, in practice, repriced for a variety of reasons, some exogenous to the asset in question, or perhaps even for no real reason at all, then volatility may be understood as the dramatic aspect of a serious problem: how to foster the quality of price discovery. Is a given repricing a collective reassessment of an asset's fundamentals, or something else?

Volatility can be dangerous—causing liquidity problems, undermining confidence, and so forth, and in extreme cases, causing the failure of institutions—failure that, if prices are inefficient, may be unwarranted. Indeed, some such understanding informs the traditional lender-of-last-resort function of central banks, which should intervene to support fundamentally solvent banks that face a liquidity crisis. The classic problem of a run on a basically sound bank implies that on occasion, investors (depositors) may be collectively irrational. Although lender-of-last-resort policy has its roots in Walter Bagehot and other nineteenth-century thinkers, orthodoxy in central banks and elsewhere over the long boom has emphasized marketplace efficiency, and hence has been relatively unconcerned with volatility. Until, of course, the rough weather of late 2007 forced the Federal Reserve to open the discount window—to extend the lender-of-last-resort service—to investment banks. And in 2008, investment banks blew up anyway.

For some time now, the idea that market inefficiency is common enough to make volatility a serious concern seems to have been gaining some ground against the dominant conception of ubiquitous financial market efficiency. Since the 1987 market break, we have seen a few efforts to restrain excessive volatility, notably circuit breakers on exchanges. The recent temporary bans on short selling certain companies, and consideration of readoption of the uptick rule, indicate a growing impulse to restrain—not eliminate, but dampen—trading activity, presumably in the belief that more sober trading is more likely to foster price discovery. Although the theoretical difficulties inherent in trying to distinguish between "good" and "bad" trading are substantial (insurmountable within the late paradigm), the idea that volatility may itself pose a problem is gaining credence.

It needs to be said, of course, that efforts to dampen short selling and the like may also reflect political efforts to protect asset prices, to use regulation to support a bubble, at least long enough for smart money to get out. And the targets of short selling will almost always deny the rationality of the short positions, for the same reason that the management of takeover targets typically argue that the price offered for their company is too low. These are expected biases, not to be taken seriously even if sometimes true. So it should be kept in mind that sometimes downward volatility is fundamentally efficient, even if its timing and ferocity reflect less-than-judicious reconsideration of well-thought positions. Enron is a good example. That said, even in a case such as Enron, questions of price inflation, timing, and so forth should not be "answered" by an easy presumption of informational efficiency.

Along with central banking (and for related reasons involving the value of money itself), international monetary policy has long been concerned with volatility (expressed in business terms as currency risk) and therefore has been relatively suspicious of pricing. In the recent crisis, as in the East Asian currency crisis of 1997–1998, we saw deleveraging of major players in developed countries and, once the crisis had begun, a flight to quality (mostly U.S. Treasuries) by global investors, resulting in substantial damage to currencies of developing countries. In many cases, the disinvestment from developing countries did not reflect any considered judgment on the fundamental soundness of the investments or even the macroeconomic policies of the countries in question.

A now classic (intellectual) response to this problematic is the Tobin tax, essentially a tax on currency exchanges, designed to discourage such exchanges without blocking them altogether. Because such a tax would make it relatively expensive for investors to change currency, they might be expected to do so only when they were serious—that is, when they had made a considered judgment about the investment in question. The idea is that investment—or trade in the financial markets—would only be done for fundamental reasons. Rephrased, a Tobin tax would be a sort of sin tax, with the sin in question being speculation, or simple economic unseriousness; a Tobin tax would be designed to discourage frivolous monetary transactions, much like a tax on alcohol or tobacco is designed to curtail consumption.

At least to date, the idea of the Tobin tax has not gone anywhere, not least because no international authority with the power to impose such a tax exists. Substantively, moreover, economic transactions have been generally assumed to be serious, because the unserious would be weeded out. By extension of the same logic, in the age of deregulation it was thought that financial transactions did not need to be regulated because financial markets were efficient—that is, they generally reflected fundamental truths (folks who traded on half-truths would be eliminated, because a fool and his money are soon parted). But suppose we came to believe, on recent evidence provided by such names as Citibank and even Goldman Sachs, that the supply of fools is virtually boundless, that foolishness may be a large part of the human condition, and certainly of humans operating in groups. Then trading activity may reflect mass foolishness, and volatility may be a real problem, because markets may inadvertently make silly decisions. We may be drinking heavily at the polling places without knowing it.

It is worth considering the possibility that the end of the investment banking industry was brought about, at least in part, by the fact that investment banks were subject to professional full-time trading, and associated volatility, on both their asset portfolios (things owned *by* the companies) and their equity (ownership interests *in* the companies). If these markets are informationally efficient, then the price of bank equity ought to reflect the value of the bank portfolio (and other aspects of the bank's business) going forward. In that case, if Bear Stearns goes out of business, then that is the market operating as it should, and good riddance. If, however, Mr. Market sometimes errs low, then we have the possibility that the bank's portfolio assets, and equity in the bank itself, will be simultaneously underpriced. Monster waves have giant troughs. Although a precipitous decline in stock price is unproblematic as a matter of a corporate balance sheet (bracketing issues such as compensation, for which stock might be paid as medium term, at worst), in practice low-priced equity might be fatal in a number of ways. A corporation whose traded share price plummets may be subject to a call for new collateral, a credit rating downgrade (often an event of default on outstanding debt), or a simple refusal to roll over or extend new credit—and like the song says, boom boom, out go the lights! Perhaps some investment banks would have survived in their present form had they been more privately held.[2]

Two additional thoughts support this notion. First, institutions that had survived far worse business climates, notably the Depression, were driven out of business, or forced to convert to commercial banks, in the current crisis. Although Lehman Brothers was a very old company, however, it had only been publicly traded since 1994. Another very old company, Goldman Sachs, had only been publicly traded since 1999. During the Depression and other hard times, partners could not sell their positions—the businesses had nowhere to go. Once investment banks became publicly traded, while remaining highly leveraged businesses dependent on daily access to credit from counterparties and others, then they had little ability to survive even brief periods of balance sheet insolvency. Even rumors might be fatal. In this regard, the partnership structure is just more robust, in part because it is only subjected to marketplace volatility on its assets, not also on its equity.

Second, as investment banks collapsed or were forced to become retail banks, it quickly became (the new) conventional wisdom that retail banks had a fundamentally more sound business model, because retail banks had access to credit (deposits) that was simply less flighty than the capital available to investment banks and other financial institutions. Putting aside the ancient history of bank runs, and the fact that for the past few decades investment banks have been far sexier than retail banks, it is true that bank depositors rarely bother to withdraw their funds. Bank deposits are, after all, insured with the FDIC, which also ensures that banks are solvent. Two lessons would seem implicit: First, the volatility of equity markets can deviate, often substantially, from sound price discovery; and second, regulation can lead to more judicious investment, or, more to the point, sales.

So, if we are concerned with volatility, and believe that appropriate regulation might lead to more judicious market activity, what might be done?

1. *Direct impediments to trade.* The closest analogy to a Tobin tax is an impediment to trade. As noted above, such impediments are not new in the securities markets. For example, short sales have been limited by the uptick rule (requiring short sales to be consummated only upon a rise in the stock's price). Sudden drops in stock market prices have, since the 1987 market break, triggered temporary halts to trading activity on exchanges—in theory allowing investors time to figure out what they think rather than selling into a falling market in the (panicky) fear that their positions will otherwise lose all value. And the SEC in 2008 imposed temporary bans on short-selling stock in financial institutions. Such impediments, it has been hoped, suffice to avert the tendency of quickly moving markets to become recursive, that is, for trades to be made on the basis of market position rather than assessment of the investment's fundamentals.

2. *Efforts to ensure the quality of trades.* One might also approach the problem of volatility as a problem of lack of confidence in one's own trading positions. This is a problem built into the structure of global financial markets, in which trades are done at great speed, with regard to very abstract and perhaps ephemeral claims of legal right, over global distances. All that is solid melted into the air some time ago, and at this altitude, the air itself is quite thin. Up here, faith—confidence—is a precious

commodity. People may suddenly become unsure of their own positions and trade quickly on their change of heart. And so we have seen companies implode, markets simply drop, and people suddenly refuse to trade.

If we understand volatility to be symptomatic of a lack of confidence, then measures to ensure confidence should suppress volatility (should make price changes more reasonable). Fortunately, we have systems in place that in many cases do inspire confidence in incredibly abstract and ethereal investments. We regulate publicly traded "securities" in order to ensure transparency (as noted in Chapter 4, this is the core of the Securities Act of 1933 and the Securities Exchange Act of 1934). By simple legislative fiat in the Commodity Futures Modernization Act of 2000, Congress decreed that derivative contracts were not securities, and that therefore their trade did not trigger the transparency mechanisms of the securities laws.[3] In principle, it would be a simple matter for Congress to decide that a derivative, which is, after all, an investment contract made with an expectation of profit through the efforts of others, to paraphrase a famous definition, is a "security" within the meaning of the great securities laws.[4]

In much the same vein and in the same act, Congress decided that credit default swaps are not insurance contracts.[5] This is a bit odd, because a CDS agreement at least superficially seems to have the same economic function as an insurance contract: The seller agrees that, if a bad event happens, the seller will make a payment to the buyer of the contract. Moreover, the CDS market was and is justified as a form of insurance, a way that debt holders can reduce the risk of default on their debts, which is important for the responsible management of pensions, endowments, mutual funds, and other large, socially significant portfolios. Thus, it has been argued, preservation of the CDS market was one more tool in the never-ending quest to protect widows and orphans.

However, the vast majority of CDS contracts (estimates range to 80 percent) during the boom and into the crisis were naked—that is, they were bought by investors who did not own any debt of the company in question.[6] In most cases, therefore, CDS contracts were not functioning as insurance, hedges on other positions, but were simply ways to take a short position on the company in question without working through the bother of the public equity markets, with their tiresome transparency requirements. So perhaps it was correctly decided that CDS contracts were not insurance contracts. Be that as it may, the legal declaration that CDS contracts were not insurance meant that the issuers of CDS contracts, most notably AIG, were not legally required to reserve capital against the possibility that they might lose. And so AIG—which inexplicably went long and unhedged on an enormous number of very dodgy companies and SPEs—blew up and had no capital to support its positions.

However, in many cases, CDS contracts *do* serve as insurance. Indeed, if one has a substantial debt position, it might be irresponsible not to hedge the position by buying a CDS contract. Even if "only" 20 percent of the positions in the CDS market are actually hedges, that means that enormous positions are taken in reliance on the availability of CDS payouts in the event things go very wrong. And here, again, the adoption of risk-management practices increases systemic risk. To see why, suppose that an institution relies on the income from a $100 million portfolio of corporate debt, sensibly hedging the investment with a CDS on each of the corporations issuing the debt. Having hedged its positions, the institution is then free to take positions in reliance on that income stream—that is, to commit its other revenues. And then one day the institution realizes that it is unhedged on its $100 million investment, and that if several of the debt-issuing corporations fail, then the institution will be unable to meet its obligations when they become due. And just suppose that the institution bought a fair amount of debt issued by companies in the financial or automotive industries, or in housing. Thus, as AIG failed, the knowledge that there was no capital in the CDS markets had ramifications throughout the financial markets, contributing mightily to volatility. These effects could not—in light of lack of time and general uncertainty—be attributed to any knowledge of actual positions. Fortunately, one is forced to suppose, the U.S. government pumped untold billions of taxpayer money into AIG's idiotic positions, the already wealthy were remunerated, and trading calmed. As we go forward, a simple place to start thinking about volatility would be to think about considering a CDS contract as a form of insurance and regulating their issuers as insurance companies, perhaps under national insurance legislation.

3. *Shifting the division between private and public.* The CDS problem discussed immediately above is an important example of a much larger question that must be continually renegotiated: Which aspects of business should be "private," and which aspects "public"? Political economy must manage reciprocal aspects of the marketplace and the household, the public and the private, the generally known and the individually lived—or, as we would say in contemporary regulatory terms, the transparent and the proprietary, that which must be disclosed or otherwise made official in the name of public confidence and legitimacy, and that which may be withheld, kept secret, often for advantage.

The reciprocal relationship between public and private is unstable, dynamic. In a time of great uncertainty, we expect to see calls for more light, regulation that makes our relations to one another more public. So the great securities acts of the 1930s required what had been relatively "private" enterprises to register their companies and their transactions with a government agency, thereby disclosing to the markets at large a great deal of what had been "their" business. Private enterprises became "publicly traded" companies.

Even in the heyday of the Roosevelt administration, however, nobody expected a few joint venturers in some local development to go to Washington, D.C., to file reams of information about their business, this transaction, and the risks they imagine they collectively face. By the same token, the patriarch who extends credit to his relatives is not thereby a bank and is not regulated as one.

To generalize, a structure of (public) requirement and (private) exemption runs through financial regulation and thought. The requirements make up a literally public network, whose ligaments are published in places such as the Code of Federal Regulation. The products of this network are public, based on disclosure, transparent.

In short, the requirements define an official space. In contrast, the exceptions to the rule define a more informal space. Enterprise within the informal space is more flexible and less costly to operate than in the official space, because enterprises within the informal space do not have to comply with the requirements of the regulatory regime from which they have been exempted. And there are often business advantages to secrecy.

The informal space mirrors the public space:
- private placement/public offering
- CDS/insurance policy
- derivative position/equity position
- hedge fund/mutual fund
- IRA or 401(k)/pension fund
- money market fund/retail bank
- commercial paper/commercial bank
- shadow financial system/financial system

Over the years, relatively more nationally and even internationally significant business has been done in the informal space, a grand development perhaps epitomized by Chrysler becoming a privately held company in 2007. From the perspective of the business actors involved, such developments were always, and by definition, sensible at the time—transactions were structured privately rather than publicly, because private transactions, with lower compliance costs, were believed to be more profitable. From the perspective of society as a whole, such developments were thought to be beneficial because markets were thought to be efficient and self-regulating, and therefore the formal requirements of the public space were considered a waste of time and resources. So it was argued, and in good times, there was much to such arguments.

When times become uncertain, as at the present, the arguments for doing business in the private space ring hollow. The systemic problem is uncertainty, lack of knowledge, especially knowledge about the positions of fellow economic actors (counterparty risk). Thus we can expect to hear, and are hearing, calls to regulate that which had not been regulated before, virtually the entire left side of the set of oppositions listed above. It is difficult to maintain confidence in something that cannot be seen, and so, in times of crisis, business is moved into official channels, which makes financial networks more visible. As of this writing, people around the globe are trying to reassure themselves that they understand their own networks and that the system is safe and sound. We are trying to convince ourselves to participate, to get back in the game.

Protecting Nodal Points

While thinking about the stresses running through the financial system, expressed as volatility, we might also think about how those stresses are localized, or may emanate from important locations. We may think about the protection of nodal points in the network, or about what, in conservation, is called the protection of indicator species.[7]

Institutional Formalism. As discussed in Chapter 1, over the past several decades, it was argued that the financial industries would regulate themselves; it was presumed that corporations were rational actors that would act in their own long-term interests.[8] This presumption is no longer plausible. The current crisis thus teaches, in a financial context, that the form of an institution matters to the way the institution behaves.[9] Institutions built to take on risk may be expected to take on risk. As noted, changes in the structure of Wall Street institutions, from privately held partnerships to publicly traded corporations, suggest that the financial system was being operated in increasingly risky fashion. It would have been wise (perhaps preternaturally wise) to understand that such changes in institutional governance should have been matched by increased government oversight, at least for institutions central to the operation of the financial system.

Diversification (Glass-Steagall Revisited, Redux). If we think about financial institutions as inhabitants of a system, then we might worry about the diversity of the institutions, on the analogy of biodiversity. An agricultural monoculture such as wheat, or a genetically homogeneous species such as the cheetah, is vulnerable. A disease that can kill one is likely to be able to kill any or even all members of the species. There is safety in variation. This notion—that institutional diversity is prudent—is closely related to both market segmentation (discussed above) and the scale of financial institutions (discussed below).

What "diversification" might mean for thinking about financial institutions is, however, hardly clear. Traditionally, different financial industries were considered different. Insurance simply was a different industry from retail banking, which was different from asset management. Consequently, when the structure of modern financial regulation was established, largely in the 1930s, it was natural to use various laws to establish separate agencies that would regulate the distinct industries, different social practices.

As noted above, it was a major achievement of finance to use the objective and quantifiable concept of risk to understand what was common among these various enterprises. And so we began to think less and less about what made different businesses different. Financial conglomerates, "financial supermarkets," became commonplace. An enormous number of institutions that varied in many ways (unions, pensions, cities, universities, insurance companies, operating companies of various sorts, and so on) found themselves alike in being fund managers, often exposed to the same markets.

Yet, as a principle for designing a sound financial system, diversification will probably prove to be less of an answer than one might hope. First, finance is, in some important ways, the same enterprise across industries. This is, to some extent, a question of the appropriate level of analysis, of the altitude or granularity with which the issue is to be analyzed. Biology is, after all, the same across vastly different kinds of living things. Second, diversity may not matter, or may not matter enough. Very different kinds of businesses failed in both the Depression and the present crisis— diversity does not guarantee survival. Once the economy (or the ecosystem) crashes, many of the inhabitants will not make it.

Those things said, the issue on the table is how to foster robust financial institutions. At a finer level of granularity, the level of business practice, as opposed to theoretical finance, important differences among financial industries remain. Devising a trading platform and algorithm through which to exploit subsecond arbitrage opportunities is hardly the same as negotiating and valuing commercial real estate loans. The businesses require different sorts of people with different skill sets. Understanding that there are important differences among the sorts of people and activities in different financial markets raises questions of management. How are different groups of different sorts of people, doing different sorts of things, to be managed? At what point do the disparities within the organization impair the ability of the organization to manage itself? Both Citigroup and AIG seem to have become unmanageable, at least by the teams of humans charged with that task.

Moreover, can it be hoped that truly different companies, each with its own perspective, might do a better job at fostering independent (or at least contrarian) judgment than we have seen in recent years from financial conglomerates? It may be impossible to demonstrate with any force, but it is worth considering whether diversification within each conglomerate has led to homogeneity among conglomerates. Certainly the age of financial conglomerates has seen a great deal of unfortunate collective action: herd behavior, bubbles, "runs" on banks and nonbanks alike, and ultimately, systemic risk. Thus, in designing robust institutions, a degree of specialization, heterogeneity, and, one hopes, independence seems desirable. In the old days, financial industries were understood to be different in kind, and therefore industries could be regulated; that is, the differences among them were assumed by law and regulation. In this era, we may come to understand industry differentiation as an objective, a prudential safeguard. We might hope that financial industries engage in certain businesses, and only those businesses, not because they could not do otherwise, but in order to think clearly.

Scale. Financial crises often occasion government intervention on behalf of particular "private" institutions, a policy familiar as "too big to fail." So we have seen, in the past few years, massive corporate bailouts, some of a direct, but more often of an indirect, nature; in these transactions, the government brokers deals, extends financing, takes on risk, and generally encourages (perhaps that is the word) transactions that would not otherwise occur.

Economic crises also tend to be times of market consolidation. Some institutions are stronger than others. And in providing funds (or in absorbing risks or simply guaranteeing outcomes), government picks winners and losers. As a matter of business opportunity, and sometimes deliberate public policy, winners buy losers or their assets. Consequently, financial crises tend to increase the concentration of financial markets and the dominance of relatively few firms. Thus intervention in a time of crisis, under the rubric of "too big to fail," combined with opportunity, leads to fewer, larger institutions, thereby exacerbating the "too big to fail problem." In intervening on behalf of major institutions, the government doubles down on its own exposure to the financial markets. And so Bank of America buys WaMu and Merrill and still needs more cash (because those acquisitions carried with them substantial problems). But suppose we (or, more precisely, the administration and those who believe the administration will, in the public interest, use tax dollars to cover their risks) lose faith in Bank of America? At some point, too big to fail becomes too big to be rescued. It is one thing to throw a rope to a drowning swimmer. It is another to tie oneself to a sinking ship.

If we understand markets in integrated, systemic terms, then the sheer scale of institutions—nodal points in the network—becomes a matter of prudential concern. It follows that we should limit the size of critical financial institutions. This would, admittedly, be a substantial shift from contemporary law. Antitrust, called "competition law" in other countries, fines, limits, or even breaks up firms that achieve market power and abuse that power to extract economic rents. That is not the issue here. If the point of financial market regulation is to protect the financial system as a system, and the possibility of ruinous uncertainty is assumed, then institutional overconcentration, without misbehavior, poses a danger to the system.

To what size, the lawyer immediately wants to know, should financial institutions be limited? Surely financial institutions that are too big to be rescued are too big to be tolerated. The more interesting question is whether institutions that are too big to fail should be permitted. Doing business in markets requires that basic principles of markets—for uncontroversial example, respect for property rights and contract rights—be followed. Sometimes the health of a given market requires the activity to be conducted on a certain scale. So, enterprises are not legally allowed to manufacture drugs, operate an airline, or engage in prime brokerage without being fairly large. By the same token, if the health of financial markets requires a degree of decentralization, then financial firms should be limited to a maximum size. It will be said that we regulate certain industries for safety reasons, and that only incidentally does such safety regulation mandate that corporations be of a certain minimum size. Indeed— it is safety that is at issue. We have no qualms about regulating airlines and drug companies for safety, even though we have never had a major international economic downturn caused by drug companies or airlines. Financial institutions should also be regulated for safety, which in some cases will dictate a maximum size. If safety recommends that we divide large institutions (some, like Citigroup and AIG, are already undergoing division), so be it.

It should be emphasized that this is not a question of limiting wealth, redistribution, or even, horrors, "populism." (One of the minor but really sad things about the current crisis is that "populist" has become a dirty word. A democratic people should be, by definition, populist, and proud of it.) At least for the purposes of this argument, there is no limit on the wealth of an individual. A major stockholder in a company deemed too large, and therefore split, would find himself or herself a major shareholder in several companies (as is, indeed, prudent and usually the case with great fortunes of any age). Individuals may find themselves diversified, as they would in a corporate spinoff, but so what?

Reforming the Administrative Structure

In 2008, as a paralyzing lack of confidence, deleveraging, and the need for cash or other collateral spread the crisis from one financial market to another, and the prices of asset class after asset class fell accordingly, it became broadly evident that nobody was in charge of risks across entire markets and among markets—systemic risk. Consequently, there has been a great deal of talk about the need for a systemic risk regulator, even a prudential macroeconomic systemic risk regulator. What might this mean?

Authority to regulate finance in the United States is divided in sundry ways: among the federal government and the many states; among various once separate but now intertwined financial industries; and among professional associations and government bureaucracies. Sometimes, the responsibilities of these institutions overlap, often creating waste, confusion, and turf wars. In other instances, no authority truly regulates financial activity—hedge funds and nonbank mortgage originators being obvious examples. And so, when a crisis convulses the entire system, no authority clearly has jurisdiction. In this crisis, ad hoc arrangements too ephemeral and numerous to follow have been made, sometimes under dubious legal authority, as the Federal Reserve, the Treasury, the White House itself, and various administrative agencies worked to coordinate an effective set of responses. And the sky has not fallen.

Even before this crisis, the structure of financial regulation in the United States was felt to be in need of rationalization.[10] It is difficult not to be cynical about the tendency to respond to the excesses of debt, of complex arrangements and the swirl of data, with still more paper. But what else are bureaucracies to do? As suggested in Chapter 5, it would be foolhardy for an intellectual to try and divine which parts of which plans will become law, and even more presumptuous to put forth still another master plan. But perhaps something should be said about what it might mean to think seriously about structural reform of U.S. financial regulation.

To begin simply, in light of the magnitude of the crisis, substantial legislative action, and some effort at structural reform, is inevitable. As with Enron and the accounting scandals that gave rise to the Sarbanes-Oxley Act, and indeed, the New Deal that established so much of U.S. financial regulation, some sort of governmental response is politically imperative. It is quite possible, as perhaps after Enron, that the very political pressure that makes some type of reform inevitable may result in rushed decisions. Nonetheless, some structural reform is substantively desirable.

Much of this crisis—but by no means all of it—is rooted in institutions or practices that effectively were unregulated, the so-called shadow financial system. Calls for more extensive regulation therefore seem sensible. And the existing hodgepodge is too complicated.

But policy is hardly half, and it is the easy half, of politics. The difficulty of achieving meaningful reform in a polity as vast as that of the United States, even in a time of relative consensus on the need for change, should not be underestimated. For example, it has long and widely been argued that the SEC and the Commodity Futures Trading Commission (CFTC) should be unified—they address many of the same actors and markets, and the questions of jurisdiction among the agencies are too complicated. Nonetheless, that merger has not happened for years, and as of this writing looks like it may not happen this year either, in part because agriculture committees oversee the CFTC, and finance and banking committees control the SEC.

But the difficulties are not just substantive—What is to be done?—or even practical—Can agreement be reached? Policy thinking, the stuff of the inevitable stream of white papers, is a problematic enterprise. Rearranging the alphabet soup of agencies may help, but it also reflects the lawyer's piety that structure and process produce justice. It can be difficult to distinguish meaningful reform from rearranging the deck chairs.[11] Thus, after 9/11, we needed to reorganize the bureaucratic structure of the intelligence community. And the relationship between structure and substance is, well, what? Similarly, reorganizing the institutional structure of financial regulation is unlikely to address the real problems, which tend to lie deeper, in our practices and even imaginations of finance.

And without being impolite, it is safe to say that the ostensibly more modern financial authorities of other countries have not handled this crisis very well, either. There is reason to doubt that the United States would have avoided the crisis if only it had a regulatory structure like, to name some recent suggestions, that of Australia, the Netherlands, or the United Kingdom. Unfortunately, the failure of the U.S. regulatory structure, or the failure of regulators in other countries, for that matter, is not as instructive as one might hope. In a big enough storm, both well-built and badly built ships will sink. If all the ships sink, however, one has little evidence about which ones were well built. Regulatory structures of various sorts have not prevented the crisis, and so it is difficult to learn much about what works well and what does not.

Regulatory reform in the United States will almost certainly be centralizing, for the simple reason that the United States is very decentralized. The desire to create a more centralized bureaucratic structure for financial regulation raises a fundamental conundrum of design. On the one hand, institutional specialization can lead to "stove-piping" or "silos"—information is not shared, important issues fall through the cracks, and so forth. This factor, arguably, both describes the existing structure of financial regulation in the United States and contributed to the crisis (although the problem seems to have been more nonregulation than regulation at cross purposes). On the other hand, centralized systems of information (and, inevitably, authority) encourage consensus, a more polite word for group-think, which is hardly different from herd behavior—and which clearly contributed to the crisis. And in many political questions, most notably the federal structure of our Constitution, the United States has followed a path of decentralization and redundancy, at some cost in clarity. It is a tradition with its advantages.

Moreover, this chapter has argued for a more heterogeneous, diverse, ecological understanding of our financial markets. From this vantage point, there is a certain attraction in a similarly redundant, flexible, and even fragmented understanding of administrative structure. At the very least, and taking these considerations together, we might think about a systemic risk regulator a bit more modestly, albeit with an open mind. The question is not whether some government office should not be tasked with thinking about systemic risk; no doubt this would be a worthwhile use of government resources. But we may be skeptical of the proposition that creating a government bureaucracy to think about the not-yet-thinkable, and to impose its necessarily hazy notions on other government organs, will be very successful. We might instead hope that the issue of systemic risk becomes part and parcel of how financial market regulators of all stripes think. "Systemic risk" might become a concept, like "progress" or "efficiency," that broadly organizes thought.

Chapter 10

The Old Questions, the Old Answers

In RETHINKING OUR FINANCIAL MARKETS, WE OUGHT TO REMEMBER FROM SAMUEL Beckett that there is nothing quite like the old questions, the old answers. The fact that financial regulation failed, and that finance, as a discipline, is something of an embarrassment, does not mean that nothing was learned in all those years—human enterprises often fail, and we should try to smile at our embarrassments as opportunities. In particular, we may not be able to eliminate or even fully identify marketplace danger, but in our efforts to invest in and cope with the future, transparency and risk management still matter. The hubris was in imagining that injunctions to tell the truth, or a bizarre combination of mathematical arrogance and contractual naïveté, could represent more than touchingly incomplete solutions.

Transparency

As suggested in Chapter 4, transparency cannot prevent the sort of financial crisis we are enduring. Language is difficult. The structure of a market, in which private actors—nodal points—enjoy autonomy, including proprietary information, precludes more than translucency. Our efforts to manage risk by shifting it to third parties thicken the network, thereby further occluding vision. So transparency cannot save us.

Moreover, even if we knew, we might still fail. (Most of us know our limitations, to say nothing of vices.) Knowledge is neither wisdom nor discipline—bubbles may be entirely transparent. The Silicon Valley bubble happened out in the open, and houses are the most transparent of investments imaginable, because they can be physically inspected, touched. Much the same can be said of the leverage cycle, the willingness to extend credit, which can both inflate and be driven by a bubble. The fundamental questions of political economy with which this book is ultimately concerned, questions of confidence and uncertainty, hope and anxiety, tend not to be objective, and therefore amenable to logical demonstration, but subjective, matters of interpretation and persuasion, and at the end of the day, social and in that broad sense political, not merely individual.

Although perfect transparency cannot be achieved, a reasonable degree of transparency should be sought. Lack of transparency may contribute to destabilizing uncertainty and, what is worse, may prevent the alleviation of such uncertainty and the reestablishment of confidence. While it seems impossible to quantify, surely the opacity of various financial institutions contributed to counterparty risk, and ultimately to lack of faith in entire markets, and hence to withdrawal from the markets and the contraction of the real economy.

The question of participation in markets—willingness to play the game, with the specter of deflation as an alternative—is not merely material. The financial system is part of our government, and taxpayer dollars will be used to rescue the system in a crisis. We need transparency for financial institutions for the same reasons we need transparency for other sorts of politics, as a form of accountability and, more deeply still, in order that we may understand our government as our own, feel allegiance. So regulatory reform should endeavor to increase the transparency of financial markets, just as doctors attempt to increase health.

Admittedly, "more transparency" is a somewhat old-fashioned and hardly perfect prescription for what has ailed us lately. Indeed, the last major effort to increase the transparency of financial markets, the Sarbanes-Oxley Act of 2002 (SOX), has been widely criticized. Criticism of SOX following its passage, however, was focused on the costs imposed by the act on reporting companies, costs that perhaps would make other capital markets more attractive than the United States. Although these concerns no longer seem so pressing, SOX does not seem to have accomplished its fundamental purposes, at least not to any great extent. SOX certainly did not prevent the bubbles leading into the current crisis, and many of the institutions that have failed so spectacularly were reporting in compliance with the law's disclosure requirements. Perhaps the ultimate insolvency of badly run companies means that the system of disclosure worked, even if belatedly. But this is cold comfort at best. Disclosure and market discipline did not foster good management at Bear Stearns or Lehman Brothers, to say nothing of Citigroup or AIG or General Motors.

And yet cold comfort is some comfort; limited transparency is worth something. Investors have not altogether lost their faith in the financial markets, which indicates a widespread belief that enough information is available to make prudent investment possible. In particular, investors have not lost all faith in accounting, which seemed to be a real possibility in the wake of Enron and the accounting scandals that occasioned the passage of SOX. Moreover, even after the damage caused by this crisis, the nation has remained willing to rescue large companies and therefore has a right (and in some cases, an obligation to the taxpayer) to demand information about these, and similarly situated, companies. So, while transparency is hardly a panacea, it seems wise to require institutions in which society is deeply invested to make information about themselves publicly available.

It may be helpful to think about transparency in terms of a three-part structure: the transparency of financial institutions; the transparency of financial instruments; and the transparency of risk.

Transparency of Financial Institutions

An obvious place to start is the so-called shadow financial system. Many institutions report very little. If, as suggested above, the exceptions that run throughout financial regulation are narrowed, then many institutions that significantly affect the financial system will be integrated into existing regulatory structures. Since disclosure requirements, the effort to make institutions transparent, are at the heart of such regulatory regimes, then many of the institutions now in the shadow financial system, including hedge funds, proprietary trading operations, and so forth, will become simply part of the ordinary financial system. In making it more difficult for financial institutions to do business as "private" entities (particularly if the public bears the risk of their failure), law makes such entities more "public," and transparency is appropriate.

Transparency of Financial Instruments

As discussed in Chapter 3, much of modern finance can be understood as a collective effort, over several generations, to make property rights more liquid. The securitization of home mortgages is an important part of this historical development. The great advantage of liquid forms of property, by definition, is the ease with which they may be traded—like money, liquid investments can be moved quickly and widely, to whomever is willing to pay. The great disadvantage of liquid forms of property is also the ease with which they may be traded—in times of stress, it is difficult to know what one really owns. Financial products approach money, and like money, they can be disconcertingly ephemeral.

A host of contemporary, many quite sensible, proposals for reviving the securitization market, and financial products markets generally, should be understood as making such products a little less like money and a little more like property—a little more concrete, a little easier to value when times get rough. A few strategies for doing so have emerged, including the following:

Skin in the Game. One of the neat and dangerous things about money is that its transfer tends to be final; payment in full extinguishes relationships. Similarly, transfer of most financial products is, in most circumstances, nonrecourse. Which means, in practice, that transfer of a financial product is also transfer of all the risk associated with the product. Which further means, in practice, that the seller of a financial product has little exposure to the risk of the product and therefore limited incentives to know, much less monitor or disclose, the risks of the investment.

A simple and not insignificant example can be found in mortgage lending. If, on one hand, a (traditional) bank makes a thirty-year loan, expecting the house to refinance or sell in, say, eight or nine years, then the bank may be expected to lend with some care. If, on the other hand, a bank plans to sell the loan within a month, the risk of default on even a very risky loan is negligibly small. And so very many very bad loans were made and sold and mixed into complex instruments, making those instruments difficult to price. At the same time, retail banking was transformed from a form of investment that profited on the lending of money at interest, with due regard for risk, to mortgage origination, the sale of loans, with profits driven by fees that were directly correlated to the number, but not the quality, of the loans made.

The lesson seems to be that transfer of 100 percent of the risk of a financial instrument is bad for the financial system: It encourages the creation of instruments, and therefore institutional positions, with hidden risks. Sale of such instruments constitutes fraud, or negligence that has much the same economic effect. And knowledge of the existence, but not the scale, of such exposure creates counterparty risk. Therefore, the question is how to ensure that instruments are priced with due regard to their underlying risks, and that marketplace actors are reasonably confident in the pricing.

One strategy is to have the originators of a financial instrument retain a financial interest in the instrument ("skin in the game"). Tactically, there are numerous ways to achieve this goal:

- Banks could be prohibited from transferring 100 percent of a given loan, or could be required to invest in any securitization of their debt.
- Fund managers (including managers of hedge, private equity, and money market funds) could be required to have substantial equity positions in their funds.
- The creation of nonrecourse SPEs could be prohibited or severely restricted, or the sponsor of an SPE might be required to carry insurance on the SPE. One could imagine recourse under various legal standards that would make it relatively harder, or easier, to wrap up chains of obligation. In designing such systems, one must keep in mind that such recourse would reduce liquidity and

presumably raise the cost of capital somewhat—but expensive capital has not been much of a concern lately.

- Securitization of mortgage debt could be replaced by a covered bond system, in which banks sequestered a pool of assets (loan obligations) and held the pool as collateral for a bond issuance. The money generated by the sale of bonds could be used to buy loans. Such a system, long used in Europe, could in theory transpose the benefits that the United States received from the securitization of mortgages and other loans into another class of financial instruments, bonds. From the perspective of investors, a covered bond system would have the added benefit, over the system of securitization used in the United States, of making the originator liable, and making collateral actually available.

One could go on, but the general point of such "skin in the game" schemes is to use risk to give some teeth to disclosure requirements and, indeed, to the underlying construction of investment vehicles. If institutions bear risk, it may be hoped that they actually understand the investments that they are selling, and that therefore the information they provide to the marketplace will be fundamentally sound.

A word of caution is in order. Merrill Lynch, Bear Stearns, and several of the other more spectacular failures had skin in the game. A number of investment banks and other institutions sought vertical integration in the securitization of mortgages, and therefore bought or established mortgage origination capacity. In a number of high-profile cases, at least, such retention of risk does not seem to have led to more prudent risk management.

Limiting Complexity. Over the past few decades, financial engineers have devised a host of complex financial "products" that can be priced with a fair degree of confidence insofar as their fundamental assumptions hold true. One of the lessons of the current crisis is that if the assumptions on which the instruments are based are not true (for example, if house prices are falling), it may be very difficult to figure out the discounted value of the instrument (or even impossible, pending bankruptcy proceedings).

One way to limit the complexity of a securitized instrument is to limit the diversity of the debt streams of which it is composed. The creation of a homogeneous pool of debt was the purpose of the Fannie Mae loan. Fannie Mae would buy mortgage loans from banks and securitize them if the banks made the loans in conformity with Fannie Mae's guidelines. Banks were thus given a buyer for their loans, and Fannie Mae was assured of a supply of loans that were homogeneous and for which risk, and thus price, could be assessed with considerable accuracy.

The system broke down in at least three ways relevant here. First, mortgage loans were made that did not conform to Fannie Mae's guidelines, because they were higher risk and hence "subprime" in retail banking parlance. Second, the risk of subprime loans, or any other debt stream, was managed not by pricing the individual obligation, or even a pool of like obligations, but through the repayment structure of the security (the "tranche" structure of CDOs and other sophisticated debt instruments). Belief that financial engineering of the instrument could handle diverse risks led to the blending of various risks as well as to derivative structures that mirrored actual obligations, making fundamental analysis that much more difficult. Third, once the housing market truly collapsed and credit dried up, even conforming loans were underwater, and many securities based on such mortgages failed.

The lesson would seem to be variations on the old KISS (Keep It Simple, Stupid!) rule. Debt instruments should be based on underlying positions; that is, synthetic instruments should be disfavored. The debt streams that make up a pool should be of known quality; "low doc" or "no doc" loans also should be disfavored. And the pool should be comprised of debt streams of relatively consistent quality. Rephrased, financial engineering may be moving from a baroque to a neoclassical phase.

Exchanges and Clearing. It is widely believed that much of the counterparty risk—or more to the point, uncertainty regarding counterparty positions in times of stress—stemmed from general knowledge that critical actors had substantial Over The Counter (OTC) positions, without specific knowledge of what those positions actually were. For example, an institution that knew only that its counterparty was exposed to AIG, and that AIG was in trouble, rationally might decline to pay—systemic risk loomed. In recognition and response, a general enthusiasm for exchange-traded instruments, in lieu of OTC instruments, has arisen.

Exchange-traded instruments offer at least four prudential advantages over OTC instruments:

- Exchange-traded products are priced in real time, and therefore institutions may mark them to market on a daily basis. In contrast, OTC derivatives are often only valued at some point in the future, often at the option of one of the parties. The values of such contracts on a daily basis, then, are somewhat indeterminate.
- The price, and oftentimes the trading activity, of exchange-traded products is public. As a result, traders on such markets know where they stand and have a fairly good idea of where their counterparties stand.
- Perhaps most important, trading is done through a clearinghouse that is collateralized by its traders.
- In many exchanges, traders settle accounts at the end of each trading day. They are solvent, or not. Extensive webs of obligation to fundamentally insolvent parties are not established.

That said, in certain circumstances it makes sense for one firm to shift risk to another, or to seek financing from another. It makes sense to contract. Some such contracts may be derivative in structure, that is, an obligation to pay may arise from a specified event without the transfer of property. So OTC contracts may serve an important economic function—but they should be used with caution. One possibility would be to require institutions to post their OTC positions—the terms of the contract—either publicly or perhaps with a regulator, so that there was some outside assessment of the risk taken on by each institution.

Note that whereas Chapter 9 argued for the heterogeneity of marketplace actors, this chapter is inclined toward the simplification of contractual relations.

Transparency of Risk

Let us begin from the unobjectionable proposition that the investment world is very complex. Investors, therefore, often use third-party analysts, sometimes called "gatekeepers," to help them steer toward sound investments and away from hidden dangers. In the securities world, industry analysts are supposed to understand which companies within an industry are likely to be successful. In the even larger world of debt investments, credit rating agencies are supposed to be able to judge the quality of debt, thereby helping investors decide whether to buy or sell it, and at what price.

As with several aspects of the current crisis, the problem with gatekeepers began to receive widespread attention in the wake of the Enron scandal. Simply put, the gatekeepers said that Enron was a great company when it was not. Even after serious and substantive doubts emerged about the company in the financial press, gatekeepers urged the purchase of Enron's securities. Gatekeepers seem to have become, in effect, touts. An important legal analysis of the Enron scandal, by *éminence grise* John Coffee, was entitled "It's About the Gatekeepers, Stupid."[1]

As is often the case with failings, it can be difficult to distinguish stupidity from cupidity. With regard to stupidity, it should be acknowledged that what gatekeepers claim to do, analyze the risk of a business, is truly difficult, and because it is difficult, mistakes will be made. Indeed, the likelihood of making mistakes is no small part of why investors are willing to pay (or at least, let their funds pay) for analysis done by others. That said, incompetence must be a large part of the problem. So many mistakes were made in the leadup to this crisis, many of them contrary to the received wisdom of the market or the opinions of prominent commentators; the rating agencies should have been on notice of possible weaknesses in the companies they were rating, but they nevertheless rated them highly. Moreover, particularly with regard to credit rating agencies, there is reason to believe that people with a real talent for this work might find significantly better-paying jobs doing much the same thing, perhaps for a private equity fund or a trading operation.

The second problem, cupidity, results from conflicts of interest created by the way that analysts and credit rating agencies are paid. Perhaps most important, investment banks, which seek to sell a debt security, must get it rated by a credit rating agency. The number of both investment banks and credit rating agencies is small. Credit rating agencies are licensed by the SEC, and the industry is dominated by three agencies. The arrangements, as in any good cartel, are cozy. Credit rating agencies know not only that a good rating is more valuable to the bank than a bad rating, but also "if one of the three got objectively truthful, the remaining two would get all the business."[2] Similarly, analysts, who often work for investment banks and/or brokerage houses, tend to extol stocks that are either owned by, or offered for sale by, their employers. And downgrades of corporate debt are often events of default on the debt spelling insolvency for the issuer of the debt (and no more business for the agency!). In short, conflicts of interest abound.

In light of the difficulty of the underlying problem of assessing the future of a business, and the doubt cast on gatekeeper probity by their conflicts of interest, why would any investor seek the advice of gatekeepers? First, many fund managers are required by statute, general fiduciary duty, or the structure of the fund to invest only in "investment" or other high-grade securities. More generally, it is a complex world, aswarm in possible investments, many of them quite bad. Fund managers, chief financial officers, and trustees of various sorts need to cover their own asses. The scale of the investment world, coupled with the need to justify investments that might go badly, seems to require gatekeepers, flawed as they no doubt are.

To view the matter structurally, the gatekeeping function shifts the burden of risk assessment onto independent, that is, less responsible, third parties. The investments in a portfolio of investment-grade debt, then, are putatively transparent, but may or may not have been examined in fact. The investments are made up of allegedly "investment-grade" debts, but the party that has rated the debts, for whom the investments are allegedly transparent, is not liable for its representations, except in extreme cases such as fraud and perhaps in some fuzzy sense of reputational cost. Presumably, however, fund managers rely on the soundness of the ratings and may be expected not to reserve, to obligate income, and otherwise to rely on the proposition that they have made sound investments. That is, in a world in which free cash and other reserves are positively correlated with confidence in investment, the gatekeeping function contributes to what emerges, in a crisis, to be excessive leverage and, collectively, hyperintegration, and hence systemic risk.

What is to be done? At least three approaches have gained some credence.

1. *Reform.* The existing industry could be reformed to eliminate, or at least reduce, conflicts of interest, perhaps through a tax on investment banks and other financial institutions that use, or benefit from, gatekeeper functions. At the same time, competition among gatekeepers must be encouraged.

2. *Government service.* Recognizing that, at least for certain fiduciary investments of great social effect, such as pensions, impartial analysis of creditworthiness is worthwhile, the government could ensure the provision of credit ratings. This could be done directly by a government agency (in much the same way that the Food and Drug Administration seeks to ensure the safety of drugs), or the government could sponsor an organization (or organizations) to provide publicly available credit ratings (in much the same way that the government once sponsored, and now again owns, institutions that securitize mortgage debt).

3. *Radical deregulation.* The existing system could be abandoned, and investors and financial industries could take responsibility for their actions rather

than trying to shuck decisions off onto third parties. Investors would be free to seek advice from whomever they pleased, but receipt of such advice would not relieve them of statutory or other responsibility. The sound operation of socially important investments, such as pensions, could be secured through heightened personal liability for fund managers coupled with a requirement that funds carry insurance against investment losses (insurance obtainable, presumably, through a chastened CDS market).

Portfolio Theory/Risk Management

Any business association may be understood, in balance sheet terms, as a collection of assets and liabilities, a way of collecting the social energies that we broadly refer to as "capital," and in that capacious sense, "a portfolio." In the case of a financial institution, which mostly invests and owns rather than operates, it is especially natural to understand the firm as a portfolio. Among highly leveraged and tightly integrated financial institutions, loss of confidence in the portfolio of a crucial institution raises systemic issues. Thus, as discussed in Chapters 3 and 4, although portfolio management is a *defense* against the dangers of the marketplace, this crisis teaches that portfolios can also be a *source* of marketplace danger.

The idea that a portfolio is itself dangerous may seem a little odd. Marketplace danger is often imagined in terms of markets, such as the stock market of 1929, or the more recent Silicon Valley bubble, or even the East Asian currency crisis or Sunbelt real estate. Conversely, the middle-aged and middle class manage portfolios for their children's education, their retirement, and their health—and so tend to think of the well-balanced portfolio as a shield and among the most worthy of institutions. But if, as suggested above, any corporation may be thought of, in balance sheet terms, as a collection of obligations and hence like a fund, then conversely, any fund may be thought of collectively, as an endowment or foundation, itself an entity, and hence like a corporation. And the idea that the firm is the source and focus of marketplace danger, and even systemic risk, is not entirely new. Two of the very first bubbles, the Mississippi scheme and the South Seas bubble, were bubbles in the obligations of a company. In our own time, Enron can be understood in similar fashion. Most important, the most familiar of systemic risks, the loss of faith in banks, is best understood as a problem stemming from the structure of the bank's portfolio, and therefore as posing a problem in, literally, portfolio management.

So, if managing a portfolio is widely necessary, difficult, and inadequately addressed by "risk management," then how are we to begin rethinking? Notwithstanding recent failures, banking law is a good place to start. Since the 1930s, banking law has regulated deposit-taking institutions. Since depositors can demand their money at any time (that is, banks borrow on a short-term basis), and banks make long-term loans so that people can buy homes and other things (that is, banks lend long), banks are exposed to the danger of a "run on the bank." In a run, a substantial number of the bank's depositors (the bank's creditors) demand their money at once. The bank does not have sufficient cash on hand to pay them, and the bank fails. What is critical to understand is that the problem arises from the fact that the bank's obligations are temporally mismatched. As a borrower, the bank owes in the short term; as a lender, the bank lends in the long term. This temporal asymmetry makes banks, by their very nature, vulnerable to runs, weak—a problem famously enacted in the film *It's a Wonderful Life*. In response to this structural infirmity at the heart of banking, the federal and state governments license banks, insure deposits, provide emergency lending, mandate reserve requirements, and otherwise seek to ensure the soundness of the banking industry and, by extension, the financial system.

For most of the years since the Depression, this system of regulation seems to have been fairly successful. With the partial exception of the savings and loan crisis, not just banks but the financial system as a whole, has seemed quite sound up until this crisis. Recently, however, federal intervention has been considered necessary for a host of nondepository institutions. In some of these institutions, citizen/taxpayers have no direct interest, but they are told that they must pay nonetheless, lest the financial system collapse. For examples, the federal government has made emergency lending open to investment banks (in December 2007); guaranteed the assets of Bear Stearns, thereby enabling the sale to JPMorgan; (re)nationalized Fannie Mae and Freddie Mac; propped up AIG, an insurance company; facilitated the sale of Merrill Lynch, a brokerage and investment bank; extended deposit insurance to investors in money market funds; guaranteed the debt offerings of Goldman Sachs (now a bank holding company, albeit doing business under exceptions to the pertinent regulations); and so forth.

If we assume, for the sake of argument, the wisdom of such interventions, it is clear that the policy issue underlying such banking-style interventions on behalf of nonbanks is the danger that these institutions pose for the financial system if they experience a liquidity crisis brought about by borrowing short and lending long. The policy issue at hand is protection of the financial system from such danger, not consumer protection in any direct sense, and certainly not the protection of depository banking per se, as Timothy Geittner, then chair of the New York branch of the Federal Reserve argued last summer. In hindsight, it appears that banking regulation did such a good job of protecting the financial system for so many years because, during that time in the U.S. economy, banks dominated the financial landscape, and bank deposits and bank loans were an adequate proxy for borrowing short and lending long. With the emergence of the shadow banking system, however, the systemic raison d'être for banking regulation could be found in a wide variety of institutions. If the fundamental problem of banking—asymmetry of the temporal horizons of assets and liabilities makes an institution vulnerable to a liquidity crisis even when it is solvent—is widespread, then we might begin thinking in much more general terms about "banking" regulation.[3] In short, because of the structure of their portfolios, institutions across the financial industries should be regulated more or less like banks.

Since a stitch in time saves nine, a government that cannot let an institution fail precipitously would be prudent to regulate the institution before problems arose. The following four ideas—the last three drawn directly from traditional banking regulation—might provide a template for deeper consideration.

1. As elsewhere in financial regulation, in banking it is preferable to demand performance rather than to specify design. So, for example, the stress testing and even reserve requirements of traditional banking regulation sensibly leave unspecified the particulars of how the institution's business is conducted. That said, performance regulation has its temptations and difficulties, illustrated by the widespread willingness among regulators, codified in Basel II, to let financial institutions estimate their own risks and determine the measures necessary to manage these risks. The thinking was that nobody knew the environment of sophisticated financial institutions better than the institutions themselves. Yet risk management is expensive, and so it is hardly surprising that, during the course of this crisis, risks have been underestimated, and reserves and other measures repeatedly proven to be inadequate—banks failed, and they failed in ways that regulators enabled.[4] The fact that financial conglomerates did not constitute themselves safely, however, does not make the question—What sorts of capacity to withstand what sorts of crisis do we wish such institutions to have?—go away. In this context, "performance" is a rather difficult concept, perhaps, like the "readiness" of the military, the subject of endless planning yet impossible to specify very well.

2. The traditional way to ensure that banks can perform under stress is to require banks to maintain capital reserves. Endless learning surrounds how much, and what kind, and under what circumstances, but a few points are worth mentioning here.

First, banks and perhaps other financial institutions should have to meet objective requirements for holding some simple form of capital in reserve. Simple is not always bad. Reserves should be verifiable, and more generally, compliance with reserve requirements should be transparent. Banks typically have business incentives to maintain fewer reserves and to use more complex (less liquid or accessible) forms of capital toward their capital requirements, and typically argue that they have managed their risks adequately, demonstrating Basel II in microcosm. From a systemic perspective, however, the issue is not merely the bank's direct relationships with its depositors, or even its other investors, such as shareholders. Bearing in mind that financial institutions are all leveraged, and that their creditworthiness is constantly being rated, it is crucial for the maintenance of confidence that financial institutions be able to demonstrate, not just claim, ongoing access to liquidity. Thus, in the current environment, maintaining rather traditional capital reserves can help financial institutions (1) cope with uncertainty (as opposed to "managing risk") and (2) encourage confidence in the institution, and hence the creditworthiness of the institution.

Second, reserve requirements probably should be countercyclical, that is, banks should be required to adopt "dynamic provisioning." In good times, banks (and other financial institutions acting as banks) are likely to lend enthusiastically and to be repaid almost all of the time, which makes them all the more willing to lend—that is, to lend on smaller and smaller margins.[5] In short, in good times, credit is easy, sometimes too easy, and both investors and banks may overcommit themselves. In such cases, bank reserves are correspondingly low because bank assets are overvalued, and the bank may be at risk.

In bad times, banks are likely to understand their positions as risky and therefore to hold capital in reserve. Credit becomes difficult to acquire, and banks will only lend on large margins and against very sound collateral, which distressed individuals and businesses are less likely to have. Even government money, provided to secure the financial system and stimulate bank lending, is likely to be used to bolster bank balance sheets. Thus, as already discussed, the leverage cycle tends to enlarge the bubble: Credit is easy and reserves are low in good times, and credit is hard and reserves are strengthened in bad times. So the idea of dynamic provisioning requirements is to make banks work against the leverage cycle, that is, their own cycles of enthusiasm and anxiety. In good times, reserve requirements would be raised, which would have the effect of giving banks a war chest for bad times, dampening their willingness to lend. In bad times, reserve requirements would be lowered, which should help banks extend credit, thereby stimulating the economy. Reserve requirements (and indirectly, margin rates) would become much like interest rates in monetary policy, a way of steering Mr. Market toward the middle path of virtue. This approach has apparently been tried with great success in Spain, which, despite a shattering housing bubble, has not suffered a banking crisis.

3. *Insurance and resolution.* Banks still fail, and sometimes should (if they are badly managed), but sudden "runs" on banks have become quite rare. Depositors generally are confident that they can withdraw their money even if the bank fails, that the bank will not "run out" of cash because other depositors have already withdrawn their money. Depositors know this because the government insures their deposits, a message drummed home through decades of advertising. Depositors are also likely to know that the federal government will seize a distressed bank and fix it, sell it, or liquidate it—in any event securing the orderly operation of ordinary functions, such as managing deposits.

A number of more general lessons may be useful for regulating the nonbank institutions that make up the shadow financial sector, including at least the following:

A. Mistakes may be due to panic, and insurance may have a calming effect. Even in the absence of panic, it makes sense to insure certain actors who, like depositors, are exposed to various forms of marketplace risk, but who are only incidentally "investors." When critical social services are provided by endowed institutions that are dependent on solid performances in financial markets, government insurance should be considered as a backstop for failure. Since the widespread adoption of defined contribution retirement plans, we have not seen a sustained bear market—and already, people are not retiring because there is not enough money in their 401(k) and similar plans.

The instances in which insurance is appropriate are probably fairly limited. It is generally inappropriate for the government to take on uncompensated risks, even when it seeks to use private investment to "leverage" public funds—by and large investors should not have their risks guaranteed, for the simple reason that investing is about taking risk. It is worth noting that the FDIC is not uncompensated for its insurance, but has been paid by taxes on the banking industry.

B. Resolution authority is critical. As discussed in Chapter 8, the issue is not so much the failure of a given institution or even the losses of its counterparties. The issue is how players continue the game in light of the failure of the institution. The success of the FDIC in resolving bank failures has meant that other banks are confident in transferring money and otherwise doing business with a bank even as it is in receivership—business is not interrupted. The challenge is to build this sort of systemic resilience into the shadow banking system, where failure is not unknown.

C. "Depositors" should be treated differently from "investors." Although it is important that business is done with and around institutions even as they fail, it is also important that investors who make bad investments lose their money. In banking regulation, it is fairly easy to separate shareholders in a bank—ordinary investors—from depositors in the bank. In general (at least until this crisis), the economic interests of a failing bank's shareholders are not protected, except perhaps indirectly, such as through lender-of-last-resort functions that may save an otherwise doomed bank. In contrast, the economic interests of a failing bank's depositors are protected up to (currently) $250,000. This separation seems natural enough, because depositors are only with effort considered "investors" in the bank. Depositors are typically thought to be parking their money, using the bank account as a way to store value or "save." Depositors are traditionally expected to use the money in their account for something else, though they may pick up a little interest on the side. Real investors, in contrast, expect their money to make more money, to work for them. So the law has no difficulty segregating depositors from investors and protecting only the former.

However, in hedge funds, investment banks, and the like, and even in money market funds, there are no real analogues to depositors. In many situations, it will not be easy to separate the system, with its need that business continue even though an institution fails—that is, that parties continue to obligate themselves—from an institution's investors, especially its creditors, who should take a loss if the bank fails. Judgment calls will be required, often along a temporal axis. Trading positions, which may be expected to change and clear relatively quickly, create more uncertainty and are more tightly intertwined than longer-term obligations. But, at least from this vantage, such distinctions are far fuzzier than the admittedly imperfect distinction between depositors and shareholders. It bears remembering, however, that the purpose is not to construct the perfect game. The purpose is to construct a game that people want to play, even when things get a little rough.

* * *

Again, we will not somehow outgrow our need to manage portfolios—and so a chastened portfolio theory and risk management will remain. Despite this crisis, we will still amass property, insure our positions, and in sundry ways seek to protect our children. But our understanding of what a portfolio, or better still, an endowment, is, our relationship to our wealth and our designs for it, may shift in history. For many years and in many places, the endowment has been understood as something that grows out of the past, an accumulation of prior efforts that could be passed on, a patrimony or legacy. Those not fortunate enough to be well born, but fortunate enough to be in the middle classes, might still be encouraged to save for a rainy day, for misfortunes unspecified. Thus property was and is understood as a way of coping with uncertainty.

As a matter of intellectual and indeed economic history, portfolio theory, in the guise of risk management, shifted these relationships, at least for significant elites, but also for the broad middle classes. Legally, and as discussed in Chapter 3, we may say that portfolio theory moved wealth from an emphasis on property to an emphasis on contract. Domestically, we moved from a house that was paid for to a house that was leveraged to its present value, with the money put to work elsewhere, or commercially, from a business with substantial cash reserves to a corporation that funded its operations in a short-term paper market. The very epistemology of the wealthy shifted—from seeing the world as a place where prudence dictated that resources be hoarded for eventualities, to seeing the world as known and therefore to be confronted with confidence (or the hubris of a Master of the Universe, as Tom Wolfe put it). Risk had not been eliminated from this bright shiny world, but it had been identified, priced, and hedged. This financial crisis marks the swing of the pendulum away from a world in which so many of us were confident in collective wisdom, the edifice of risk management—and in which we even presumed our dealings were in some sense efficient, toward a world widely perceived as more mysterious, where we are uncertain. And in our "new" world, we are again painfully aware that contracts may not pay, and it is prudent to save.

Conclusion

Fears and Other Possibilities

ALL POLITIES PROTECT THEIR ELITES, AND MOST READERS SHOULD BE THANKFUL for that. And since at least Athens we have known that commercial polities tend to oligarchy. Indeed there is no clear line between a democratic republic, which will of course have its privileged classes, and a polity designed to serve those classes, but perhaps structured as a democratic republic. Citizens and officials of both may profess the virtues of a democratic republic. The elites in both sorts of polity may even honestly believe that, in serving their own interests, they are serving the common interests, as they are, after all, leaders. To make matters worse, sometimes serving the interests of elites—for example, by using tax dollars to keep badly run businesses from failing—does in fact benefit the polity as a whole. Sometimes, what is good for General Motors, or Goldman Sachs, is good for America. But depending on who is speaking, the idea can be awfully self-serving, and thus suspect. Which is to say that not only may we be corrupt, we may be unaware of the extent of our own corruption. We may be as innocently rotten as an old barn on the edge of collapse, probably too damp for fire. It is worth worrying over.

At this point, the naïveté of Americans appears to be incurable. So, for example, from 2006–2008 Larry Summers, currently chief economic adviser to the president, spent one day each week learning about the trading strategies of the large hedge fund DE Shaw, for which education Summers might have been expected to pay a fair amount of money. (Hedge funds do not typically take it upon themselves to educate others in their strategies.) For his last year of service, DE Shaw transferred (neither "paid" nor "gave" seems quite right) $5.2 million to Summers. Although it raised eyebrows, the transfer was presented as payment for work, instead of what it was, an investment in political access (Citigroup already had Robert Rubin). Asked about these matters by the paper of record, DE Shaw has made much of the fact that the failed president of Harvard and former practicing economist is very intelligent, at least in some ways. We are told that Summers passed the firm's entrance exam, a series of mathematical puzzles. Putting aside the offensiveness of such "argument," and the extent to which firms who buy political influence are to be trusted, one must admit that the hedge fund seems to have invested wisely: Summers, treasury secretary under Clinton, has become consigliere of the administration's economic policy and some form of hedge fund regulation looks likely; DE Shaw's purchase of political risk insurance seems quite savvy, a bargain at the price. To make matters funnier, at least one commentator thought it good that Summers had spent some time learning about hedging strategies, because now, during a financial crisis, Summers knows how things work.[1]

Such arrangements are generally beneath us, the kind of thing for which we rightly mock the Russians. Corruption in the United States tends to be more subtle and less blameworthy, more or less innocent fraud, as John Kenneth Galbraith put it. In such cases, the word "corruption," at least as it is currently used, is overly moralistic, misleadingly suggesting variations on the theme of bribery. We are not entirely above that sort of thing, but our real problems lie deeper. Our elites are so deeply educated into (ideologically informed by) what they think they know about financial markets that they truly have difficulty standing apart and thinking critically. In some serious sense, our leaders have not been intellectually prepared for political economy, because they do not think politically about markets. Markets, after all, are opposed to politics, or else the polarity between left and right through which their world is organized would make no sense.

When, as now, the economy is in crisis and our government is forced to act, our elites discover they have few principles through which to think, much less explain why they exercised power as they did. And so there is much unfocused talk of the necessity of doing something. The end (saving the economy) not only justifies the means (the intervention du jour), the end substitutes for sustained thought about how the means will work at all.

In this relatively unprincipled milieu, trust—access—is everything. And so some companies have done very well, some have been maintained on life support, and others have been allowed to die. Some investors have been rescued; others have been pressured to surrender hitherto valid claims. Decisions have been made and articulated in lawyerly fashion, but the sense of principled purpose, considered policy, and fundamental fairness evoked by the phrase *rule of law* are absent, and we are left to hope that our governing classes retain their general altruism.

Perhaps chilly laughter is appropriate. Two administrations, of different parties, have responded to the financial crisis in ways that bear farcical resemblance to the marketplace practices that generated the crisis—a "hair of the dog" approach to financial policy.

Consider the following:

- The Federal Reserve, acting under Section 13(g) of the Federal Reserve Act, has established off-balance-sheet special purpose entities (Maiden Lane I, II, and III) in order to bail out Bear Stearns and AIG. (Who says we learned nothing from Enron?)
- In exchange for funding the Maidens, and various failed entities, with cash, the government has received notes.
- Whenever and to the extent possible, the administration has maintained that the firms in question are independent, and that therefore their liabilities are off the balance sheet. Despite owning 80 percent of AIG, for example, the firm's operations are not on the federal budget.
- The government has supported weak or failed institutions with low-cost loans and guarantees in lieu of cash, thereby encouraging private participation and, no doubt, fostering genuine market transactions. Key institutions have thus become the functional equivalents of SIVs (or Fannie Mae), operating with below market cost of capital, and therefore, cheap leverage, and available to do the government's bidding.
- Recapitalization of financial firms has been attempted through complicated and opaque transactions, many structured as if they were commercial transactions. The transactions vary, but the "commercial" appearance of the deals is vitiated by government funding, subsidies, and adoption of risk; the lack of attention to corporate governance; and, allegedly in some cases, the lack of choice given to recipient institutions.
- Rather than manage assets directly, the government has outsourced the job, often to the firm Blackrock, best known for pricing CDOs and largely owned by Bank of America, a major recipient of government money. The terms of most such contracts have not yet been made public.
- Despite the foregoing, our government is perfectly transparent. Web pages and acronyms abound, but how much money has been spent, and who really benefits, is far from clear.
- Despite the talk of a deeply flawed system requiring profound change, the last two administrations have worked very hard to preserve the existing system. Although numerous institutions failed, many were saved in substantially existing form. Trading patterns were saved; the personal fortunes of many of those involved were saved. Although various temporary programs have been established, there has not been substantial new regulation, and no major new laws.[2]
- As the stock market decline appears to have stopped, and the unemployment rate's fall has at least slowed substantially, elites in the business and policy community are beginning to congratulate themselves on averting another Depression, weathering the tsunami.

Do we care? Some folks might believe that the nation means more than the fortunes of its executive class. But aren't such republican sentiments a bit hard to take too seriously, in these late days?

And some folks might believe that we are losing a market worth playing in, a usually exciting and sometimes joyous game of honest toil, obligations kept and efforts rewarded, and that instead we are building the sorts of markets we associate with weapons procurement or even kleptocracies, in which connections and influence determine success—a market of courtiers, where people expend their energies seeking favors and concessions and are willing to pay in advance for the support of the powerful. But isn't this objection just a little too entrepreneurial, a little too Norman Rockwell meets Schumpeter?

Is there any reason we cannot have a courtier economy, with the role of cavalier played by the new breed of banker, currying favor on Lafayette Park? It cannot be said that oligarchy is inherently unstable. The United States perhaps has come closer than anywhere else in the modern era, but even here we have not achieved, and will never achieve, the Jeffersonian dream of an agrarian republic. The pure republic does not exist, and we should make some peace with the world's shortcomings. And for most of us, some peace should not be too hard to make. I realize that not everyone teaches finance, but the vast majority of folks well educated enough to have read this far in a book this difficult are, or could easily be, well-protected mandarins, beneficiaries of our less-than-perfect meritocracy. So we can speak freely, here among our kind.

But even if we are content to take our place in the courtier economy—this meritocratic oligarchy that seems most natural to advanced knowledge economies—we might nonetheless worry that our regulatory state has come to resemble Citigroup before its fall. Oligarchies may sometimes be durable, but is ours? Are we Venice? We should not forget that Citigroup failed miserably. It was not close, and at least in hindsight and broad outline, it does not seem that hard to understand. Recall that bureaucrats, meaning modern politicians, typically seek to avoid responsibility. Jobs overseeing socially vital functions may be operated as mechanistically as possible and, whenever possible, shifted to another organization altogether, perhaps one that is entirely unaccountable, a hedge fund, an SPE, one of the Maiden Lanes, the Financial Products division of AIG, a monoline, an auction that may or may not be held. Of course, we need to preserve the independence of GM and Chrysler, so that we will have somebody to blame when they, too, fail. And so important work does not get done. Risks are not actually managed. Neglected structures collapse—with luck, in slow motion, so that people have time to get out of the way, and fewer are hurt less than would be the case if the edifice collapsed suddenly. If society's hurt gets bad enough, political will is mobilized to tax, or inflate, and the cycle begins again.

Such sophisticated corruption, best contemplated with a martini in hand (again strangely correct, because the times again call for poisonous clarity?), is not merely a question of decadent behaviors in unhealthy markets. The creation of the courtier economy is fundamentally in tension with the liberal trading regime that the United

States has struggled to erect since the end of World War II, in the belief that protectionism lay at the root of the militarized nation-state that proved so effective at slaughter. We may complain about globalization, but we should not forget the very real peace and prosperity, and even certain joys, in the City of Gold. The difficulties of contemporary global politics are dwarfed by the nationalist horrors of the twentieth century, and the surest way to awaken those monsters is to redefine economies in aggressively national terms.

The problem is that nationalism is built into the structure of political intervention in the response to economic crisis. Corporations may live globally, but they die—or are rescued—nationally. Once insolvency proceedings begin, officials are legally obligated to preserve the assets (and tax base) of creditors within the jurisdiction—that is, nationally. More broadly, a government moved to intervene, to spend taxpayer money, will be under pressure to secure a benefit for those taxpayers and for the national economy. So for example, because the U.S. government rescued Citigroup, U.S. taxpayers must hope that Citi does well, which is likely to mean that other, perhaps more deserving banks, perhaps HSBC, do not take Citi's market position. On the morning GM filed for bankruptcy, there was talk of which U.S. plants would be closed and which non-U.S. operations would be supported by U.S. taxpayers. Thus financial crisis may force us to think economically in national terms; in so doing, we may begin to unwind globalization.

Some things have been learned. Another Smoot-Hawley Act—or even a vigorous "Buy American" campaign—is unlikely. Far more likely is a decline of global trade, coupled with inflationary policies that will, not incidentally, aid exports (and make imports more expensive), a quasiconscious form of the beggar-thy-neighbor policies of the late 1930s, albeit perhaps more subtly and gradually enacted. If mutually adopted (and why would they not be?), such policies could lead to the disintegration of integrated markets. Renationalized economies lead to renationalized politics and social perspectives. Serious militarization might ensue.

This is a nightmare, of course, but not an impossible one. I sincerely doubt this year 2009 is like 1933, with new idealists in office who are incapable of keeping a stalled global economy from beginning its death spiral. That said, the structures of our integration, financial and otherwise, are more delicate than many thought just a few years ago while we were living so large. From here, we can see at least one way the current order might end. Adepts of a political economy worthy of the name, practitioners of a mature and generous capitalism, would think hard about such horrors and struggle to avert them.

* * *

It is still too soon to tell, from here in the midst of things, what this crisis will mean for thinking politically about financial markets. But we have possibilities. This book has explored three interconnected ways through which we may very literally rethink our financial markets.

First, objectively, we may stop thinking of markets and governments as antithetical conceptions. We might develop a more nuanced and realistic political economy, in which markets are an often preferred way of doing politics. We might conceive our markets in more organic terms across many social structures, few of them national. It might become bad taste to be so squeamish, or so triumphant, about economic life. Over two hundred years after Adam Smith, political economy might grow up.

Second, politically, the easy bifurcation between the partisans of administration, the left, and their opponents on the right, that has done so much to stultify thinking since the French Revolution, finally might give way. This could be a time in which we find a third way, our passage to India. It is just possible that a less servile understanding of how markets are played could foster a spirit of generosity. A deeper understanding of how we construct society through civil, largely marketplace, interactions could make us sensitive to our own roles, particularly those of us who are finance adepts in business, government, and yes, the academy.

Third, intellectually, the contemporary intermingling of things that had been thought separate and even opposed, "the market" and "the government," presents a great chance for better thinking. Recent events should have instilled a certain modesty about the uses of Reason and a desire for critical acuity. Political economy might finally take the turn to interpretation and even be understood as, at the end of the day, a humane science.

*   *   *

Admittedly, such changes in mind and spirit are unlikely, though one may hope. Perhaps this crisis is already ameliorating, and the opportunity for changing our patterns of thought is declining accordingly.

Which is not to say that we will not muddle forward. The United States and other nations, working alone and with each other, will arrive at some set of inelegant but workable compromises for our financial institutions, our businesses, and so for large parts of our social and individual lives. Surely we will see more regulation, combined with an underlying confidence that markets are the appropriate mechanism for constructing and governing much of social life. And maybe a reaffirmation of that stance, reminiscent of Roosevelt, will be all that emerges, though I have of course urged more.

I have faith that, along the way, this nation and most others will do a fair job of helping those who need it most. A residual sense of republican decency, lubricated by traditional hypocrisies, will probably keep our oligarchical tendencies within more or less seemly bounds. Despite the threats of nationalism entailed in financial crises, I believe we will protect global integration and the possibilities for peace and even civilization that our new politics affords. So there is much that may be hoped, even if we fail to rethink our financial markets, and much for which we should be grateful.

To close with a thought for policy intellectuals: It should be remembered that while reflexive critical analysis is a prerequisite for a mature political economy, such analysis is highly acidic. Even when our financial markets fail, our economies falter, and our officials stumble, it is important to find the sweetness in society, to remember the reasons to love our world and our nation, while we think about losses and opportunities.

Appendix

A Note on Recent U.S. Monetary Policy

Hindsight is twenty/twenty, or as intellectuals like to say, the owl of Minerva flies at dusk, but the question of whether monetary policy was too loose in the first decade of the twenty-first century should be considered in ways that proved to be a distraction from the task of rethinking how we go about financial policy but that are important for assessing recent history. Bubbles by definition involve the undue inflation of asset prices, and easy credit almost always aggravates the height of the bubble, and so the severity of the crash. That said, it bears remembering that bubbles almost always have their reasons, and all that easy financing often accomplishes something very real. For example, although the Silicon Valley bubble "destroyed" more than 60 percent of the value indicated by the NASDAQ Index, it also helped build the modern information economy. In the long bull market of the last few decades, a great deal got done. China and India and other places, especially in Asia, modernized. The world became networked. These are historically significant developments, and on balance, good things—at least from the perspective of the new world.

Perhaps too much was purchased at Wal-Mart, and we no doubt have too many lake houses and SUVs and angus steaks and Starbucks and iPhones and soccer moms in folding chairs. But consider, by way of example, a handsome woman, drinking excellent coffee, while watching her children play soccer some dewy Saturday morning—this vast bourgeois experiment has much to recommend it. The building of an elaborate material culture is not everything, but it is not nothing, particularly not in an already developed economy. The joie de vivre that has marked much of American life during this last long bull market, fueled yes in part by credit (as capitalism always is), is nothing to sneeze at, especially if we consider the ennui of other countries.

Now that our ride is over, it is quite easy to suggest that the air might have come out of the national hot air balloon at almost any time around the turn of the century. Consider the following: In 1997, a currency crisis started in Southeast Asia and quickly spread to Latin America and Russia. Shortly thereafter, Long-Term Capital Management (should have) taught us a lesson in systemic risk and the vulnerability of our financial system. At almost the same time, the Silicon Valley bubble popped, destroying huge amounts of faith in the nation's premier industry. There was not much time to focus on that, however, because terrorists destroyed the World Trade Center, the very symbol of our financial markets, and even attacked the Pentagon and took out a fourth jet for good measure, all on our own soil. Two wars followed, along with a massive expansion of the federal government and deficit spending (inflation appears to have been kept under control by free-floating anxiety). Enron and the accounting scandals reminded us that we had no real idea of what our investments were worth, and hence little reason for confidence in our retirements or a host of civil institutions, because corporations are just too big and accounting is just too shaky an enterprise. In short, during this entire period, it made at least as much sense for U.S. investors to lose faith in their financial markets as it did circa 1929. Under those circumstances, and even in light of the present crisis, I have a hard time being sure that the Federal Reserve, bless Alan's Keynesian soul, was wrong to be so free and easy with the money in the early years of this decade. We didn't lose our confidence, at least not then. (And now that we have lost so much of our confidence, even very cheap money does not make us lend, or borrow, much.)

My support of first-decade monetary policy is less than wholehearted, however, because of even darker facts. As suggested, China—whose recent history evokes both great admiration and real horror—remains unfree in no small part because of the government's ability to manipulate markets. I worry that our monetary policy has abetted the retardation of Chinese political development. Less subtly, and as mentioned, after 9/11, the U.S. government undertook a massive expansion of its security apparatus, mostly under the unsettlingly Germanic banner of "Homeland Security." We also embarked upon hot wars in Afghanistan and Iraq. The Bush administration was ideologically opposed to both taxes and the institutions of government, that is, the military and diplomatic capabilities at the government's disposal were relatively low. Moreover, the Bush administration thought in terms of business (that waging war might be an essentially public matter in a republic does not seem to have crossed the mind of anybody higher than a G-15). At any rate, the United States tended to outsource much of the cost of the wars and pay its quickly mounting bills with debt. A loose monetary policy and low interest rates on government borrowing were, shall we say, convenient for the execution of our fundamentally irresponsible security policy.

Notes

Notes for Preface

1. Joan Didion wrote: "All numbers in El Salvador tended to materialize and vanish and rematerialize in a different form, as if numbers denoted only the 'use' of numbers, an intention, a wish, a recognition that someone, somewhere, for whatever reason, needed to hear the ineffable expressed as a number. At any given time in El Salvador a great deal of what goes on is considered ineffable, and the use of numbers in this context tends to frustrate people who try to understand them literally, rather than as propositions to be floated, 'heard,' 'mentioned'" (Joan Didion, *Salvador* [New York: Simon and Schuster, 1983], 61).

2. See Jordan A. Schwarz, *Liberal: Adolf A. Berle* (New York: Free Press, 1987), vii. Berle is remembered for the idea that the separation of ownership from control is the key characteristic of the modern business corporation, which is a pretty big structural insight that remains influential in corporate law. See Adolf Berle and Gardner Means, *The Modern Corporation and Private Property* (New York: Macmillan, 1933). That said, Berle did not in fact become a grand systemic thinker; he became a consummate Washington insider.

Notes for Introduction

1. In testimony to the U.S. House of Representatives Committee on Oversight and Government Reform, October 23, 2008, Greenspan's second sentence ended with "because the data input into the risk management models generally covered only the past two decades, a period of euphoria." Neither Congress nor Greenspan himself was satisfied with this answer.

2. John Kenneth Galbraith, *The Affluent Society* (Boston: Houghton Mifflin, 1998), 17 (first published 1958).

Notes for Chapter 1

1. Jerry Mueller, "Our Epistemological Depression," *American: The Journal of the American Enterprise Institute* (January 29, 2009).

2. Even in the case of Lehman Brothers, the administration intervened. Not only was the government deeply involved in efforts to broker a "private" deal, the administration provided well over $100 billion—the details remain unclear—to close out Lehman's trading positions. See Andrew Ross Sorkin, "How the Fed Reached Out to Lehman," *New York Times,* December 16, 2008, B1.

3. See Vikas Bajaj and Michael Grynbaum, "Eager Investors Buy U.S. Debt at Zero Yield," *New York Times,* December 10, 2008, A1.

4. Ben Bernanke, Address at the 2009 Commencement of Boston College School of Law, Newton, Massachusetts, May 22, 2009.

5. I have heard it said that, in the real world, the symmetry does not hold—long positions seem to perform better.

6. Fisher Black, who coinvented the derivatives pricing model and who left MIT for Goldman Sachs, is reported to have said that "markets look a lot less efficient from the banks of the Hudson than from the banks of the Charles." Peter Bernstein, *Against the Gods: The Remarkable Story of Risk* (New York: Wiley, 1996), 6–7.

7. See Frank H. Knight, *Risk, Uncertainty and Profit* (Gloucester, UK: Dodo Press, 2008) (original printing 1921).

8. It is bad manners in the academy to make too much of our lack of critical reflexivity, but I will say that the financial academy in the United States is in desperate need of its Bourdieu. See generally Pierre Bourdieu, *Homo Academicus* (Palo Alto, CA: Stanford University Press, 1988).

9. One of the reasons this crisis was called so late, by so many, is that regulators must take care not to weaken confidence. Most other commentators are on the sell side, or paid by the sell side. Conversation with Nouriel Roubini, February 26, 2008.

Notes for Chapter 2

1. The fourth problem is more subtle and hardly received wisdom. Banks generally have to reserve capital against the loans they hold. Investors in the bank, and ultimately in the bank's portfolio of loans, are somewhat protected against the nonperformance of the loans by the bank's capital reserves. In securitization, however, bank loans are transferred to a special purpose entity, which is not legally required to maintain capital reserves, for the simple reason that the SPE is not a bank. Thus, the move from a bank holding a portfolio to the securitization of the same portfolio involved an increase of risk to investors in the portfolio—a risk that was realized, and to some extent absorbed by the government through the TALF program, when the securitization market essentially evaporated.

2. Financial Services Authority (UK), "The Turner Review: A Regulatory Response to the Global Banking Crisis," March 2009, 93.

3. Committee on the Budget, Republican National Caucus, "Roots of the Financial Crisis: The Role of Government Policy," January 8, 2009.

4. See the appendix for more on monetary policy.

Notes for Chapter 3

1. One can elaborate on this story: Consider the large number of quite traditional and conservative home loans, especially for first-time buyers (or, lately, buyers who cannot sell their houses), in which the borrower makes a smaller down payment, giving the bank a smaller margin, and

therefore more risk. In order to be induced to make the loan, the bank demands that the borrower buy "private mortgage insurance" (PMI) against the event of the borrower's default. Now suppose that the borrowers, who buy with little money down near the top of the market in a difficult economy, begin to default in substantial numbers. For how long can the PMI companies pay benefits under their policies? Presumably, the existence of PMI figured in the bank's own risk assessment, so that the insolvency of a PMI company ought to make a bank's assets riskier ... small-town AIG.

2. Sam Roberts et al., "Slump Creates Lack of Mobility for Americans," *New York Times,* April 23, 2009, 1.

3. Notably, in his critique of the Case-Shiller numbers Thomas Lawler ends up with the same 35 percent drop between the peak of the housing market and May 2009. See James R. Hagerty, "Outlook for Home Prices Clouded by Spat over Historical Trends," *Wall Street Journal,* April 24, 2009, A11.

4. See Ruth Simon and James Hagerty, "House Price Drops Leave More Underwater," *Wall Street Journal,* May 6, 2009, A3 (estimating that 21.9 percent of U.S. houses were worth less than the mortgage). Note that this number does not take account of the considerable transactional costs associated with an actual sale. See also Reuters, "About Half of U.S. Mortgages Seen Underwater by 2011," *New York Times* (online), August 5, 2009.

5. Serena Ng and Liam Pleven, "An AIG Unit's Quest to Juice Profit—Securities Lending Business Made Risky Bets; They Backfired on Insurer," *Wall Street Journal,* February 5, 2009, C1.

6. The traditional justification for finance—venture capital fostering material progress—can also be understood in roughly these terms, as the capitalization of an idea for a new business. The difference, at least in the ideal case, is that the pure idea may never be realized at all, and may therefore be worthless, if it does not receive financing.

7. It is worth remembering that Basel I (which was said to be too conservative) required banks to have a 4 percent tier-one capital-to-asset ratio; that is, for every \$1 of capital (largely equity), banks were expected to make \$25 in loans and to have \$24 in debts. (This is an oversimplification, ignoring "tier-two" capital and other things, but the point stands.)

8. This book is concerned, however, with politics, the worldview that might emerge from the present crisis, and so more philosophical (creative, idiosyncratic?) speculation awaits another book. Perhaps.

9. See Niall Ferguson, "Wall Street Lays Another Egg," *Vanity Fair* 50 (December 12, 2008): 190.

10. Henry Sumner Maine, *Ancient Law: Its Connection with the Early History of Society, and Its Relation to Modern Ideas* (New York: Dorat, 1986 [1861]).

11. Property: uncertainty : : contract: risk.

12. The thinking in this paragraph owes more than a little to George Williams.

13. Robert J. Shiller, "Challenging the Crowd in Whispers, Not Shouts," *New York Times,* November 2, 2008, BU5.

14. Traders may establish correlations among markets and put mechanisms in place for monitoring the markets and trading when conditions are right, often without human intervention. The tiny margins and high speed of such transactions mean that, in order to make money, they must be done on a grand scale. Hedge funds and other institutions therefore deploy vast amounts of borrowed money—leverage—to turn relatively small opportunities into substantial returns for the equity participants. For example: Various structured investment vehicles (SIVs) sponsored by Citigroup borrowed money in the commercial credit market and reinvested it, at slightly higher rates, in the debt markets. And so forth—access to credit is built into the business operations of contemporary financial institutions. Without the leverage, the transactions are not profitable, the deals make no sense.

15. The Merrill Lynch deal was done under the widespread belief that Merrill was next. Chief

executive of Goldman Sachs Lloyd Blankfein likened the sequence of insolvencies in investment banking in 2008 to a giant wave sweeping up Wall Street institutions, the weakest first, but soon enough it was unclear that Morgan Stanley and even Goldman Sachs were safe. When the "crisis" began to give way to the new status quo (quite profitable for the survivors), the firm unsurprisingly began to sing a different tune. See Jenny Anderson, "Despite Bailouts, Business as Usual at Goldman," *New York Times*, August 7, 2009, B1.

16. Federal Reserve Board, "Remarks by Chairman Alan Greenspan: Finance: United States and Global," at the Institute of International Finance, New York, New York (via videoconference), April 22, 2002.

17. As the text is meant to suggest, these lessons should have been learned from Long-Term Capital Management, if not the portfolio insurance aspects of the 1987 market break.

Notes for Chapter 4

1. In the interest of brevity and personal comfort, the focus here is on securities law. The argument with regard to banking would be a little different, because banking law operates differently, but would be essentially parallel.

2. I have asked students in China, Suppose you wished to explain to me, a sympathetic listener and with all goodwill, face to face and over a table, what you thought your individual future would be. Now suppose you were to tell me, or perhaps a distant stranger, about an institution with which you are intimately familiar, and in writing. What would you write? Could you be transparent? Fraud is hardly the greatest bar to communication.

3. For more on transparency, see "Telling All: The Sarbanes-Oxley Act and the Ideal of Transparency," *Michigan State Law Review* 441 (2004).

4. Paul Samuelson, "Farewell to Friedman-Hayek Libertarian Capitalism," Tribune Media Services, October 15, 2008.

5. As discussed below, in the last decade, the industry also attempted to price the risks underlying a given product by using a so-called copula function that correlated the pool's risk to another asset class for which better data existed. If this were done well, bothersome diversification might not be necessary. Or so, at any rate, the ratings agencies thought.

6. David Li, "On Default Correlation: A Copula Function Approach," *Journal of Fixed Income* 9: 43–54 (2000). A good explanation is available in Felix Salmon, "Recipe for Disaster: The Formula That Killed Wall Street," *Wired* 17, no. 3 (February 2009).

7. Not that notable people are not trying to solve the problem outright. For example, the father of modern portfolio theory, Harry Markowitz, somewhat ironically but rather touchingly has recently argued that what the world needs now is more transparency. L. Gordon Crovitz, "The Father of Portfolio Theory on the Crisis: Harry Markowitz Says Valuation Is the Critical Step," *Wall Street Journal*, November 3, 2008, A17. Michael Lewis has argued that what is needed is less conflict of interest, and for folks on Wall Street to take a longer-term perspective. Michael Lewis, "The End," Portfolio.com, December 2008. And former Federal Reserve chair Volcker and the Group of Thirty have argued that what is necessary is massively increased government participation in the decisionmaking processes of financial firms, many of which the government, after all, now owns. Group of 30, "Financial Reform: A Framework for Financial Stability," January 15, 2009. Such views are sensible enough, but they hold forth the hope that traditional financial policy thinking, once more, with feeling, will be adequate.

8. As a corollary, this crisis may mark the beginning of the end for the Enlightened imagery of "left" and "right" echoed in talk about regulatory responses, government intervention, moral hazard, and so forth.

9. This is a common preoccupation among anthropologists who are attempting to come

to grips with the global contemporary. For my take on these efforts, see David A. Westbrook, *Navigators of the Contemporary: Why Ethnography Matters* (Chicago: University of Chicago Press, 2008).

Notes for Chapter 6

1. I am not making a partisan argument here. For these purposes, the differences between the Obama and the Bush administrations are not important. The legal scholar in me is tempted to say "the executive." An underlying problem is that the obligation of the executive branch to respond to economic crisis has been well established since Roosevelt, but the role is hardly well defined.

2. The administration has had less problem simply giving away guarantees, access to the discount window, and other commercially valuable, but noncash, forms of support.

3. Congressional Budget Office, "The Troubled Asset Relief Program: Report on Transactions through June 17, 2009," June 2009, 6.

Notes for Chapter 7

1. A typo (?) in this book's draft read "Goldman Sax," which seemed just right to at least one of my readers, if a little too Brecht and Weil.

2. For an example of such thinking, see Richard Bookstaber, *A Demon of Our Design* (New York: Wiley, 2007) chap. 10, "Cockroaches and Hedge Funds."

Notes for Chapter 8

1. The first bailout of Chrysler worked, for a while. And the bailout of Lockheed worked, although it could be argued that using tax dollars to transform a company into a monopsonistic supplier of military hardware, or perhaps a government sponsored entity, does not teach much about the restoration of healthy markets.

2. AIG's financial products group was in some economic ways functioning as an insurance company, but its business was conducted with the speed of and otherwise much like a hedge fund or other trading operation.

3. The flaws in the PPIP appear in many other plans as well. I've chosen to discuss PPIP because it is an important example of contemporary thinking.

4. Absent exogenous good news, hardly on the horizon at midsummer 2009, PPIP is likely either to wash out altogether (what if they gave an auction and nobody came?), or to prove to be only an expensive cash infusion producing short-term modest gains for bank equity holders. Investors in PPIP may be expected to take short-term long positions on the banks that will receive taxpayer money, thereby freeing themselves of the need to profit from their positions in the plan itself. It is also said that firms may be willing to participate in PPIP in order to be seen by the administration as good soldiers. Eventually, a government with over a trillion dollars in debt will hold a serious garage sale, and firms with access are likely to make a killing.

Notes for Chapter 9

1. The first Glass-Steagall act, the Banking Act of 1932, Public Law 72–44, liberalized Federal Reserve rules so that the Fed could hold government paper as collateral (allowing for

substantial increases in the money supply) and makes gold reserves available for loans. The second Glass-Steagall act (usually called "Glass Steagall"), Public Law 73–66, was part of the Banking Act of 1933 and established the Federal Deposit Insurance Corporation (FDIC). As discussed in the text, and although the details are torturous, generally speaking, Glass Steagall separated commercial banking from investment banking, a separation enforced and extended (notably to include insurance activities) by the bank Holding Company Act of 1956, Public Law 511.

2. Note that the point here—the volatility of trading—is distinct from the rationality of investment banks discussed in Chapter 1.

3. See Commodity Futures Modernization Act of 2000, Pub. L. No. 106–554, §§302, 303. The CFMA was passed by reference in an omnibus spending bill and was not debated on the floor of either house. The Senate version, which passed unanimously, was introduced the day before the Christmas recess.

4. See *SEC v. Howey*, 328 U.S. 293 (1946). In Howey an "investment contract" for purposes of the securities laws was an investment in a "common enterprise." To call an interest rate swap a common enterprise might be too much of a stretch for the courts, but would pose no impediment to Congress.

5. See Commodity Futures Modernization Act of 2000, Pub. L. No. 106–554, §117. The story is a bit more complicated. States traditionally regulate insurance companies. Bets on the direction of prices traditionally were not thought of as insurance, but instead have been regulated under so-called bucket-shop and gaming laws. What §117 explicitly did was preempt states from regulating derivatives, including CDS, under such laws. This seems to have been universally understood as prohibiting regulation of CDS by state insurance authorities. See Statement of the National Conference of Insurance Legislators (NCOIL) Before the Committee on Agriculture, U.S. House of Representatives, Hearing on "Derivatives Markets Transparency and Accountability Act of 2009," February 4, 2009.

6. I have been unable to determine how good this estimate, based on largely proprietary information held by many different actors, is. Suffice it to say that the vast majority of swaps are naked.

7. As with consideration of the network, such "nodal" concerns for institutions will overlap with, and benefit from, institutional design conducted in the name of traditional strategies of transparency or portfolio management, which are sketched in the next chapter.

8. As an aside, within that sub-branch of the legal academy devoted to corporation law, it was heatedly argued (with more heat than light) that the institution known as a body, or corpus, should be "really" understood exclusively as a nexus of contracts. A footnote to the present crisis, after so much has been done to prevent the disaggregation of corporations along present lines, is that the powers-that-be are quite committed to the idea that corporations are entities.

9. This is a rather odd lesson for Americans, with their profound belief in constitutionalism—in the power of form to generate good politics—to have to learn. And it is an odd lesson for lawyers to learn as well, with their traditional belief in process. I think the rediscovery of process has to be understood in terms of three great obstacles to clear thought: (1) the profound divide, in American minds, between "the government" and "the market," coupled with (2) a nearly religious commitment to the idea of marketplace efficiency, without which so much would seem so wasteful, and (3) the sheer difficulty of conceiving of this bubble (the difficulty with every bubble).

10. In March 2008, the Treasury put out a white paper entitled "Blueprint for a Modernized Financial Regulatory Structure"—a project begun in 2007, when folks in Washington had the luxury of worrying about competitiveness, whether people were making more money in New York or London. While the "Blueprint" was being written, however, the financial world began to melt down. Since then, and as one might expect, numerous additional proposals for regulatory reform have appeared. In October 2008 at the London School of Economics, Harvard Law School

Professor Howell Jackson presented a centralized regulatory structure loosely modeled after the United Kingdom's Financial Services Authority. Former Federal Reserve chair Paul Volcker and the Group of 30 announced a plan that would, among other things, involve government in the corporate governance of major financial institutions. See Group of 30, "Financial Reform: A Framework for Financial Stability," 2009 ("G30 Financial Reform" hereafter). The Congressional Oversight Panel released a report in January 2009 titled "Special Report on Regulatory Reform." More reports are listed in the bibliography of this book.

11. More subtly but in the same vein, arguments for institutional reform tend to overindulge the dominant trope of the legal academy, that bureaucratic structure and laws generally are expressions of an underlying normative rationality, fortuitously my own normative rationality, instead of a messy tangle of political compromises made under the circumstances. See David A. Westbrook, "Pierre Schlag and the Temple of Boredom," 57 *University of Miami Law Review* 649 (2003); David A. Westbook, *Navigators of the Contemporary: Why Ethnography Matters* (Chicago: University of Chicago Press, 2008).

Notes for Chapter 10

1. John C. Coffee, "It's About the Gatekeepers, Stupid," *Business Lawyer* 57 (2002): 1403.

2. Paul Samuelson, "Farewell to Friedman-Hayek Libertarian Capitalism," Tribune Media Services, October 15, 2008.

3. See Timothy F. Geithner, "Reducing Systemic Risk in a Dynamic Financial System," Remarks at the Economic Club of New York, New York City, June 9, 2008. Geithner goes on to argue, in the conclusory fashion expected from regulators, that the decisions made by the Federal Reserve up to that point (notably the Bear Stearns intervention) were wise, and that going forward, a much more centralized system of regulatory oversight, with the Federal Reserve playing a key role, ought to be established.

4. Humorously enough, in hindsight, there was a brief period at the beginning of the crisis when it was said that the problems of some big U.S. banks could not happen in Europe, because Europe had already implemented Basel II.

5. As discussed in Chapter 3, this was obvious during the housing boom, when banks required less and less of a down payment (homeowner equity in the house/margin) in order to make loans and essentially relied on increases in home prices to secure the loans on their books (or on their ability to sell the loans to someone else).

Notes for Conclusion

1. Louise Story, "A Rich Education for Summers (After Harvard)," *New York Times*, April 6, 2009.

2. By way of comparison, by midsummer of the first year of the Roosevelt administration, the Securities Act of 1933 and the Banking Act of 1933 (the second Glass Steagall Act), inter alia establishing the FDIC, had been passed.

Bibliography

It is not obvious how to write a "bibliography" for a book like this, concerned with whether and how an important *Geist* of our *Zeit,* the financial imagination of our political class, will change his mind. Surely minds change for many reasons besides the reading of books, or even articles, newspapers, blogs, listening to policy remarks and talk radio, and the dim recollection of instruction long ago, the cultural stream in which we swim. The text of this book, therefore, cannot really be said to be "based" on the materials referenced here.

Rather than dispense altogether with a bibliography, however, I have listed a number of texts for a variety of reasons. Some materials are listed simply because they were mentioned in the book's text, though not everything mentioned is cited. Some entries represent materials that were in fact important to the writing of this book, and that may or may not have been mentioned. Other entries acknowledge friendship, in some small way repay debt, perpetuate the tribalism of academia, or perform some combination of these indispensable tasks. A number of materials are listed because they are fashionable, or even influential in the intellectual world that I inhabit, perhaps along with some readers. Omission of such references might reflect badly on me; inclusion might be convenient for somebody who wants to do further reading.

Commercially published materials have been cited in conventional fashion. For the sake of appearances, in the beliefs that links break and nobody retypes, and in reliance on search engines, web addresses have not been provided.

Books

Ackerloff, George A., and Robert Shiller. *Animal Spirits: How Human Psychology Drives the Economy, and Why It Matters for Global Capitalism.* Princeton, NJ: Princeton University Press, 2009.

Ahamed, Liaquat. *Lords of Finance: The Bankers Who Broke the World*. New York: Penguin, 2009.

Beckett, Samuel. *Endgame*. London: Faber and Faber, 1976.

Benjamin, Walter. *Illuminations*. New York: Harcourt, Brace, 1968.

Berle, Adolf, and Gardner Means, *The Modern Corporation and Private Property*. New York: Macmillan, 1933.

Berman, Harold. *Law and Revolution: The Formation of the Western Legal Tradition*. Cambridge, MA: Harvard University Press, 1983.

Bernanke, Ben. *Essays on the Great Depression*. Princeton, NJ: Princeton University Press, 2004 [2000].

Bernstein, Peter. *Against the Gods: The Remarkable Story of Risk*. Hoboken, NJ: Wiley, 1996.

Bookstaber, Richard. *A Demon of Our Own Design: Markets, Hedge Funds, and the Perils of Financial Innovation*. Hoboken, NJ: Wiley, 2007.

Boorstin, Daniel. *The Mysterious Science of the Law*. Cambridge, MA: Harvard University Press, 1941.

Bourdieu, Pierre. *Homo Academicus*. Stanford, CA: Stanford University Press, 1988.

Breyer, Stephen. *Regulation and Its Reform*. Cambridge, MA: Harvard University Press, 1982.

Bruner, Robert F., and Sean D. Carr. *The Panic of 1907: Lessons Learned from the Market's Perfect Storm*. Hoboken, NJ: Wiley, 2009 [2007].

Buffett, Warren. *The Essays of Warren Buffett: Lessons for Corporate America*. Edited by Lawrence Cunningham. New York: Cunningham Group, 2001.

Cohan, William D. *House of Cards: A Tale of Hubris and Wretched Excess on Wall Street*. New York: Doubleday, 2009.

Cooper, George. *The Origin of Financial Crises: Central Banks, Credit Bubbles, and the Efficient Market Fallacy*. New York: Vintage, 2008.

Didion, Joan. *Salvador*. New York: Simon and Schuster, 1983.

Downey, Greg, and Melissa Fisher. *Frontiers of Capital: Ethnographic Reflections on the New Economy*. Durham, NC: Duke University Press, 2006.

Ferguson, Niall. *The Cash Nexus: Economics and Politics from the Age of Warfare through the Age of Welfare, 1700–2000*. New York: Basic Books, 2001.

Fisher, Irving. *Booms and Depressions: Some First Principles*. New York: Adelphi, 1932.

Fox, Justin. *The Myth of the Rational Market: A History of Risk, Reward, and Delusion on Wall Street*. New York: Harper, 2009.

Friedman, Milton, and Anna Schwartz. *A Monetary History of the United States 1867–1960*. Princeton, NJ: Princeton University Press, 1963.

Galbraith, J. K. *The Affluent Society*. Boston: Houghton Mifflin, 1998 [1958].

———. *The Economics of Innocent Fraud: Truth for Our Time*. Boston: Houghton Mifflin Harcourt, 2004.

———. *The Great Crash, 1929*. New York: Penguin, 1992 [1955].

Goodhart, Charles. *The Regulatory Response to the Financial Crisis*. Northampton, MA: Edward Elgar, 2009.

Graham, Benjamin. *Security Analysis*. 6th ed. New York: McGraw-Hill, 2008.

Keynes, John Maynard. *The General Theory of Employment, Interest, and Money*. Rockford, IL: BN Publishing 2009 [1935].

Kindleberger, Charles, and Robert Aliber. 6th ed. *Manias, Panics, and Crashes: A History of Financial Crises*. New York: Palgrave Macmillan, 2010.

Knight, Frank H. *Risk, Uncertainty, and Profit*. Gloucester, UK: Dodo, 2008 [1921].

Krugman, Paul. *The Return of Depression Economics and the Crisis of 2008*. New York: Norton, 2009.

Kuhn, Thomas. *The Structure of Scientific Revolutions*. 3rd ed. Chicago: University of Chicago Press, 1996 [1962].

Lastra, Rosa M. *Legal Foundations of International Monetary Stability*. New York: Oxford University Press, 2006.

Lewis, Michael. *Liar's Poker: Rising through the Wreckage on Wall Street*. New York: Norton, 1989.

Lewis, Michael, ed. *Panic: The Story of Modern Financial Insanity*. New York: Norton, 2008.

Lowenstein, Roger. *When Genius Failed: The Rise and Fall of Long-Term Capital Management*. New York: Random House, 2000.

Mackay, Charles. *Extraordinary Popular Delusions and the Madness of Crowds*. Radford, VA: Wilder, 2009 [1841].

Mackenzie, Donald. *An Engine, Not a Camera: How Financial Models Shape Markets*. Cambridge: Massachusetts Institute of Technology Press, 2008 [2006].

McDonald, Lawrence G. *A Colossal Failure of Common Sense: The Inside Story of the Collapse of Lehman Brothers*. New York: Crown, 2009.

Minsky, Hyman. *Stabilizing an Unstable Economy*. New York: McGraw-Hill, 2008 [1986].

Morris, Charles R. *The Trillion Dollar Meltdown: Easy Money, High Rollers, and the Great Credit Crash*. New York: Public Affairs, 2008.

Moss, David. *When All Else Fails: Government as the Ultimate Risk Manager*. Cambridge, MA: Harvard University Press, 2004 [2002].

Partnoy, Frank. *Infectious Greed: How Deceit and Risk Corrupted the Financial Markets*. New York: Times Books, 2003.

Posner, Richard A. *A Failure of Capitalism: The Crisis of '08 and the Descent into Depression*. Cambridge, MA: Harvard University Press, 2009.

Ramsey, Robert Lee, and John W. Head. *Preventing Financial Chaos: An International Guide to the Legal Rules and Operational Procedures for Handling Insolvent Banks*. The Hague, Switzerland: Kluwer, 2000.

Schiller, Robert. *Irrational Exuberance*. Princeton, NJ: Princeton University Press, 2000.

Schlegel, John. *American Legal Realism and Empirical Social Science*. Chapel Hill: University of North Carolina Press, 1995.

Schwarz, Jordan A. *Liberal: Adolf A. Berle and the Vision of an American Era*. New York: Free Press, 1987.

Taleb, Nassim Nicholas. *The Black Swan: The Impact of the Highly Improbable*. New York: Random House, 2007.

———. *Fooled by Randomness: The Hidden Role of Chance in the Markets and in Life*. New York: Norton, 2001.

Tett, Gillian. *Fool's Gold: How the Bold Dream of a Small Tribe at JP Morgan Was Corrupted by Wall Street Greed and Unleashed a Catastrophe*. New York: Free Press, 2009.

Wessel, David. *In Fed We Trust: Ben Bernanke's War on the Great Panic*. New York: Crown Business Publishing. 2009.

Westbrook, David A. *Between Citizen and State: An Introduction to the Corporation*. Boulder, CO: Paradigm, 2007.

———. *City of Gold: An Apology for Global Capitalism in a Time of Discontent*. New York: Routledge, 2004.

————. *Navigators of the Contemporary: Why Ethnography Matters.* Chicago: University of Chicago Press, 2008.

Wolfe, Tom. *The Bonfire of the Vanities.* New York: Picador, 2008 [1987].

Zaloom, Caitlin. *Out of the Pits: Traders and Technology from Chicago to London.* Chicago: University of Chicago Press, 2006.

Zandi, Mark. *Financial Shock: A 360° Look at the Subprime Mortgage Implosion, and How to Avoid the Next Financial Crisis.* Upper Saddle River, NJ: FT Press, 2008.

Articles, Speeches, Testimony

Bartley, Timothy, and Marc Schneiberg. "Regulating and Redesigning Finance: Observations from Organizational Sociology." Paper presented at the Tobin Project Conference, April 2009.

Bernanke, Ben. Remarks at the 2009 Commencement of the Boston College School of Law, Newton, Massachusetts, May 22, 2009.

Carpenter, Daniel. "Confidence Games: How Does Regulation Constitute Markets?" Paper presented at the Tobin Project Conference, February 2008.

Coffee, John. "Understanding Enron: It's about the Gatekeepers, Stupid." *Business Lawyer* 57 (2002): 1403.

Eisner, Marc. "Markets in the Shadow of the State: An Appraisal of Deregulation and Implications for Future Research." Paper presented at the Tobin Project Conference, February 2008.

Ferguson, Niall. "A Long Shadow: The 'Great Repression' to Curb Downturns Could This Time Fail." *Financial Times,* September 22, 2008, 13, 19.

————. "Wall Street Lays Another Egg." *Vanity Fair* 50, no. 12 (December 2008): 190.

Fisher, Irving. "The Debt-Deflation Theory of Great Depressions." *Econometrica* 1 (October 1933): 337.

Geithner, Timothy. "Reducing Systemic Risk in a Dynamic Financial System." Remarks at the Economic Club of New York, New York City, June 9, 2008.

Greenspan, Alan. "Finance: United States and Global." Remarks at the Institute of International Finance, New York, New York, April 22, 2002.

Holmes, Douglas R. "Economy of Words." *Cultural Anthropology* 24 (2009): 381.

Johnson, Simon. "The Quiet Coup." *Atlantic* 303, no. 4 (May 2009): 46.

Kuttner, Robert. "Financial Regulation: After the Fall." Report for Demos, January 8, 2009.

Lewis, Michael. "The End." *Conde Nast Portfolio* 2, no. 12 (December 2008): 114.

Li, David X. "On Default Correlation: A Copula Function Approach." *Journal of Fixed Income* 9, no. 4 (March 2000): 43.

Lo, Andrew. "Hedge Funds, Systemic Risk, and the Financial Crisis of 2007–2008: Written Testimony for the House Oversight Committee Hearing on Hedge Funds," November 13, 2008.

Markowitz, Harry. "Portfolio Selection." *Journal of Finance* 7 (1952): 77.

Morgenson, Gretchen et al. "The Reckoning." *New York Times,* September 28–December 28, 2008.

Muller, Jerry Z. "Our Epistemological Depression." *American: Journal of the American Enterprise Institute* (January 29, 2009).

Partnoy, Frank. Testimony in Hearings before the U.S Senate Committee on Banking, Housing, and Urban Affairs Assessing the Current Oversight and Operations of Credit Ratings Agencies, 108th Cong., March 7, 2006.

Salmon, Felix. "A Formula for Disaster." *Wired* 17, no. 3 (March 2009): 74.

Sirri, Erik R. Municipal Bond Turmoil, Impact on Cities, Towns and States: Hearing before the Committee on Financial Services, 110th Cong., 2008.

Westbrook, David. "Corporation Law after Enron: The Possibility of a Capitalist Reimagination." *Georgetown Law Journal* 61 (2004): 92.

———. "Pierre Schlag and the Temple of Boredom." *University of Miami Law Review* 57 (2003): 649.

———. "Telling All: The Sarbanes-Oxley Act and the Ideal of Transparency." *Michigan State Law Review* 441 (2004).

Institutional Reports

Basel Committee on Banking Supervision. *Principles for Sound Liquidity Risk Management and Supervision*, September 2008.

Bloomberg, Michael, and Charles Schumer with McKinsey and Company and New York City Economic Development Corporation. *Sustaining New York's and the U.S. Global Financial Services Leadership*, January 2007.

Centre for Economic Policy Research. *The Fundamental Principles of Financial Regulation: Geneva Reports on the World Economy II*, July 2009.

Committee on Capital Markets Regulation (CCMR). *Interim Report of the Committee on Capital Markets Regulation*, November 30, 2006.

———. *Recommendations for Reorganizing the U.S. Financial Regulatory Structure*, January 14, 2009.

Congressional Budget Office. *The Troubled Asset Relief Program: Report on Transactions through June 17, 2009*, June 2009.

Council of Institutional Investors. *Some Investor Perspectives on Financial Regulation Proposals (Cunningham White Paper)*, September 2008.

Counterparty Risk Management Policy Group (CRMPG) III. *Containing Systemic Risk: The Road to Reform*, August 6, 2008.

Dewey and LeBoeuf. *Waiting for Regulation L(iquidity)*, Client Alert, January 27, 2009.

Enron. *Report of Investigation by the Special Investigative Committee of the Board of Directors of Enron Corp.* ("Powers Report"), February 1, 2002.

Financial Services Authority (United Kingdom). *The Turner Review: A Regulatory Response to the Global Banking Crisis*, March 2009.

Financial Services Roundtable (FSR). *The Blueprint for U.S. Financial Competitiveness*, November 2007.

Financial Stability Forum (FSF). Report of the Financial Stability Forum on Enhancing Market and Institutional Resilience and the Follow-Up on Implementation, April 7, 2008, and October 10, 2008.

Group of 30 (G-30). *Financial Reform: A Framework for Financial Stability*, January 15, 2009.

———. *The Structure of Financial Supervision: Approaches and Challenges in a Global Marketplace*, October 2008.

Institute of International Finance (IIF). *Final Report of the IIF Committee on Market Best*

Practices: Principles of Conduct and Best Practice Recommendations—Financial Services Industry Response to the Market Turmoil of 2007–2008, July 17, 2008.

International Organization of Securities Commissions Technical Committee (IOSCO). *Report on the Subprime Crisis,* May 2008.

———. *The Role of Credit Rating Agencies in Structured Finance Markets,* May 2008.

North American Securities Administrators Association. *Proceedings of the NASAA Financial Services Regulatory Reform Roundtable,* December 11, 2008.

President's Working Group on Financial Markets (PWG). *Policy Statement on Financial Market Developments,* March 2008. http://www.ustreas.gov/press/releases/hp871.htm.

———. *Progress Update on March Policy Statement on Financial Market Developments,* October 2008.

Republican Caucus Committee on the Budget. *Roots of the Financial Crisis: The Role of Government Policy,* January 8, 2009.

Securities Industry and Financial Markets Association (SIFMA). *Recommendations of the Securities Industry and Financial Markets Association Credit Rating Agency Task Force,* July 2008.

Senior Supervisors Group (SSG). *Observations on Risk Management Practices in the Recent Market Turbulence,* March 6, 2008.

U.S. Chamber of Commerce Commission on the Regulation of U.S. Capital Markets in the 21st Century. *Report and Recommendations,* March 2007.

U.S. Congress, Congressional Oversight Panel. *Special Report on Regulatory Reform,* 111th Cong., January 2009.

U.S. Department of the Treasury. *Blueprint for a Modernized Financial Regulatory Structure,* March 31, 2008.

U.S. Government Accountability Office (GAO). *Financial Regulation: A Framework for Crafting and Assessing Proposals to Modernize the Outdated U.S. Financial Regulatory System.* GAO-09-216. January 2009.

U.S. Securities and Exchange Commission Staff. *Summary Report of Issues Identified in the Commission Staff's Examination of Select Credit Rating Agencies,* July 2008.

Index

About the Author

David A. Westbrook is Floyd H. & Hilda L. Hurst Faculty Scholar and Professor of Law at the University at Buffalo, the State University of New York, and Visiting Professor of Law at the University of Kansas and Washburn University. His books include *Navigators of the Contemporary: Why Ethnography Matters* (University of Chicago Press 2008) and *Between Citizen and State: An Introduction to the Corporation* (Paradigm 2007).